Design
for
Children

Design for Children

Kimberlie Birks

Play
Ride
Learn
Eat
Create
Sit
Sleep

Φ

Small in Size but Big in Ideas
Kimberlie Birks

As philosopher Alain de Botton has suggested, 'all designed objects are propaganda for a way of life.'[1] Nowhere does this seem more relevant than with design for children, as the things with which we surround them become central to their experience and perception of the world. The stuff of childhood is abundant: anyone who is a parent or has spent time in the presence of a toddler knows that to be around a young child is to have any semblance of a modern minimalist lifestyle upended. As the tide of children's products continues to rise, design-minded parents are increasingly looking for objects that showcase aesthetic and material quality, craftsmanship and adaptability, and will not only stand the test of time, but also offer visual reprieve from the onslaught of garish, blinking, beeping sanity-testers. Thankfully, as this survey shows, designers have long been applying their skills to just this end, creating noteworthy objects that advocate for a different, more harmonious way of life.

While we rarely question our notion of childhood as a time of innocence and playful exploration, it is in fact a relatively modern concept. For the vast majority of history, children were regarded as incomplete adults. The belief that childhood should be treated as an independent life-phase would only take root in the eighteenth and nineteenth centuries, during the Age of Enlightenment and Romanticism. With it came the emergence of a new range of child-centric objects, such as furniture, which the famous Viennese brand Gebrüder Thonet began selling in 1866. While intended for children, these items were merely downsized adult designs. Children would have to wait until the Progressive Education movement of the late 1800s, and the spread of Maria Montessori's pedagogy in the early 1900s, to have their particular design needs addressed. With improvements in child labour laws, the twentieth century would see design for children become an unparalleled preoccupation. Nevertheless, objects created for children by the era's pioneering designers – from Gerrit Rietveld (1888–1964) and Marcel Breuer (1902–81), to Charles (1907–78) and

Ray Eames (1912–88) and Ladislav Sutnar (1897–1976) – have remained downplayed within the context of both their careers and the wider design narrative. Though diminutive and often light-hearted in nature, design for children should not be underestimated or denied serious consideration: in the eloquent words of Charles Eames, 'toys and games are the preludes to serious ideas.'[2] This historically underrepresented area of design not only provides new insight into familiar figures, but also sheds light on a range of individuals equally deserving of recognition.

Children's objects are often a signal of the times, reflecting both the evolution of the design industry and shifts in public perception. As the items on these pages attest, much of the design history of the twentieth century can be traced through the developments in its output for children. This central role in the historical narrative becomes evident through the use of children's furniture and products as a testing ground for prototypes and technological advancements, albeit on a smaller scale. From the wood and tubular steel constructions of the Bauhaus in the 1920s, to the plastic pioneers of the 1960s, the remarkable technical, material and aesthetic innovations made in designs for children reflected – and at times led – the wider design field.

Alvar Aalto's (1898–1976) cantilever chairs for children from the early 1930s can be seen as precursors of his famous adult versions. Similarly, the Eameses' 1944 collaboration with Evans Products Company produced a run of 5,000 children's chairs, stools and tables, marking their first attempt to fabricate their three-dimensional plywood furniture in larger quantities, and as such, paving the way for their later plywood lounge chairs for adults. In the 1960s, when material advances made plastic affordable for daily use, Walter Papst (1924–2008) gave the world its first piece of furniture made from a single piece of fibreglass reinforced polyester, in the form of a children's table. Marco Zanuso (1916–2001) and Richard Sapper (1932–2015) followed closely behind, with the K 1340 stacking chair for kids, the first to be built entirely from injection-moulded plastic.

The malleability afforded by new materials and technology further liberated mid-century designers from previous limitations, allowing for a greater inventiveness in children's objects and inspiring some of the century's most progressive designs. Concurrently, the 1950s and 1960s saw a growing interest in traditional craft practices and well designed objects amongst well-educated, middle-class parents in both Europe and America. The belief that thoughtful design not only enriches daily life, but also stimulates a child's creativity sparked a range of now-iconic toys produced by the likes of Kay Bojesen (1886–1958), Fredun Shapur (1929–), Kurt Naef (1926–2006) and the American company, Creative Playthings.

This book is by no means a definitive compendium of design for children. It is instead motivated by a desire to promote an important and growing field of design, worthy of critical attention. Loosely assembled around the categories of play, ride, learn, eat, create, sit and sleep – each of which is denoted with its own icon throughout these pages – Design for Children presents a selection of children's objects filtered through the lenses of craftsmanship, exceptional design and modern aesthetics. Aspiring to celebrate a sense of timelessness, the book does not address the dynamic and rapidly changing landscape of technological toys. Instead, the objects in this collection attest to the fact that despite significant social, cultural and technological shifts, many qualities of good design remain unchanged. Beyond the purely aesthetic, this volume reflects the belief that noteworthy toys stimulate creativity, encourage a child's development and are largely gender neutral. Similarly, exceptional children's furniture caters to the specific needs of youth, adapts to their growth, and provides the child with a sense of security and comfort. Happily, recent years have seen this area of design steadily inching further into the spotlight, with respected brands, including Kartell, Magis and Vitra, enlisting high-profile designers to create children's furniture that embodies the sophistication of their adult offerings. Similarly, important exhibitions such as *Zappel, Philipp! Die Welt der Kindermöbel* (*Fidgety Philipp! The World of Children's Furniture*) at the Imperial Furniture Collection, Vienna, *Century of the Child: Growing by Design 1900–2000* (2012) at the Museum of Modern Art, New York, and *Giro Giro Tondo: Design for Children* (2017) at Milan's Triennale Design Museum, mark a growing recognition of the importance of the subject. While small in scale, children's design can be big in ideas. This survey hopes to pay tribute to those who have shaped the field – and by extension the world – while adding its voice to the chorus of growing advocates for more thoughtful, innovative and exceptional design for children. We will all benefit.

Design for Children Matters
Lora Appleton

How children learn to perceive and interact with the world is critical to their social and emotional development. And at the heart of this discovery is play, an activity which represents a significant educational experience, one that is imperative for a child's creativity, cognitive growth and healthy development. Unlike (most) adults, children take exploration and play very seriously, they also have highly specific needs that aren't typically supported by design made for adults.

Through creating design that is both thoughtful and functional, it is possible to cultivate the creativity, autonomy, critical thinking and language that children need in order to fully develop their social and emotional skills. While design made specifically for children is not a new concept, these objects reflect the historical shifts in perspective – both pedagogical and sociological – that continue to evolve about childhood: the specificities of material, form and function often being strongly indicative of both when and where a design was produced. When furniture and objects are designed with the intent to be more than simply miniaturized adult versions, designers encourage a deeper engagement between a child and their environment. Through thoughtful interactions, as well as by rich visual and sensory explorations into the built environment around them, children are more likely to turn into forward-thinking, creative adolescents (and – all too quickly – adults). Seeing, feeling and interacting with different materials and varying types of functional design prompts children to begin thinking about and discussing how things are made, by whom, and why – leading to a dynamic learning environment and a child's independent discovery of the designed products around them.

The mid-twentieth century saw a proliferation of designers really begin to consider children's products as a valuable market, and also start to analyze their users' needs in a more focused and rigorous way. Following World War II, the child's place within the new modern city became an important consideration as part of the reconstruction efforts both in Europe and beyond. Being able to work on a small scale and for a young audience gave these designers (many of whom are now considered iconic) the space to experiment without fear of wasting expensive materials, or of criticism.

However, public interest in pieces designed exclusively for children had already begun several decades earlier. As early as 1900, designers created innovative toys and furniture, experimenting with avant-garde interpretations of contemporary trends. Play objects and toys incorporated new forms to engage mini-users in ways that had not previously been explored. As Modernism took root, designers such as Gerrit Rietveld (1888–1964), Jacobus Verzuu (aka Ko Verzuu, 1901–71), Jean Prouvé (1901–84) and others were working professionally to design simple and practical school environments, while also creating one-off pieces for family and friends. Materials such as tubular steel, washable paint, bent wood and plywood were all utilized for their hygienic properties, lightness and ease of care, while also fostering imagination through their capacity to create new and open forms. During this time, many now-seminal pieces were brought to life, from Rietveld's De Stijl-inspired Child's Wheelbarrow of 1923 (148) to Prouvé's perfectly engineered, enamelled-steel School Desk from 1946 (172). Modernist designers had chosen to follow one simple theory: items in a room should be functional and inspirational, not purely decorative. Children's furniture must serve specific purposes related to certain activities, such as play (in all its various forms), mobility, learning, sleeping and interacting with peers. Thoughtful design should also address children's age-appropriate needs and consider how these might change over time; for example, levels of stimulation and interactivity, but also security and hygiene.

One notable piece of mid-century children's design is the Schaukelwagen (438), an ingenious, multifunctional play piece by Hans Brockhage (1925–2009) and Erwin Andrä (1921–), which was manufactured by Gottfried Lenz in Germany in 1950. This interactive piece functions as both a pedal car and, when flipped over, an unconventional rocking chair, being innovative in both its design and its versatility. The form and features of the Schaukelwagen are wholly unique: a technical triumph for any period, let alone the 1950s. First, a child must figure out how to use the toy. Then they might ask themselves, 'Should I get in?' Next, they notice the wheels – therefore it must move! Once inside, they quickly realize that their feet can push and 'pedal' to make the wagon move. Finally, after a little more experimentation, they discover that it can be turned over and a completely new function appears – the car is now a rocking chair.

Rietveld similarly reinvented traditional structures by creating forms that were almost entirely new, yet still based in the familiar. Now widely admired for its prominence within the Dutch artistic movement De Stijl, the Rietveld joint – an overlapping joint of three battens in the three orthogonal directions – features a revealed straight architectural edge, a typically dovetailed seam. The acclaimed Rietveld High Chair (270) showcased this joint, making it the focal point of the design. In deconstructing each element of a typical high chair, before reassembling them into something visually and structurally different, Rietveld's High Chair was not merely a childhood necessity: while still successfully serving its original intended function, it also proved extremely innovative in its form and construction. This inspired approach can also be seen in Rietveld's Child's Wheelbarrow, which was only manufactured in larger numbers in 1958 as a result of the post-war economic boom, once factories were no longer solely focused on the war effort but were able to use new technology in the production of commercial objects instead.

During this period, designers and architects were suddenly able to take advantage of the phenomenal opportunities afforded by mass manufacturing.

Twentieth-century masters such as Alvar Aalto (1898–1976), Charles (1907–78) and Ray Eames (1912–88), Isamu Noguchi (1904–88) and Verner Panton (1926–98) seized the opportunity to create child-sized versions of their iconic furniture designs, and also introduced rockers, play tables and miniature desks into their repertoires. The Finnish designer and architect Aalto was recognized as one of the most influential architects of Nordic Modernism and had a very strong impact on design for children. His N65 Children's Chair (432) was created in 1935, and featured curved legs of bent-birch veneer with no sharp edges, perfect for any nursery or child's room. Charles and Ray Eames's impact on modern design, meanwhile, was rooted in play. They believed that toys were the forerunners to great ideas, and their work stimulated creative and imaginative responses in both adults and children. Even the simplest of their designs, such as the Child's Chair of c. 1944 (429), which was an inexpensive, lightweight plywood chair and designed to enable a child to move autonomously, acknowledged innocence and sentiment with a cut-out heart shape in the back.

For many reasons, materiality carries special importance in design for children. From the 1920s through to the 1940s, wood forms predominated. Formal experimentation and the simplicity of materials and production were emphasized, most frequently seen in the choices of paint and lacquer, or in the additions of leather or textile seating. In the 1960s and 1970s, plastic became the material of choice, with iconic designers creating collections in moulded plastics, such as polyurethane, that represented a radical design departure both practically and stylistically. Just a decade before, in the 1950s, this same material had still been thought of as quite unconventional for domestic furniture.

In 1963, the pioneer of plastic, Kartell, founded its Habitat division for furniture design. A year later, Marco Zanuso (1916–2001) and Richard Sapper (1932–2015) produced the K 1340 children's chair (14), the world's first to be made from a single piece of injection-moulded plastic, and the winner of the Compasso d'Oro in 1964. It was constructed from high-density polyethylene, an inexpensive semi-rigid plastic, and produced in a variety of bright playful colours. To encourage creative play, the legs of the K 1340 could be removed from the slatted back and the parts rearranged like building blocks. In 1967, Marc Berthier (1935–) led a small revolution in the field of design, creating the first complete series of affordable plastic furniture, the famous Ozoo collection. The all-in-one Ozoo 700 Desk (419), developed for Roche Bobois, was constructed from a single sheet of glass-reinforced polyester. Also introduced at the end of the 1960s was powder-coated tubular steel in bright colours. Hard-wearing and tougher than conventional paint, the finish was better suited to the active play environments of children. This rough-and-tumble coated steel is still popular for these qualities today, appearing frequently in pieces for children. The Roche Bobois Twenty Tube Desk (422) of 1972 by Berthier and the Lazy Basketball Chair of 2013 (286) by Emanuele Magini (1977–) for Campeggi are just two examples of the innovative application of this material in designs for children. With an imaginative form, and playful yet functional use, both pieces show a clear movement towards structured play in home design, and an attempt to bring both humour and narrative-based design to a child's environment. In another contemporary reinterpretation of the material, Rogier Martens (1978–) used a steel-rod frame coated in polyester powder to develop the Trotter for Magis (02) in 2015. This much-desired, wheelbarrow-inspired children's chair debuted to great acclaim.

The contemporary market for children has never been as strong as it is today. There is a heightened interest in using new materials in innovative ways. Who better to experiment for than the discerning child, the mini-client who feels the benefit of play and fun in their daily lives and likewise in their furnishings? Many high-level designers who have been successful in the global market are now turning their attention to design for children. As some begin to start families of their own, the refocusing of attention on children's needs is inevitable, and perpetuates the core cycle of this area of design. There is freedom, excitement and experimentation in this market, and it breathes life into an often limited industry.

On the side of the consumer, as more young families are coming to value design and reject big-name brands, we inevitably see more creativity in the drive for sustainability – not only in terms of recycleability but also in the desire to create products that will endure and evolve with the family, and retain their usefulness beyond the early childhood years. The Caravan Crib (88), by Los Angeles-based Kalon Studios, was designed with precisely this evolution mind. Featuring two mattress heights, and the ability to convert from a crib to a toddler's bed, then once more into a divan or a low, backless couch, the timeless elegance of this transforming set is retained (even enhanced) as it shifts from one function to the next – not an easy feat.

Treating children's furniture as disposable is passé. As we move towards the future, it is essential that we continually reassess the ethics and motivations of design and ensure that our spirit of experimentation and resourcefulness is not lost. Good design teaches us about the types of lives we want to lead and the legacy of objects we leave behind, not only for our children, but also for the generations that follow them.

Today, curators and designers with a focus on children's furniture and products are drawn to industrial and recycled materials, including concrete, foam, industrial rubber, waste paper, recycled paper, repurposed construction scraps, and new types of engineered fibres and mixes, which allow for innovative ways of designing and manufacturing. Progressive designers and studios, such as Maarten Baas (1979–), Doshi Levien, Kamkam, and Bobles are pushing the limits of material sourcing, creating highly conceptual pieces that draw inspiration from the most unlikely places. As with their predecessors, the innovative material choices and forms made by these designers function as their calling card, helping them to express their unique points of view, inspirations and motivations.

The most successful projects in contemporary design for children are more than merely chic, sophisticated and clever; they also make bold statements about the industry (through form and innovative materiality) and the world at large (through social commentary). As part of a design life contract, the designer Lucas Maassen (1975–) has employed his three sons, Thijme, Julian and Maris, to work for him in their own family 'furniture factory', in which he designs and produces the furniture that the children then paint (319). Due to Dutch child labour laws, the boys are only permitted to work for three hours each week, their signature slapdash painting aesthetic created out of a consideration for production speed. The first pieces in their collection were simple in construction, but large in conception and design; engaging a dialogue surrounding the boys' design education, manufacturing practices, creative control and more, reaching well beyond the pieces' basic functions.

A designer whose social commentary echoes Maassen's is Gaetano Pesce (1939–), an Italian innovator who is known for his fantastical work with resin (439) and whose designs call into question the nature, form, function and permanence of furniture itself. Pesci's depictions are some of the most imaginative and inspired pieces in the history of design for children, including his iconic UPJ Chair (440) for B&B Italia in 2014. While design for children is often unsuccessful when it is simply a scaled-down version of an adult product, the UPJ's playful character is instead enhanced by its diminutive size. Pesce's feminist critique about women's roles in society, made with the original adult version of his so-called 'ball-and-chain' chair, becomes distinctly playful, and even a bit cheeky, when shrunk down to the child's version.

As a mother, designer, curator and gallerist, I have worked to engage the design community in learning about the incredible, and largely overlooked, niche in the industry that is design for children. I have endeavoured to inspire the same dedication and reverence given to the furniture used by children as to that used by adults. There is clearly a universe of beautiful furniture and objects designed for adults: I want to make it my goal to motivate this same universe to be similarly filled with incredible design for children of all ages, too. As part of a community of designers, I hope to support the development of innovative collections of furniture and objects, which can be used throughout a child's primary education and well into maturity, each piece an heirloom, intended to be repurposed throughout the home over many years.

In the past five years, I have seen a major refocusing of attention towards, and interest in, handcrafted pieces, as opposed to objects that have been mass-produced; more and more people are now choosing quality over quantity, filling their homes with only the necessary items. I've made it my mission, in both my business and my life, to engage a level of superior craftsmanship in new productions, putting value on long-term use and sustainability. I hope to continue to encourage people and designers worldwide to increase the demand and interest for this necessary shift in how we live with children. Because, put simply, good design equals smart and happy kids.

Play

Ride

Learn

Eat

Create

Sit

Sleep

01 🪑 🛴

Puppy, 2005
Eero Aarnio (1932–)
Magis

Though now in his eighties, Eero Aarnio is still at work, creating objects that are as playful as ever. With Finnish design so often characterized by its use of wood, Aarnio has long employed plastic in order to distinguish his work from the traditional craft practices of his home country. The vivid colour, organic form and youthful spirit of Puppy are characteristic of his oeuvre, which stretches back to the 1960s. Well-known to design-savvy adults as a coveted sculptural piece with Pop-like flair, Puppy stands with one paw firmly in the art world and the other in the realm of functional design. Aarnio's abstract dog follows on from Pony, his boundary-pushing equine creation of 1973 (229). Originally produced in two sizes, and now available in four, Puppy can live happily either in the bedroom or back garden, serving as a conversation piece, a diminutive place to sit or a child's fellow adventurer.

02 🪑 🐻

Trotter, 2015
Rogier Martens (1978–)
Magis

Most chairs are designed for sitting still in, but Trotter is instead made for freewheeling fun. Its steel-rod frame fuses the distinctive angles of a wheelbarrow with the form of a seat, creating a chair that begs to be carted around. This offbeat item is the brainchild of Dutchman, Rogier Martens. Conceptually, it's the younger sibling of a wheeled wooden bench that Martens launched in 2009, although this children's version features a more playful application of colour and materials. Like other products in the Me Too children's collection by the Italian design company Magis, the Trotter is bright, robust and overflowing with buoyant charm. The wheels and handles are made of rotational-moulded polypropylene (one of the hallmark manufacturing processes of Magis), which is lightweight, durable and easy to clean. As its name indicates, Martens designed the Trotter in response to a child's natural desire to be active.

03 ✎

SumBlox, 2014
David Skaggs (1979–)
SumBlox

The idea for SumBlox came about as designer David Skaggs struggled to help a young student learn addition and subtraction. At the time, Skaggs was studying for a Master's degree in digital game development, yet he turned to a timeless, non-digital toy to find a solution – wooden blocks. For children, mathematics can seem abstract when numbers are just unfamiliar symbols. SumBlox are beech blocks in the shape of numbers, with the height of each number corresponding to its value. For example, when two blocks of the number five are stacked vertically, they reach the same height as the number ten, thus providing children with a tactile way to learn the value of each number through constructive free play. Skaggs started out carving each SumBlox set by hand in his father's garage but soon launched a successful Kickstarter campaign, with the support of the Saigling Elementary School in Plano, Texas, where he first volunteered as a tutor. This innovative learning aid is now widely available, encouraging children to explore mathematics through free play.

Monkey, 1951
Kay Bojesen (1886–1958)
Kay Bojesen Denmark

Kay Bojesen's wooden monkey is arguably the most famous member of the Danish designer's marvellous menagerie. Trained as a silversmith under Georg Jensen, Bojesen was among the first to embrace functionalism in Danish crafts. The birth of his son, Otto, in 1919, inspired Bojesen to create playthings reminiscent of those his own father had made for him in his childhood. These initial figures led him to explore in earnest his interest in working with wood. Maintaining that his designs should be round, soft and feel good in the hand, he sought to create animals that had both soul and a sense of humour. The horse, Bojesen's first animal, emerged in 1930, later followed by many others. Originally conceived as an amusing coat hook, Bojesen's monkey launched in 1951, exemplifying his belief that the lines of design should 'smile'. Able to hang from either his hands or feet, this charming simian quickly swung to design fame.

Roadster Saab, 2003
Ulf Hanses (1949–)
Playsam

Playsam's streamlined and sleek aesthetic is applied to a ride-on car with this dapper Roadster Saab. Crafted from wood and coated in a glossy black finish, the vehicle was designed by Ulf Hanses, the man behind many of Playsam's most noteworthy products, including the Streamliner (131). The Roadster is based on the Saab 92001, a historic prototype known as the Ursaab (original Saab). Designed by Sixten Sason in 1946, the prototype was the first of four created by Saab AB, a Swedish airplane manufacturer seeking to diversify its product line at the end of World War II. The Ursaab's jet-inspired styling set it apart from the competition and became the inspiration for the first commercially sold Saab, as well as for many future models. Although the Playsam version of the Ursaab lacks an interior, working lights or the rear-hinge doors of the original, its metal and wood steering wheel is true to Sason's prototype.

06 🛴

Rocker, 2010
Doshi Levien (est. 2000)
Richard Lampert

The inspiration for this hourglass-shaped rocker came from the designers' observation that children are often more interested in everyday objects that are not intended for play. Entirely non-figurative, Rocker leaves its identity up to the imagination of its young rider. Established in 2000, Doshi Levien is an internationally acclaimed design studio known for its collaborations with leading companies such as Moroso, B&B Italia, Nanimarquina and Cappellini. Its work combines the unique viewpoints and interests of its founding partners: Scottish-born Jonathan Levien's fascination for industrial processes and aesthetic is integrated with Indian designer Nipa Doshi's more craft-oriented approach. Although Levien spent his childhood in his parents' toy factory, Rocker marks the duo's first design for children – most likely inspired by their transition into parenthood. Conceived for the German brand Richard Lampert, Rocker has won several awards and was included in the collection of the Museum of Modern Art, New York, in 2012.

07

Wooden Dolls, 1963
Alexander Girard (1907–93)
Vitra

Based on figures that Alexander Girard originally carved from cedar wood and painted by hand for his own home in Santa Fe, New Mexico, these wooden dolls exhibit the affection for colour and pattern that would come to define his artistic sensibility. An architect, and interior, furniture and industrial designer, Girard is perhaps best known for the more than 300 textile and wallpaper designs that he produced as the director of design for Herman Miller between 1952–75. Together with his wife, Susan, he was also an avid collector of folk art, accumulating more than 100,000 treasures from South America, Asia and Eastern Europe. His penchant for strong motifs and jubilant hues, like those seen in these figures, infuses their Modernist aesthetic with warmth and playfulness. Reproduced today from originals in the collection of the Vitra Design Museum, these characterful wooden dolls feature undulating, hand-painted bodies and a range of immediately relatable expressions.

08 🛴

Brum Brum Balance Bike, 2009
Krišjānis Jermaks (1983–)
Brum Brum

The Brum Brum bike's dramatic cantilevered frame is more than just an aesthetic detail: it also acts as an in-built suspension system that makes for a smooth, all-terrain ride. The birch and oak bicycle is designed for children between the ages of two and six, and can be adjusted to three different heights with no tools required. The Brum Brum was conceived by Krišjānis Jermaks, a lawyer by profession, who assembled a team of friends to help him design and produce it. Inspired by the sound of their father's motorcycle, Jermaks's children came up with the name for the bike. Despite the Brum Brum's apparently simple design, it incorporated a number of safety features: a limited range of steering angles, wheels without spokes that fingers might otherwise get caught in and solid rubber tyres that remove the possibility of punctures, making Jermaks's creation as easy to use as it is on the eyes.

Child's Chair, 1957
Kristian Vedel (1923–2003)
Torben Ørskov
/ currently Architectmade

'My goal was to create a combination of a child's chair and a toy, which would appeal to children's imagination and their varying physical and psychological needs,'[1] explained Kristian Vedel. Among the first to take children's furniture seriously, Vedel rejected miniaturized adult designs in favour of objects that responded to the ways in which children develop, move and play. Influenced by Kaare Klint, the father of Danish furniture design, and the Bauhaus, Vedel became known for his creative use of materials, particularly plastic and wood. The Danish designer's first successful piece, Child's Chair, is as much a building toy as a piece of furniture. Composed of a slotted half-circle of bent-plywood and four loose, slide-in planar elements, the object invites children to configure its various pieces into a seat, shelf, small table or even a rocking toy. Originally produced by Torben Ørskov, and today reproduced by Architectmade, Child's Chair can be found in several museum collections, including that of the Cooper Hewitt, Smithsonian Design Museum, New York.

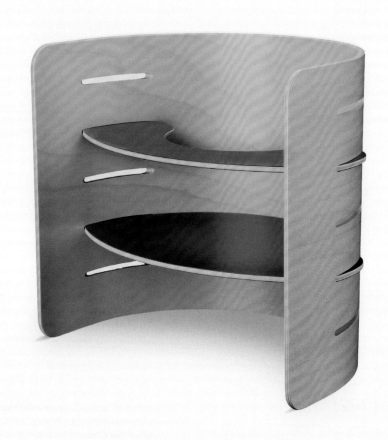

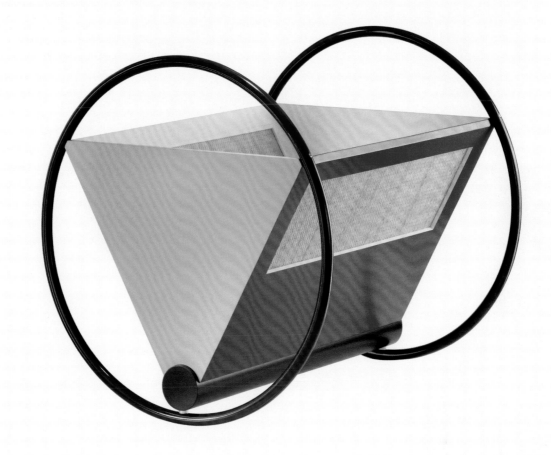

10 🌙

Bauhaus Cradle, 1922
Peter Keler (1898–1982)
Tecta

Conceived in 1922, when Peter Keler was just a twenty-four-year-old apprentice at the Bauhaus, this primary-coloured crib has come to symbolize the 'perfect' example of the school's aesthetic. Combining art with functional elements, such as wicker slats on either side for ventilation and a black dowel to weight the structure, Keler's cradle represents the beginning of a new Bauhaus style, which emphasizes a clear, simple order in which art is not seen as decorative but rather as an integral part of a unified whole. His use of the red square, blue circle and yellow triangle reflect the strong influence of his teacher, Wassily Kandinsky. Originally built for the Bauhaus's first exhibition in 1924, the cradle was never commercially produced. German company Tecta have since reissued the design as a rather more functional magazine holder.

11 🍴

Dombo, 2002
Richard Hutten (1967–)
Gispen

When the German television network RTL asked Dutch designer Richard Hutten to redesign the standard giveaway mug for its annual children's programme event, Hutten looked to his toddler son for inspiration. With a playfulness characteristic of Dutch design, Hutten created a mug that could not only be easily grasped by tiny hands, but would also comically exaggerate the act of drinking. The shape of the mug's two oversized handles – or 'ears' as they are called in Dutch – echoes the handle of his Zzzidt-object, a stool/table that the designer created for the Centraal Museum in Utrecht two years before. Originally named Domoor (Dutch for 'idiot' or 'dummy'), the jaunty mug was later renamed Dombo, playfully referencing the iconic, large-eared Disney elephant. 'For me, the best thing is that it makes people smile, and makes people happy when they see it,' Hutten says.[1] Made of injection-moulded plastic, Dombo is completely child-friendly, being unbreakable, dishwasher-safe and BPA-free.

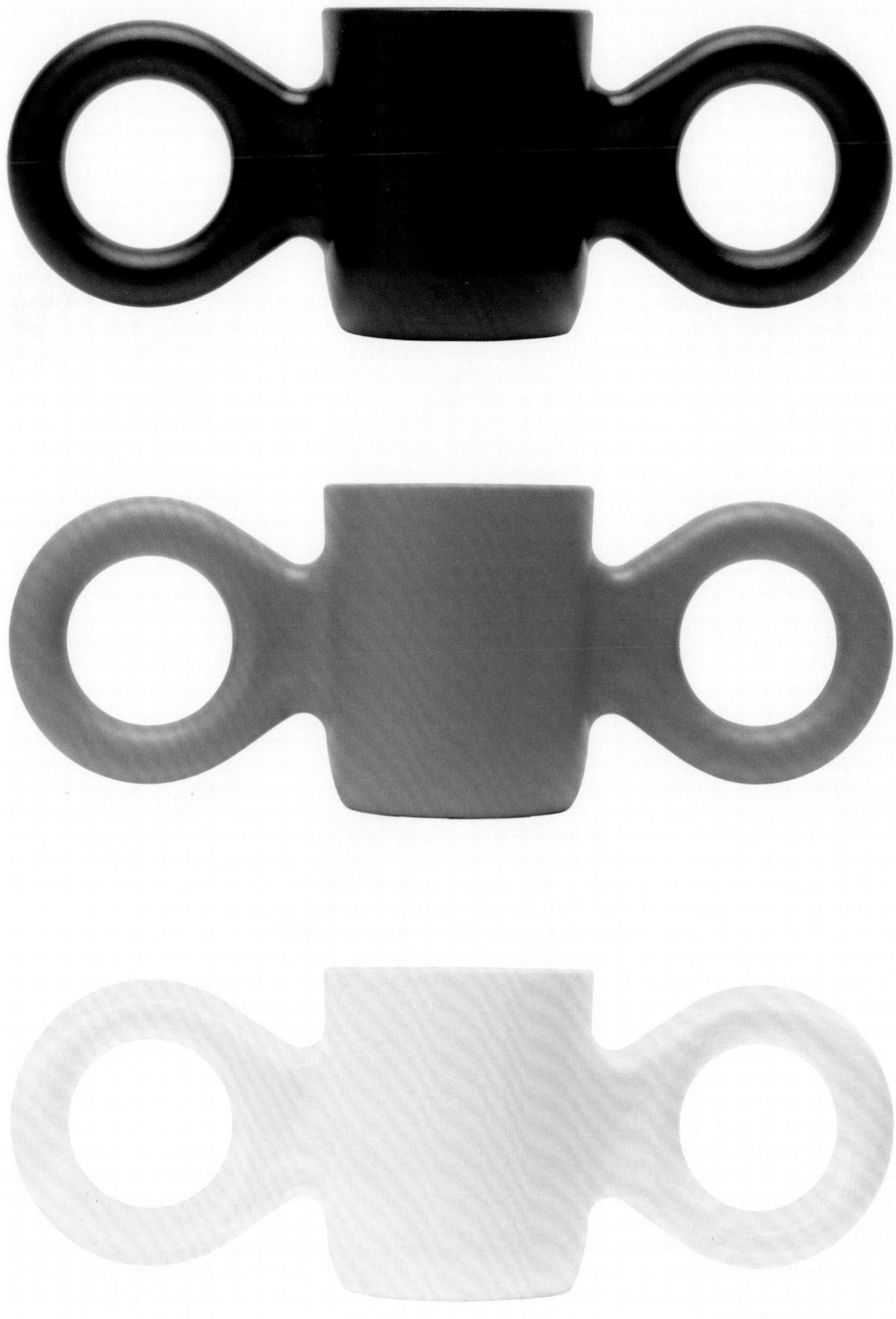

12 🪑 🍴

Children's High Chair, 1955
Nanna Ditzel (1923–2005)
and Jørgen Ditzel (1921–61)
Kolds Savværk / currently Kitani

After more than half a century, the elegant lines of this iconic high chair, by the acclaimed pioneer Nanna Ditzel, stand up against anything the contemporary design world has to offer. Ditzel trained as a cabinetmaker before going on to study furniture design at the School of Arts and Crafts (now the Danish Design School) in Copenhagen, where she met her future husband and collaborator, Jørgen. Nanna and Jørgen's partnership, in both business and life, was remarkably equal, with both parties contributing fully to their studio practice, as well as to housework and childcare. In 1955, the Ditzels introduced their High Chair with two primary designs: one version featured a wipeable vinyl seat and leather T-strap; the second model, which was geared to older toddlers, was made of solid wood with no T-strap. An adjustable footrest allowed the chair to adapt to the needs of a growing child. The Ditzel's golden-haired twin daughters appeared in the adverts for the High Chair, which received critical praise and remained popular in Danish households for many years after its release.

13 🛴

Eames Elephant, 1945/2007
Charles Eames (1907–78)
and Ray Eames (1912–88)
Vitra

Charles and Ray Eames's experiments in moulded plywood resulted not only in some of the most recognized Modernist furniture designs for adults and children, but also in the creation of a group of whimsical, sculptural animals that included bears, seals and frogs. This elephant was a particularly charming example, although it would take decades for it to reach showrooms. The Eameses produced two early prototypes of Elephant, giving one to their teenage daughter, Lucia. Unfortunately, due to a challenging fabrication process, the design was deemed not suitable for commercial production. In celebration of Charles Eames's 100th birthday, however, Vitra revived the character in 2007, producing it both in plywood and, later, in colourful moulded plastic. Eames Demetrios, the grandson of Charles and Ray, even produced a short stop-motion film of the Vitra elephant on an African safari. The perfect size for toddlers to ride, this creature's friendly eyes and pet-like proportions suggest that it doesn't need much taming.

14 ♯ 🐻

K 1340, 1964
Marco Zanuso (1916–2001)
and Richard Sapper (1932–2015)
Kartell

This jaunty children's chair, with its cylindrical legs and ribbed back, revolutionized chair design in 1964. Following four years of studies in technology and pedagogy, Marco Zanuso and Richard Sapper began their collaboration with Kartell, a firm founded by the chemical engineer Giulio Castelli in 1949. Together, they produced the first piece of furniture made entirely from injection-moulded plastic. Lightweight, stable and durable, the K 1340 was one of the earliest designs responsible for convincing people that plastic was an appropriate material for the modern home. Able to be stacked like large building blocks and available in yellow, red, blue and white, the chair was both playful and functional. It immediately won the Compasso d'Oro, awarded by the revered Milanese department store La Rinascente, and remained in production until 1979. The first of many successes for both Zanuso and Sapper, the designers would each go on to have remarkable careers, continuing to collaborate until 1977.

Miffy Lamp, 2011
Jannes Hak (1973–)
and Lennart Bosker (1974–)
Mr. Maria

Under the studio name Mr. Maria, the Dutch duo Jannes Hak and Lennart Bosker have used light to bring a beloved national icon to life, crafting a child-sized replica lamp of Miffy, the friendly white rabbit of storybook fame. Originally created in 1955 by the Dutch graphic artist Dick Bruna, Miffy went on to star in more than thirty children's books and two television series, earning herself a worldwide fan base. Uncomplicated and innocent, Miffy's character is echoed in her simplified, monochrome appearance, which varies little from one book to the next. Having always loved the character's clean lines, Hak and Lennart wanted to further enhance Miffy's peaceful presence into one of companionship and security; and the leap from bedtime story to night light seemed only logical. Their most recent version of the lamp – the Miffy First Light – won a Red Dot Design Award in 2018.

Suzy Snooze, 2016
Map (est. 2012) and Hirsch & Mann (est. 2010)
BleepBleeps

Baby monitors have come a long way since Isamu Noguchi's Radio Nurse of 1937 (389). Her sweet sleeping face and clementine colour give her a simple, child-friendly aesthetic, yet Suzy Snooze is far from asleep herself. Released in 2016 by the UK-based company, BleepBleeps, Suzy is fully integrated within the Internet of Things, providing an encrypted audio stream that enables parents to check on their sleeping children via the company's smartphone app. 'We saw this as a real opportunity to make something that was loved and useful and would grow with the child,'[1] BleepBleeps' founder Tom Evans recalls. In the dark, Suzy becomes a night light through a glowing, cool-to-the-touch LED. The unit also includes a soothing white-noise function when its 'cry sensor' is triggered, while a pop-up 'hat' encourages children to develop a regular wake-up routine. The project resulted from a hugely collaborative process, which included industrial design consultancy, Map; design and technology consultancy, Hirsch & Mann; sleep scientists, Sleepio; DJ, Erol Alkan; and app developers, We Are Hive.

17 🐼

Zoo, 2016
Ionna Vautrin (1979–)
Elements Optimal

These abstract yet endearing animals are the creation of French designer, Ionna Vautrin. Made in small and large sizes, the panda, toucan and whale are each intended to represent a natural element; earth, air and water. Describing her work as a marriage between 'poetry and industry', Vautrin seeks to create objects that are simultaneously functional and whimsical. At approximately 1 metre (3 feet) tall, the large version of Vautrin's animals encourage young children to relate to them as friends. Part plush toy, part pillow, the Zoo animals are produced by Elements Optimal out of foam and Hallingdal 65, Kvadrat's first and most successful textile, which is famous for its durability and rich colours. To celebrate its longevity and honour its pioneering creator, Nanna Ditzel, the fabric was recently restored to its original colour palette and featured in new designs, including Vautrin's Zoo collection, by a curated group of emerging designers from around the world.

18

Tsumiki, 2015
Kengo Kuma (1954–)
More Trees

While *tsumiki* (building blocks) are a familiar Japanese toy, this triangular version elevates the traditional concept to a new level. Notches cut into the tips of each lightweight cedar block allow them to be easily nested and stacked in a variety of ways, creating light, transparent structures that echo contemporary Japanese architecture. Designed by Kengo Kuma, the celebrated architect of the 2020 Tokyo Olympic Stadium, these building blocks were created in collaboration with fellow architect Shuhei Kamiya and More Trees, a forest conservation organization led by the renowned musician Ryuichi Sakamoto. The organization supports tree thinning, an eco-friendly deforestation technique, which clears weak, ageing trees from the forest to improve its overall health, allowing beautiful objects to be created from the wood that it produces. Elegant in design and purpose, Kuma's Tsumiki are sold in sets of seven, thirteen or twenty-two pieces.

19

Chalkboard Storage Cabinet, 2011
Peter Jakubik (1979–)
Prototype

Best known for addressing adult themes in his design, Peter Jakubik's clean-lined Chalkboard Storage Cabinet is surprisingly family friendly. Frequently found exploring fetishes, objectification and do-it-yourself aesthetics, the Slovakian designer is known both for his sense of irony and his provocative spirit. Entirely veneered in chalkboard, this simple, four-legged, square cabinet offers infinite decorative possibilities; users can draw directly onto its surface, changing it as often as they please. While the storage unit is certainly the most child-friendly of Jakubik's designs, which also include a BDSM Pony Girl Rocker that subverts the traditional rocking chair toy, it is consistent with Jakubik's work in its playful invitation. His light-hearted, open and mischievous approach to design is further illustrated in the Hobby Panton chair, which he made by roughly carving the shape of the famous chair into a tree trunk with a chainsaw.

 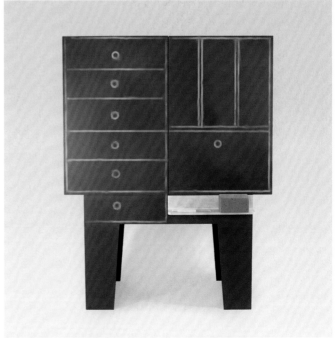

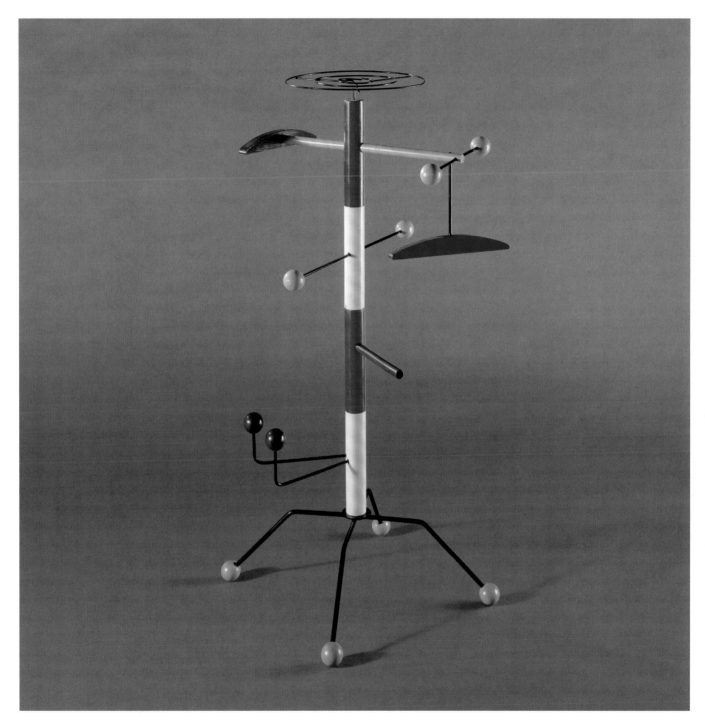

20 🖊️ 🌙

Bamboozler, c. 1953
Richard Neagle (1922–)
Manufacturer unknown

Referencing the scientific discoveries of the 1940s and 1950s, the Bamboozler clothing tree uses atomic and space-age shapes to 'bamboozle' children into thinking that the chore of hanging their clothes is fun. Its designer, Richard Neagle, sought to encourage self-discipline by creating a toy that could stimulate creativity and the imagination. Sold as a set of individual pieces, its coloured balls, cylinders and racks could be assembled in a variety of configurations, giving children agency over their environment. The design vocabulary of the Bamboozler recalls toys that emerged out of the Bauhaus in the 1920s for good reason. While at the Pratt Institute in New York, Neagle studied under Rowena Reed Kostellow, a Bauhaus member who emigrated to the United States during World War II. Neagle's creation also visibly reflects progressive shifts in attitude towards childhood, which was increasingly viewed as a stage of life during which learning could be synonymous with fun.

21

Pluï Rain Cloud, 2014
Alex Hochstrasser (1973–)
Moluk

'I think I'm lucky to have retained a sense of wonder and a fascination for the "magic" objects I had as a child,' says Alex Hochstrasser.[1] His award-winning bath toy, Pluï, demonstrates this, turning bath time into a fascinating science lesson about the water cycle. Named after the French word for rain, *pluie*, this little cloud fills with water when submerged. Children can then lift it out of the water, controlling the flow of the rain shower by covering a small hole at the top of the cloud with their finger. Phthalate-, latex- and BPA-free, the plastic toy has a hidden latching mechanism that enables easy cleaning. Hochstrasser launched the Zürich-based toy company Moluk with his sister Dora, a trained architect, in 2011. At a time when toys are becoming increasingly virtual, Moluk is committed to creating totally manual toys, which are sustainable, gender-neutral and encourage children to move and explore.

22 ☾

IO Bunk Pod, 2013
Mina Panic (1973–)
IO Kids Design

There is a touch of Stanley Kubrick's *2001: A Space Odyssey* in the award-winning IO Bunk Pod, created by Mina Panic for her company, IO Kids Design. Inspired by her daughter's love of astronomy, Panic chose to name the bed (and her studio) after one of Jupiter's 'unpredictable, surprising and ever-changing'[1] moons. This versatile design reflects that spirit: it can transform into two single beds, a combined bed and desk unit, or even separate bed and desk pieces. Its ability to evolve as a child grows makes it a sustainable piece of furniture that can adapt to the changing needs of the family. 'I think that designing for kids can be really challenging', Panic explains, 'because it's a lot about creating things which are playful, interactive, joyful and something that kids can grow up with.'[2] Drawing on the utility, clean lines and craftsmanship of Scandinavian design, IO Bunk Pod comprises a minimal number of parts, making it easy to assemble.

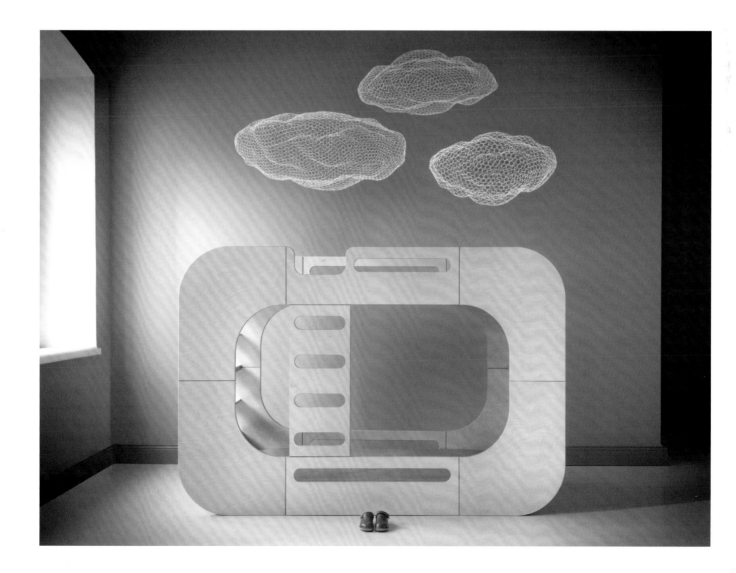

Labyrintspel, 1946
Sven Bergling (1913–97)
BRIO

Labyrintspel (Labyrinth) is a game of dexterity and visual problem-solving. Turning the side knobs, the player tilts the board to guide a steel marble from one end of the maze to the other. Along the way, the player must take care not to let the marble fall into the holes that line the route, while a cam-like mechanism on the interior of the board helps to keep it balanced. Labyrintspel is largely responsible for familiarizing a broad international market with BRIO, the iconic Swedish toy company. Designed in the early 1940s by Sven Bergling, the game was patented by BRIO in 1946, and has since become the most widely copied product in the company's line. Beyond its entertainment value, Labyrintspel was also used for therapeutic purposes in the rehabilitation of World War II pilots. This timeless game proved to be an immediate hit and remains a beloved toy to this day.

24

Rainbow, 1996
Heiko Hillig (1971–)
Naef

Colourful, sculptural and musical, Heiko Hillig's Rainbow is a multisensory triumph. Nine nesting arcs make up the design, each one consisting of layered maple wood, stained in a vibrant rainbow hue. The toy's name is, of course, based on the familiar image that the toy makes in its most basic configuration. Thanks to the shape of its wooden elements, each piece affords interesting opportunities for building and stacking; alternately, it can be connected end-to-end to create a spiralling track for a ball to run through. When turned over and struck with a small xylophone mallet, each arc produces an individual, melodic sound, instantly turning the toy into a makeshift musical instrument. Rainbow's creator, Heiko Hillig, became the chief designer at the celebrated wooden toy company Naef in 1997, a year after the toy's release. Made by hand in Switzerland, Rainbow is a testament to both simplicity and craftsmanship, as well as to the heirloom quality of Naef's product range.

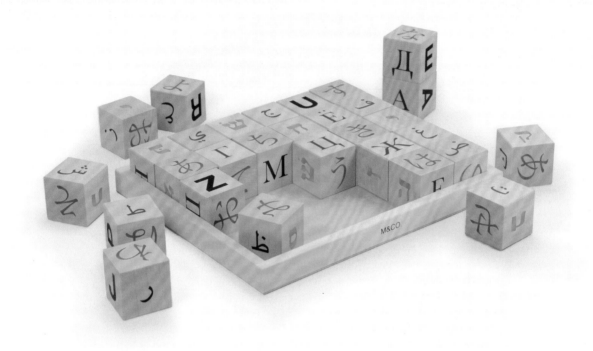

25 ✏️ ◢⬤

Global Alphabet Blocks, 1991
Tibor Kalman (1949–99)
M&Co / currently IC Design

Designed in 1991 by Tibor Kalman in collaboration with Scott Stowell, these thirty humanist blocks display five different alphabet scripts on their sides – Arabic, Cyrillic, Hebrew, Hiragana (Japanese) and Latin/Roman. An American graphic designer of Hungarian descent, Kalman's idealistic and innovative ideas about art and society influenced a generation of designers, before his untimely death at the age of fifty. Kalman, whose New York studio, M&Co, quickly rose to the top of its field, viewed himself more as a social activist than as a designer, strongly advocating that designers take greater responsibility for how their work influences culture. Perhaps best known for his role as editor-in-chief of *Colors*, the edgy, multicultural 'magazine for the MTV generation', published by the Italian clothing company Benetton, Kalman constantly sought to use his designs to promote causes like environmentalism and economic equality. By celebrating the notion of a shared human identity, these Global Alphabet Blocks elegantly embody Kalman's liberal spirit.

26 🛴

Skippy-Racer, c. 1933
John Rideout (1898–1951)
and Harold Van Doren (1895–1957)
American National Company

Streamlining – a style that featured aerodynamic silhouettes, gleaming materials and applied speed lines – was the epitome of modernity for American consumers in the 1930s. It even trickled into designs for children, like the fittingly named Skippy-Racer scooters and tricycles produced by the American National Company in Ohio. Designed (and patented) by John Rideout and Harold Van Doren, the scooter offered children the same promise of freedom and mobility implicit in streamlined products for adults. The style ushered in the profession of industrial design and Van Doren was profiled by *Fortune* magazine, alongside other seminal American figures in the burgeoning field, as an upstart of the new discipline in 1934. 'At his best, the designer is an animator, a builder of enthusiasm in others,'[1] he wrote in his book, *Industrial Design: A Practical Guide*, in 1940. With its red fenders, slim wheels and sleek handlebars, the Skippy-Racer sparked enthusiasm in many a young heart.

Clackers, c. 1969
Designer unknown
Various

Clackers (known by a myriad of onomatopoeic names, including Click Clacks, Clankers, Whackers and Ker-Bangers) swept the US and UK as a fad toy in the late 1960s and early 1970s. Simple in design, Clackers consist of two balls, each about 5 cm (2 in) in diameter, attached to a tab by a sturdy string. By holding the tab, the player can use an up-and-down motion to set the balls swinging back and forth, thereby making the loud clacking noise when they whack together that gives the toy its name. With practice, the balls can be made to bang against each other both above and below the hand. Clackers are similar in design to the *bolas*, a type of throwing weapon that the Argentinian gauchos use to capture running cattle by entangling their legs. In 2017, the toy was revived among schoolchildren in Egypt, where it was controversially dubbed 'Sisi's balls', after the Egyptian President, Abdel Fattah el-Sisi.

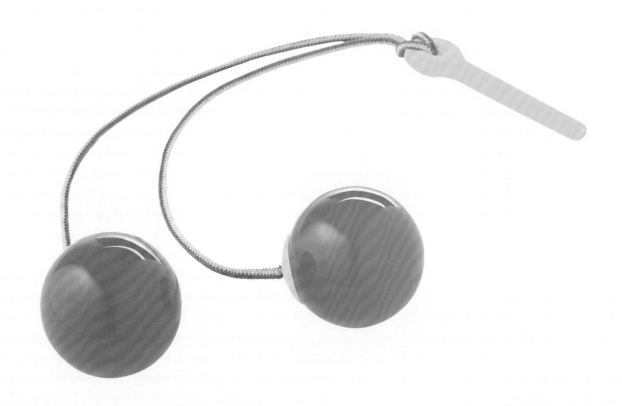

28

Dachshund, 1958
BRIO (est. 1884)
BRIO

BRIO's pull-along Dachshund rolled onto the scene in 1958, a banner year that would see the prolific Swedish company produce many of its most popular toys. When kids pull Dachsund's yellow lead, his red-wheeled legs propel him along, his head and ears pivot and his spring-mounted tail swings into action. One clever feature of this wooden dog's design is the slightly off-centre drilling of his hind legs, which produces a back-and-forth wobble in his gait. BRIO, an acronym for Bröderna Ivarsson Osby (Ivarsson brothers of Osby) began in the 1880s, establishing itself in 1908 as the premier wooden-toy company that we know today. The Dachshund was not BRIO's first hound toy. Before its debut, the company sold a number of dog-themed playthings in their line: Sampo, a push-up pup, is one that remains in production today. Still sporting his original design, Dachshund continues both to delight children and to encourage their early walking and coordination.

29 🛏 🐻

Peter's Table and Chair, 1944
Hans Wegner (1914–2007)
Carl Hansen & Søn

While seeking a christening gift for the son of furniture designer Børge Mogensen, Hans Wegner found quality furniture to be in short supply and so decided to take matters into his own hands. His resulting table-and-chair set is a fine example of knock-down design, as each item requires no tools for assembly and can be put together and taken apart with ease, like a life-sized puzzle. The absence of sharp edges makes the design safe for children, while its untreated finish, simple shapes and quality craftsmanship render it a timeless treasure that will remain beloved long after it is outgrown. Trained as both a carpenter and an architect, Wegner's name is synonymous with Danish Modernism. Over the course of his career, he designed more than 500 chairs, embracing a style known as Organic Functionalism. Among Wegner's most recognized pieces are the Wishbone Chair, the Shell Chair and the Round Chair, which turned Danish design into a cover story in the United States upon its release in 1949.

30

Lumping Rocking Horse, 2016
Alvin Tjitrowirjo (1983–)
AlvinT

Alvin Tjitrowirjo's work is deeply rooted in his Indonesian heritage. Having trained as an industrial and product designer in Melbourne and Madrid, Tjitrowirjo founded the Jakarta-based studio AlvinT in 2006. His furniture and product designs are locally crafted and built with regional materials, such as rattan, bamboo and teak. Tjitrowirjo aims to promote Indonesian values through contemporary interpretations of his cultural roots and its vernacular. The Lumping Rocking Horse, for example, was inspired by Kuda Lumping, a customary Javanese dance, in which performers re-enact a historical war against Dutch colonial forces with the help of bamboo horses. Made from rattan woven over an aluminium frame, Tjitrowirjo's interpretation maintains the spirit of movement, while also being lightweight and equally suitable for indoor or outdoor use. More than a play piece, Lumping is a celebration of indigenous customs, and is at once traditional and modern, simple and dynamic.

31 ▲▼ 🐻

Blockitecture, 2013
James Paulius (1990–)
Areaware

When James Paulius, then a student at the Rochester Institute of Technology, set out to create a toy for his university's annual Metaproject design challenge, he found inspiration in one of Brutalism's most far-out architectural designs, Moshe Safdie's Habitat 67. Built in Montreal for Expo 67, Safdie's creation comprised dozens of prefabricated modular units, piled into a seemingly higgledy-piggledy, constructed collage. For the Metaproject challenge, students were asked to produce a universal toy made from wood, with the winning design receiving its manufacturing and distribution through gift- and home-accessories brand Areaware. Paulius's winning entry consisted of a series of hexagonal, window-laden blocks called Blockitecture. The shapes of the blocks allow them to be assembled into interesting formations of sky-high verticals and cantilevered horizontals, defying the boundaries often imposed by more traditional cubic blocks. Since Areaware's release of Habitat, the initial Blockitecture set, Paulius has created add-on sets, including a Garden City line which incorporates balconies and greenery into the architecture.

32 ♯ ☾

Ami Bassinet Rocker, 2016
Chelsea J Park (1988–)
Nursery Works

While useful during a baby's earliest days, bassinets are generally only recommended for the first three to six months, or until a child is able to roll over or sit up. Such a short lifespan presents a design challenge to create furniture that can evolve after it has lost its initial value. Versatile and transformable, the Ami Bassinet Rocker is one example of a design that responds to this rapid obsolescence. Its modular structure means that the crib and seat are interchangeable and when the child outgrows the crib, it can be replaced by cushions, converting the rocker into a two-seater. The powder-coated steel frame offers a clean contrast with the rocker's plush, rounded, wool cushions, giving it a thoroughly contemporary look and feel. Created by the Swiss-based Korean designer Chelsea J Park, and produced by Nursery Works, the Ami Bassinet Rocker, as its name suggests, is friendly to the needs of both child and parent, creating a clever, adjustable solution to a common nursery dilemma.

33 🪑 ✏️

Dice, 2014
Torafu Architects (est. 2004)
Tanseisha

This aptly named, playful piece can be rolled, dice-like, to rest on various sides, allowing it to function alternatively as a toddler's desk, a child's shelving unit or an adult stool. Tokyo-based designers Koichi Suzuno and Shinya Kamuro explain that they developed the multipurpose, cuboidal shape to be 'a companion evolving with us through life'.[1] Known as Torafu Architects, the multidisciplinary design duo work across the mediums of architecture, interiors, exhibitions and products, often repurposing found materials, and finding innovative ways to create and save space. With Dice, the desk orientation enables toddlers to sit without the need for a freestanding chair. Older children may use the object as a seat, with the added functionality of shelves to display their belongings in different arrangements. Bright rubber piping protects and accents the interlocking wooden panels as they are rolled from one position to the next.

Zoo Timers, 1965
George Nelson (1908–86)
Howard Miller Company / currently Vitra

George Nelson wore many hats throughout his career, from writer to architect and furniture designer, becoming one of the most influential thinkers in industrial design. In spite of having three children of his own, Nelson rarely designed for this age group. The Zoo Timers, a characterful group of animal-shaped wall clocks produced in 1965, is a happy exception. Each clock depicts a different brightly patterned animal, complete with playfully alliterative names such as Elihu the Elephant, Fernando the Fish, Talulah the Toucan and Omar the Owl. The clock's large, easy-to-read numbers and brightly coloured hands enable it to be more easily used by young audiences. Much of Nelson's best-known furniture was produced for Herman Miller, where he served as design director for many years. However, the Zoo Timers were originally produced by the Howard Miller Company, which was founded by Herman's son. Nelson's archive now belongs to Vitra, which continues to produce a selection of his charming timepieces.

35 ⬛▲▼ 🐻

Cuboro, 1986
Matthias Etter (1954–)
Cuboro

Part block set, part marble run, part puzzle, Cuboro is a building system that challenges children to develop spatial reasoning and three-dimensional problem-solving skills. Each block in the system has been carved with different channels, both on its surface and through its interior. It is up to the player to configure these pathways into a run that a marble can travel down, free from obstruction. Designed by Matthias Etter, a Swiss mechanic and special educational needs teacher, the 'sphere rail system' is also inclusive: partially sighted children are enabled to construct the set through the use of touch rather than by relying on visual observation. First conceived in the 1970s, the game was initially released under the name of Konstrito in 1985. Since its launch, the game has grown and multiplied, and can now be enhanced with a variety of supplementary sets. Although formally simple, Cuboro poses a serious creative and intellectual challenge for growing minds.

36 🌙

Caravan Divan Twin Bed, 2014
Johannes Pauwen (1976–)
and Michaele Simmering (1978–)
Kalon Studios

According to Michaele Simmering, co-founder of Kalon Studios, designing for children is no different from designing for adults. 'All the same tenets of good design apply,' she says.[1] Simmering founded Kalon Studios in 2007 with her husband, Johannes Pauwen, when they were expecting their first child and couldn't find any furniture that suited their design sensibilities and environmental ethics. Taking their name from the ancient Greek word for beauty (both aesthetic and moral), the studio manufactures each piece in New England, using sustainable woods, finishes and materials. This Caravan Divan Twin Bed embodies their belief that good products should be beautiful, practical, versatile and sustainable. Available in six finishes, the children's bed transforms into a handsome divan as a child grows up, providing a perch for daytime play or afternoon naps. Simmering and Pauwen base their company out of their home in Los Angeles, thoroughly testing each piece on their own family.

Mobi, 2016
Ale Giorgini (1976–) and
BrogliatoTraverso (est. 2014)
MyYour

By day, this sleeping whale poses as an endearing sculpture. By night, however, Mobi glows to reveal a hidden passenger sitting patiently in his belly: our famous long-nosed friend, Pinocchio. This timeless Italian classic has been given new life by three Venetians who, having long admired each other's work, decided to collaborate in 2016. Invited by designers Alberto Brogliato and Federico Traverso to sketch something that could be translated into three dimensions, illustrator Ale Giorgini took inspiration from his childhood memories of bedtime stories. Seeking to conceive of a children's night light that could itself tell a story, the three designers were drawn to the way in which the whale's simple form could recall an iconic tale. The success of the Mobi collaboration has since expanded into the Light Tales line of table lamps, which includes Mobi XL (a larger version of the whale), Tin (inspired by *The Wizard of Oz*) and Cat (which references *Alice in Wonderland*), among others.

38 ☾

The Budding Superhero, 2003
Stig Leander (1958–)
Leander

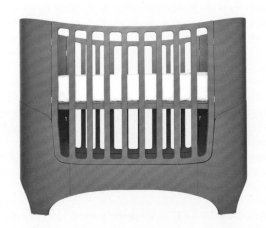

Danish designer Stig Leander was working as a blacksmith's apprentice when his sister-in-law became pregnant with twins. Thinking about the shared emotional journey of his new family members and their first-time parents, Leander became inspired to create quality furniture that could be positively associated with the first years of childhood and parenthood. Unlike cribs that only stay in the household until a baby outgrows them, Leander's cot is designed to become a staple of kids' rooms well into childhood. The moulded beech frame can be arranged in five different ways, each adapting to a new phase of development: when the child begins to stand, the bed lowers from baby position; when ready to crawl, the guardrails can be removed; when they are outgrown, the base and sides can be extended using an allen key and a few screws. And, after that, it can even be used as a sofa for a teenager's room.

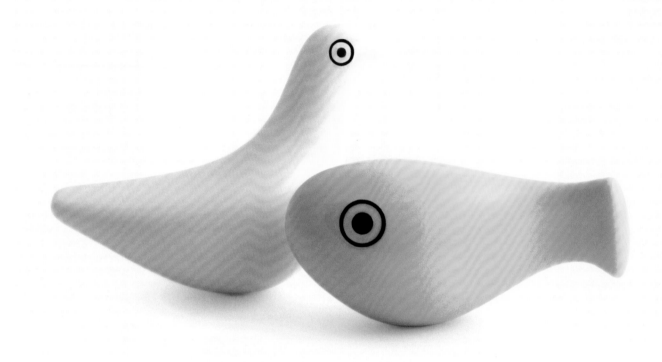

39

Bird and Fish Bath Toys, 1970
Patrick Rylands (1942–)
Trendon / currently Ambi Toys

World-renowned British toy designer Patrick Rylands produced the popular Bird and Fish Bath Toys in 1969, when he was just twenty-six-years old. Trained as a ceramicist at the Royal College of Art, London, Rylands combined his love of sculptural forms with an interest in plastics technology to produce toys that were sculptural, tactile and now iconic. 'The bird came first, based on Eskimo bone carvings in the British Museum,' he explained. 'I did some drawings, thought it would make a nice toy and whilst teaching at Hornsey College of Art, I made a prototype from plaster of Paris and decided he needed a friend, and so I designed a fish – simple as that.'¹ Internal ballast keeps the two friends bobbing upright in the water. Originally conceived as part of Rylands' line of products for Trendon, they were later reintroduced by Ambi Toys. The iconic duo is on permanent display at the Victoria and Albert Museum of Childhood, London.

Rocking Horse Rattle, 1970
Antonio Vitali (1909–2008)
Otto Maier Verlag

Antonio Vitali worked primarily in wood, yet this Rocking Horse Rattle illustrates how he also successfully adapted his simplified, sculptural forms to plastic. A streamlined interpretation of a toy type that dates back thousands of years, the rattle offers sensory stimulation for young infants, who learn to connect the sound of the toy with its movement. The central hollow of the rattle also responds to a young child's grip instinct and offers a surface for teething. In addition to the rocking horse, Vitali also designed rattles in the shape of a plastic duckling and a fish, each featuring the same distinctive curved form. The Swiss sculptor began designing toys when he became a father and was dissatisfied with the options then available on the market. He gained international fame in the 1950s for his collaborations with the renowned toy company, Creative Playthings.

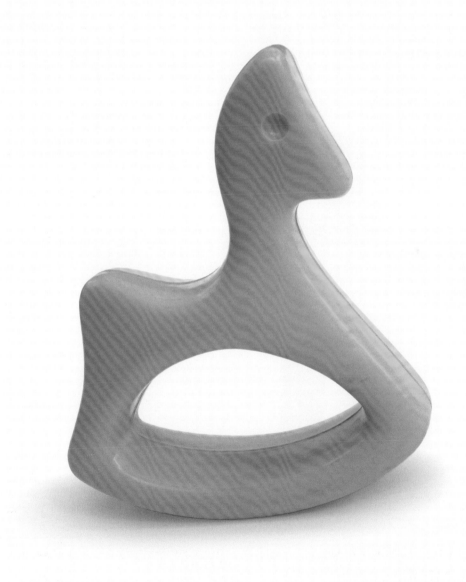

41

Balancing Blocks, 2011
Fort Standard (est. 2011)
Areaware

Born out of resourceful thinking and an entrepreneurial spirit, these jewel-like blocks emerged from the workshop of best friends, Gregory Buntain and Ian Collings. Under the moniker Fort Standard, the design duo set up shop in a temporary space in Brooklyn in 2011, with only modest supplies at hand. Using simple tools and scrap wood, they crafted their first sets of Balancing Blocks for a holiday pop-up. The public took to the faceted, salvaged-wood stacking forms with such fervour that the young studio could not keep up with demand. Sold by over seventy retailers within the first year, Fort Standard was thrilled when Areaware, a purveyor of home goods and toys created by emerging designers, offered to take over production of the blocks. Packaged in sets of ten and available both in a colourful palette and in monochrome white, Balancing Blocks enable young builders to stack horizontal and vertical elements as sturdily – or precariously – as they desire.

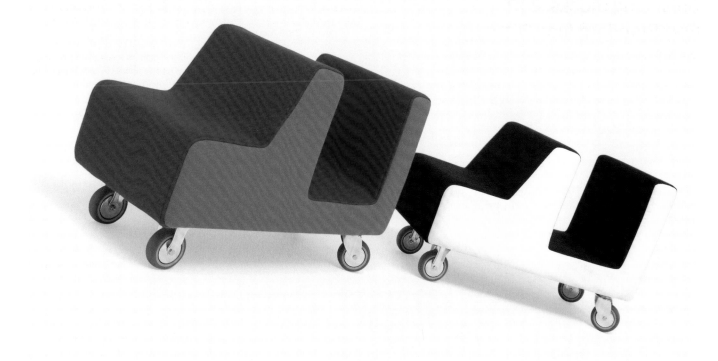

42

Pick-Up, 2002
Alfredo Häberli (1964–)
Offecct

It was a treasured childhood milestone that inspired Alfredo Häberli to design this chair, which doubles as a walking aid. The idea struck the Swiss–Argentinian designer as he watched his son take his first steps, observing that he needed to hold onto a stool to steady himself. Produced by the furniture company Offecct, Pick-Up is constructed from laminated plywood, with a cold-foam seat and back, upholstered in bold, monochrome fabrics. Häberli has described Pick-Up's function as evolving with the child as they age, allowing them to take their friends for a ride or later becoming a place to keep books. A special version of the chair was finished in blue and gold for Victoria, the Swedish Crown Princess, to match the decor of the Haga Palace in Stockholm. In addition to being favoured by royalty, Häberli has been the recipient of numerous awards, including the 2014 Swiss Grand Prix for Design.

43 🐻

Wombat, 2015
Alexander Lotersztain (1977–)
Les Basic

Since moving to Australia in the 1990s, the Argentinian-born designer Alexander Lotersztain has become one of the country's most successful designers. As head of the multidisciplinary studio Derlot, Lotersztain has collaborated with a wide range of international clients on everything from art direction to airport lounges. His most recent furniture brand, Les Basic (pronounced 'less basic'), aims to target a hyper-connected, hyper-mobile generation. Pared-down and multifunctional, each piece in the Les Basic collection has a touch of whimsy, like the Homework Sofa, which includes built-in power outlets for electronics and wooden surfaces that can be used as a table or desk. The range even includes a mascot in the form of a plush toy shaped like a wombat. Made from textile off-cuts generated from their upholstered products, this muscular, native marsupial is both cuddly and eco-conscious. With a percentage of every sale going to the RSPCA, Wombat is a friend to children, adults and wildlife alike.

Furia Rocking Horse, 2016
Front (est. 2003)
Gebrüder Thonet

The classic rocking horse gets a contemporary makeover with the Furia Rocking Horse for Gebrüder Thonet. Created by Front, the Swedish design duo comprising Anna Lindgren and Sofia Lagerkvist, Furia pushes the company's signature bentwood technique into new territory. The original Thonet brand pioneered the use of steam-bent wood in products like their loop-backed Chair No. 14 of 1859. During their collaboration, Front became fascinated with the company's nineteenth-century advertisements, which featured not only furniture but also more utilitarian items, such as walking canes and cradles. Using elements of Thonet's 1860s rocking chair as inspiration, Front sought to create a new design typology that was specific to children but elegant enough to become a family heirloom. The result was Furia, a thoroughly modern rocking horse with its seat and ears upholstered in leather, whose craftsmanship will stand the test of time.

45 ☾

Gradient Crib, 2013
Matthew Grayson (1982–)
and Eric Lin (1976–)
Nursery Works

The undulating waves of the Gradient Crib by Nursery Works make it as sculptural as it is functional. With no clear front or back, it boasts an ovular body composed of maple-wood slats, each one carved in a unique shape. Its designers, Matthew Grayson, who trained in computer science, fine art and product design, and Eric Lin, who spent a decade working in residential architecture, combined their skills to digitally sculpt a crib that is equal parts art, architecture and product. By attaching aluminium fasteners into small pockets underneath the top and bottom rails of the crib, Grayson and Lin were able to achieve a strong structure that seamlessly hides its hardware. The height of the bed platform in the crib can be raised and lowered, allowing it to transition from a bassinet to a toddler bed. Highlighting its aesthetic refinement, the Gradient Crib's advertising campaign was photographed in Pierre Koenig's iconic Modernist Stahl House.

46

Puppet Theatre, 2016
Robbrecht en Daem (est. 1975)
Valerie Objects

When Belgian architecture firm Robbrecht and Daem turned their attention to creating children's toys, they drew inspiration both from memories of their own childhoods and their professional backgrounds. Channelling the exaggerated roof angles of their famous Market Hall in Ghent (2012), Paul Robbrecht and Hilde Daem designed a puppet theatre that looks as if it would be at home in an Expressionist painting. Its wooden frame comes in a glossy red or black, and is accented with a variety of cut-out sections and shuttered windows to accommodate dynamic theatrical action. When not in use, the theatre can be folded flat for easy storage. Produced for the Belgian design label Valerie Objects, which works with designers, architects and artists to translate their signature works into tangible objects, the puppet theatre was first tested on Robbrecht's grandchildren before its official launch at the IMM Cologne Furniture Fair in 2016. Both audiences approved.

Iconic Rockers, 2016
Pia Weinberg (1985–)
and Woes Weinberg (1981–)
Maison Deux

The wooden rocker takes a unexpected turn with this quirky design from Maison Deux, an emergent Dutch brand founded by Pia and Woes Weinberg following the birth of their twin daughter and son. Turning the conventional equine form of the rocking horse on its head, the duo created a truly novel collection, including a pastel-tinted watermelon slice, a grey cumulus cloud (pictured) and a bowler hat, with echoes of the Surrealist painter, René Magritte. Each one is constructed from French oak, upholstered in a refined-wool textile from Kvadrat and topped with an easy-to-grip wooden handle. Offering children's products that blend comfortably with the aesthetics of the contemporary home, Maison Deux seeks to create items that parents will enjoy as much as their children. These rockers fit the brief perfectly.

48 🐻

I Tondotti Animals, 2006
Fabio Guaricci (1981–)
Milaniwood

Composed from merely a small range of simple, rounded forms, each of these wooden animals still perfectly exudes its own unique character and charm. Conceived by the Italian toy designer Fabio Guaricci, I Tondotti animals are produced by Milaniwood, an offshoot of Guaricci's family business, Tamil, which was established near Lake Como in 1924. Desiring to highlight wood's ability to make us feel connected to nature, Guaricci accentuated the material's natural beauty by leaving the final objects raw and unvarnished, so the colour of the toys deepens over time and through use. The collectible animals were among the first designs produced for the Milaniwood range, which was launched in 2008. In establishing the new brand, Tamil turned to young Italian designers to assist in the creation of contemporary toys using traditional wood-turning techniques. Each animal is handmade in Italy from sustainably sourced beech.

49 ☾

Timer Lamp, 2010
Industrial Facility (est. 2002)
Muji

As Muji's retained designers since 2001, Sam Hecht and Kim Colin have been the creative forces behind hundreds of the Japanese lifestyle brand's products – everything from toilet brushes to pocket notebooks. Co-founders of the British studio Industrial Facility, the pair's minimal designs can be characterized by a sleek integration of form and function: a hairdryer, for instance, features a translucent cavity for cable storage, with the plug doubling as the cavity's lid. The energy-efficient Timer Lamp is a product born of the same ingenuity and is designed to give children a better night's sleep. Made from a soft, unbreakable silicone, the lamp emits a warm, evenly distributed LED light for intervals of either thirty or sixty minutes, during which time its glow gradually dims. It can also be turned on or off manually, using an interface that is placed discreetly on its underside. As with all of Industrial Facility's work, the Timer Lamp's tactile quality was an important concern: its rounded shape, inspired by Japanese lanterns, is designed to feel natural in the palm of a hand.

Sedici Animali, 1957
Enzo Mari (1932–)
Danese Milano

The acclaimed artist and designer Enzo Mari features several times in this book, and for good reason. From toys to furniture, his sustained interest in the world of children led him to create a treasure chest of beautiful child-centric objects. Sedici Animali (Sixteen Animals) displays Mari's strong graphic sense, in which a single incision transforms a block of wood into sixteen interlocking animals, leaving virtually no unused space. Designed in 1957, Sedici Animali was Mari's first foray into toy design, however, it was not commercially produced until 1965, after being picked up by the Italian design company Danese Milano. As each piece required hand finishing, production numbers initally remained small. Danese later created versions of the puzzle in resin, allowing it to be manufactured more economically. Though the toy fell out of production in the 1970s, it was resurrected by Danese in 2003, who has fabricated a limited number in the design's original dimensions and material every year since.

51 ☾

Eco Cradle, 2003
Ruth Kenan (1970–)
Green Lullaby

Sustainability has emerged as a major theme of twenty-first-century design, impacting product life cycles, manufacturing processes and materials. Children are not exempt from this debate, with modern child-rearing being the number one contributor to our annual carbon footprint – ahead of meat eating, travelling by plane or driving a vehicle. The Eco Cradle, designed by Ruth Kenan, demonstrates that there are ways to minimize one's environmental impact as a parent. When allergies to dust and lacquer curtailed Kenan's dream of making a wooden cradle for her first child, she turned to a humbler material. Her flat-pack crib, which comes in both rocking and stationary versions, is constructed entirely from cardboard. Incredibly simple to both transport and assemble, the bassinet can be personalized by drawing on its surface and also easily recycled when outgrown. Since creating the Eco Cradle in 2002, Kenan has produced an entire line of children's furniture made from the same durable, earth-friendly material.

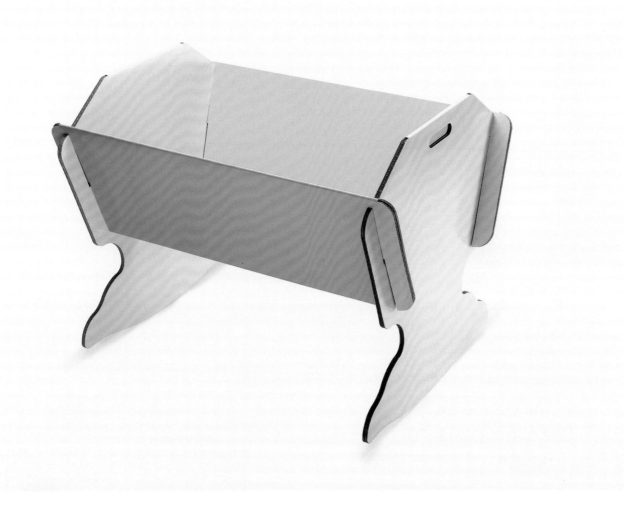

52 🪑

SE76 Children's Chair, 1953
Egon Eiermann (1904–70)
Wilde + Spieth

The clean lines and straightforward forms that are admired in Egon Eiermann's work as an architect also inflect his furniture designs. Some of these, such as the SE76 Children's Chair that he designed in 1953, are now considered classics thanks to both their enduring functionality and aesthetic restraint. Manufactured by the Dutch furniture company Wilde + Spieth, the chair was relaunched in the early 1960s as model SE18, which was available in two child-friendly sizes, the larger of which was foldable. Eiermann originally trained in Germany, but met influential figures, including Walter Gropius, Marcel Breuer and Ludwig Mies van der Rohe, during study tours to the United States, and his work reflects the influence of his fellow designers and architects. The original SE76 won a Good Design Award from the Museum of Modern Art, New York, in 1953 and a Silver Medal at the Milan Triennale in 1954.

53

Avlia Furniture Collection, 2016
Nataša Njegovanović (1987–)
Prototype

Created by the Croatian industrial designer Nataša Njegovanović, the Avlia collection turns functional children's furniture into toys. Playful design elements imbue each piece in the collection with the spirit of a domestic or farm animal: the desk hints at the shape of a cow, the stool resembles a dog, a pencil box suggests a chicken, a toy chest resembles a pig and a pushbike becomes a cat. With each design more suggestive than literal, Njegovanović injects a sophisticated sense of playfulness into otherwise ordinary objects, countering the dominant trend for character representation in toys and games. Conceived when Njegovanović was still an industrial design student at the University of Zagreb, the collection is fashioned from Slavonian oak, sourced from the Croatian village in which all of the pieces are created.

54 🪑

Sarenka Chair, 1943
Olgierd Szlekys (1908–80)
and Władysław Wincze (1905–92)
Ład Artists' Cooperative

Emerging from the milieu of the Warsaw School of Fine Arts, Olgierd Szlekys and Władysław Wincze were both members of the Polish artists' cooperative Ład, which is recognized for its distinctive modern style infused with touches of Polish folk art and traditional carpentry techniques. The pair, who formed their own company in the 1940s, designed these Sarenka (deer) chairs in 1943. They were produced in ash or burnt pine – a material that masked any flaws in the wood – and became a popular fixture in settings such as kindergartens and children's clinics. In 1945, following the occupation of Poland, Ład was revived as part of the nationwide rebuilding programme. Exported to the West during the 1960s and 1970s, and produced in the company's workshops until the 1980s, the Sarenka Chair today forms part of the Polish design collection at the National Museum in Warsaw.

55 ☾

Fox E, 2015
Pinar Yar Gövsa (1979–)
Lil'Gaea

Pinar Yar Gövsa, one of the designers behind the kids furniture brand Lil'Gaea, first established herself in the creation of its adult parent company, GAEAforms. It was following the birth of her daughter that Pinar and her husband, Tugrul Gövsa, were encouraged to turn their talents toward creating furniture for little ones, with an emphasis on the transitional nature of childhood. With this cute, versatile crib-to-bed, Gövsa has created a sleeping platform with design and safety features that can be adjusted according to the growing child's changing needs. As the crib converts to a toddler-ready bed, it retains a signature graphic element in the form of a fox, a teddy or a baby-blue bicycle – a decorative flourish that also serves as a mini sleeping rail to keep tots safely nestled in their beds. Fox E's quiet colours, emphasis on natural finishes and gender-neutral design offer an updated look to the nursery, while still retaining a child-friendly feel.

56 🪑 🛴

Hut-Hut, 2010
Johannes Pauwen (1976–)
and Michaele Simmering (1978–)
Kalon Studios

The Hut-Hut children's rocking stool, developed by the Los Angeles-based, eco-friendly furniture company Kalon Studios in 2010, demonstrates the power of a simple design solution. Despite the conspicuous lack of any of the typical representational visual cues – reins, a saddle, ears, a tail – this convex, dimensional toy clearly wants to be ridden. In fact, only the name of the design, Hut-Hut (the 'giddy-up' of the camel-riding world), makes any kind of animal reference. Its abstract form and thoughtful construction mean that Hut-Hut can be flipped, stood on its end and played with in whichever way a child desires. As children rock on its edge, they hone their balance and coordination. Kalon departed from their traditional use of wood in crafting the toy, opting instead to use a food-safe, sustainable resin. The sculptural body, which comes in a brilliant range of colours, adds an eye-catching design flourish to any nursery or playroom.

57 ⧖

Sono Kid, 2010
Dieter Paul (1964–)
Design Möbel Paul

This bright and squishy Sono Kid offers both a comfortable seat for relaxing on and a piece of versatile play furniture for boisterous fun. For children who are prone to wriggle about while seated, the chair's adaptable cushion flexes to fit the body, making for an ergonomic seat no matter what the position. Made from polyurethane foam, its lack of sharp edges means that the chair can safely accommodate all kinds of play, is easy to wipe clean and is lightweight enough for children to move it around the house themselves. Sono Kid was designed by Dieter Paul, who established his own studio in 1998 after studying architecture at the Graz University of Technology in Austria. Specializing in furniture design, Paul continues to work in Graz and his designs have been included in exhibitions at the Museum of Applied Arts in Vienna.

58 🐻

Slide, 1967
Günter Beltzig (1941–)
Brüder Beltzig

Trained as an industrial designer, Günter Beltzig began his career in 1966, designing refrigerators and vacuum cleaners for Siemens AG in Munich. However, he soon turned to the design of playground equipment, with the 1960s spirit of wanting to change the world. His first collection of moulded-fibreglass furniture included the Juniör children's table and chairs (376), as well as a sculptural seesaw and this organically shaped slide. Beltzig spent the next ten years designing plastic furniture pieces that can now be found in museum collections such as New York's Museum of Modern Art. Since 1977, Beltzig has devoted his career to playgrounds, in which he is a world-renowned expert, having designed several thousand of them across the globe. His designs are notable for abandoning the standard elements in favour of more complex climbing landscapes that feature natural components.

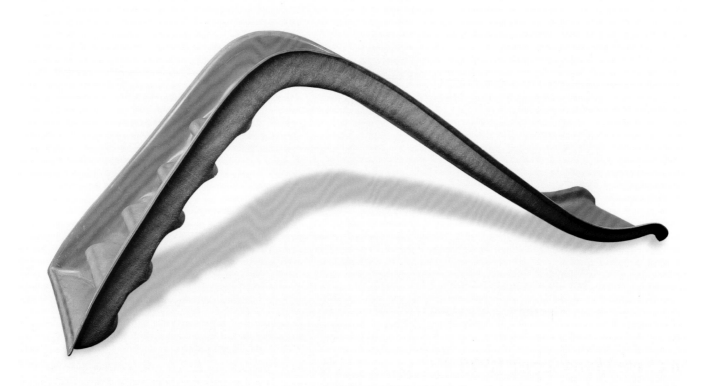

59 🛴 🐻

Plust Van, 2016
Michele Menescardi (1979–)
Plust

Italian brand Plust is known for its bold and playful designs, often characterized by their rounded forms: a standing coat hanger and a planter imitate
cacti; a sofa takes the shape of a soft, indented bubble gum; a lacquered
chair resembles a splash of paint. The company's Plust Junior collection
of toys and what they call 'imaginative items' exhibits the same tongue-in-
cheek attitude. Among the objects, which include a miniature gumball chair,
a crocodile-shaped rocking chair and a piggy bank with no coin slot, is the
Plust Van, created by the award-winning Italian industrial designer Michele
Menescardi of MrSmith Studio. The Van, made of rotational-moulded
polyethylene and wooden wheels, is a durable storage container that doubles
as a play item, carrying both children and their toys. Like its fellow Plust
Junior products, it features only smooth edges and comes in an assortment
of seven vibrant colours.

60

Little Characters
Yen Jui-Lin (1972–)
Self-produced

These delightful 'Little Characters' are masterfully carved from a variety of woods by Taiwanese artist, Yen Jui-Lin. Bursting with life, each of the figures is born of a collaboration between Jui-Lin and his two children. They begin by sharing and sketching their ideas, drawing inspiration from everyday things like onions, clouds and birds, before he brings them to life by carving each one by hand. While many become pocket-sized companions, others are made to function as wall hooks or vases. The figures are varnished and stained to highlight the natural beauty of each timber's grain, and some of the characters – like the Siamese twins – emerge from the particular qualities of a specific piece of wood. Each creation is unique, with many crafted as gifts for Jui-Lin's children. When not busy populating his universe of lively personalities, Jui-Lin also teaches illustration and carving to children.

61 ⊟ ☾

Babysitter, 1961
Björn Jakobson (1934–)
BabyBjörn

After visiting the United States in 1961, Björn Jakobson returned to his native Sweden with a 'babysitter' bouncer chair in hand. Jakobson's resolve to bring the product to the Swedish market remained undeterred in spite of repeated refusals from major department stores. Ingeniously, Jakobson appealed to paediatricians to improve and endorse the product. His wife, Lillemor, a textile designer, handled the aesthetics and their children served as product testers. The resulting chair, with its clean design and progressive medical endorsement, proved a winning formula. The Babysitter would pave the way for the 1973 Hjartenara (Close to the Heart) baby carrier, later known as the BabyBjörn, another design that was paediatrician-approved, tapping into research that suggested that parental contact fosters a closer parent–child bond. With over 25 million baby carriers sold worldwide, BabyBjörn went on to become the twentieth century's most iconic carrier, spawning an entire industry of slings and backpacks.

62 ⛩

Series E Classroom Chair, 1971
Robin Day (1915–2010)
Hille

Designed by Robin Day in 1963, the Polypropylene Chair has become so iconic that it once featured in a series of 'British Design Classics' stamps. Still in production today, it is currently the world's best-selling school chair, with nearly of 50 million units sold to date (according to the chair's manufacturer, Hille). Charged with designing a low-cost, mass-produced, stacking chair that would meet virtually every seating requirement and be affordable to all, Day conceived the Polyprop, an injection-moulded design intended to make use of the then-new material polypropylene. The thermoplastic proved ideally suited for the task, as it was cheaper, lighter and more durable than plywood, or any form of plastic then available on the market. Attentive to every technical and ergonomic detail, Day's chair was both visually sophisticated and structurally ingenious, making it a landmark of modern furniture design. Its success led the designer to release several variations, including the tots-to-teens Series E school chairs of 1971 (seen here), which came in five sizes and had a lifting hole in the back.

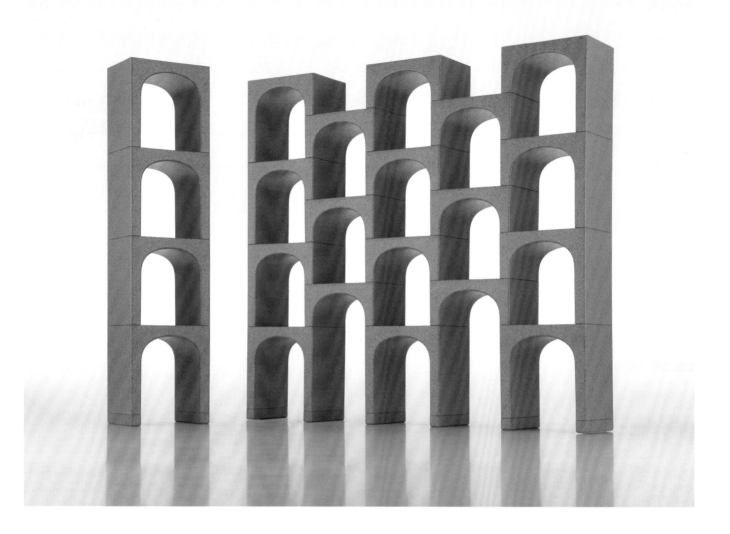

63 ✎

Eur, 2013
Giulio Iacchetti (1966–)
Magis

Giulio Iacchetti designed this modular shelving system in homage to the Palazzo della Civiltà Italiana, Rome's New Classical icon, which was built in the city's Esposizione Universale Roma (EUR) quarter in 1942. Understanding a child's desire to assemble things, he sought to create an object that would invite interaction. Comprising four types of interlocking pieces, Eur's flat-topped arches allow children to build upwards or outwards in whatever configuration they like, using the oversized building set to form shelving or benches. The resulting construction exhibits Iacchetti's fondness for recurring pattern and careful attention to the typologies of Italian art and architecture. In 2001, he was awarded the prestigious Compasso d'Oro award for industrial design and was the subject of a solo exhibition at the Triennale Design Museum, Milan, in 2009.

Flying Dutchman
Sailing Ship Kite, 2013
Emily Fisher (1979–)
Haptic Lab

As its name suggests, Haptic Lab creates objects with a wonderful tactility. Founded by Emily Fischer in 2009, the Brooklyn-based studio began making quilted maps that playfully explored the sense of touch, motivated by Fischer's mother's deteriorating sight. When an impromptu kite-making competition led to a high-profile commission for fashion brand Opening Ceremony, Haptic Lab launched itself into a new product line. 'I'm an architect by trade, and kite-making has always been a hobby of mine,' Fischer explains. 'I wanted to make kites that last longer than an afternoon [...] and become cherished objects.'[1] Fischer immersed herself in kite history and traditions, even travelling to Asia to learn from kite artisans. Each of Haptic Lab's kites, whether simple or complex, reflect her passion and knowledge of these timeless toys. The Flying Dutchman – a sailing ship outfitted with rigs, ropes and flags – is based on a design from Bali, where such kites have graced the skies for generations.

65

Rocking Beauty, c. 1965
Gloria Caranica (1931–)
Creative Playthings

Long recognized as a classic of modern design, this shapely plywood rocker was created by Gloria Caranica, a graduate of the Pratt Institute in New York. Rocking Beauty was one of Caranica's first projects for the renowned toy company, Creative Playthings, which was founded in 1945 by two former teachers. Creative Playthings sought to provide simple and beautifully designed toys to promote a child's creativity and imagination, frequently collaborating with artists and designers to promote unpainted abstract forms that emphasized shape, colour and texture. Caranica designed for children throughout her career and although she went on to increasingly work in plastic, this rocker showcases her long-held passion for woodworking. In 2006, the modern furniture purveyor Design Within Reach hired the Industrial Woodworking Corporation to reproduce Caranica's design under the name Red Ball Rocker, which featured as part of their Knú furniture collection in 2009. Sadly, the rocker has since been discontinued.

66   🛴

Hippo Rocker, 1993
Wolfgang Rebentisch (1948–)
Stokke

The little-known Wolfgang Rebentisch of Hamburg is probably most recognized for his Hippo Rocker, designed in 1993 for the Norwegian children's furniture and toy giant, Stokke. The simple design comprises just three bendable, thermo-formed plywood panels, nested to one another through two sockets, with a cylindrical red handle attached at one end. The Hippo's elementary shape comes in two sizes and in a natural beech or yellow–blue–green version, its geometric abstraction and pared-down union of form and function evoking the Dutch De Stijl movement of the early twentieth century. Initially distributed by Stokke, then later by Ergo and Timkid of Germany, the Hippo Rocker was celebrated for its sculptural simplicity and picked up several awards, including a Best in Show at the 1993 Furniture Expo in Nuremberg (which today hosts an international toy fair).

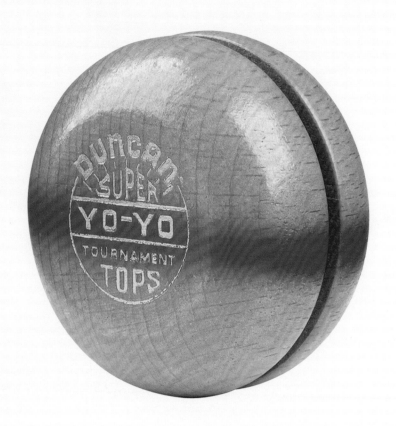

67

Yo-Yo, 1928
Pedro Flores (1896–1963)
Duncan

While our modern concept of the yo-yo dates from the 1920s, the toy itself is the second oldest in the world, predated only by the doll. Almost as old as the wheel itself, the yo-yo dates back more than 2,500 years. While it is believed to have originated in China, the first historical mention of the toy came from ancient Greece. This timeless toy has spun its simple magic around the world for centuries under a variety of names, such as the *ban-dalore, emigrette* and *joujou de Normandie*. The name *yo-yo* ('come-come' in Filipino) first gained recognition in the 1920s, when Pedro Flores brought the popular Filipino version of the toy to the United States, starting the Yo-Yo Manufacturing Company in California, in 1928. Following the success of the product, the entrepreneur Donald F Duncan released a redesigned version and, in 1932, the yo-yo became a registered trademark. Duncan yo-yos are still in production today.

Rip + Tatter Chair, 2009
Pete Oyler (1983–)
Self-produced

Riffing off the traditional club chair, Rip + Tatter celebrates the lived-in look. 'Designing for children offers a unique opportunity to embrace a wondrous and whimsical spirit, and to invoke a sense of playful curiosity,'[1] Pete Oyler explains. While exploring cardboard furniture for his graduate thesis at the Rhode Island School of Design, Oyler made a children's chair for a friend. Little did he know at the time, but it would become his breakthrough piece. Conceived for children aged two to five, the Rip + Tatter Chair is delightfully tactile and light enough for a toddler to move. Inspired by the ephemeral and imaginative nature of childhood, the industrial cardboard chair acknowledges that children's objects don't always need to be handled with care. As its name suggests, the patina of use is an essential part of this chair's design. Even more conveniently, Rip + Tatter can be put directly in the recycling bin when outgrown.

69 ◨▿◖ ✎

Kuum, 2016
Marie Uno (1984–)
Felissimo

The award-winning Kuum block set, by Portland-based creative agency Monogoto, exemplifies the company's desire to 'make logic into beauty'.[1] Its designer, Marie Uno, drew on her background in applied physics to create the 202-piece puzzle, inspired by the natural elements of her native Japan: soil, fire, flower, trees, mountains, sea, ice, stone, earth, moon, sun and sand. In Kuum, derived from *ku-mu*, the Japanese word meaning 'interlock', each element in the collection gets its own distinct unit, comprised of thirty six beech shapes, painted in multiple shades of one colour. Uno's block set aims to foster four creative skill-sets within a child: building, puzzle-solving, storytelling and art-making. Akin to poetry for the playroom, Uno sees each unique piece embodying a small fragment of nature, and likens Kuum to a haiku that channels the environment into a finite formula, in which each block interacts with the next in a pre-established harmony.

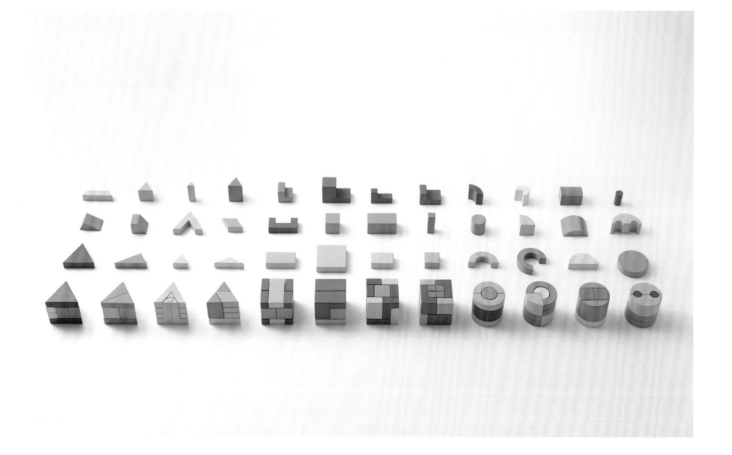

70 🪑

Elephant Chair and Table, 2016
Mark Venot (1979–)
Elements Optimal

Award-winning French designer Mark Venot didn't initially have an elephant in mind when he drew sketches for this children's chair and table set. However, when his three young children immediately spotted a gentle giant in the paper prototype that he'd made, he knew he was on to something good. 'The elephant is one of the most famous figures of the animal world for children, and it's like a dream for them to sit on an elephant head,' he explains.[1] Each chair in the natural beech set resembles a stylized elephant's head, with a trunk and tusks making up the legs, and the table completing its body. Add more chairs around the table and it becomes 'like an elephant family', Venot continues.[2] The playfulness of the chairs will excite children, while its stripped-down design will satisfy their minimalist parents, who may even detect its reference to the Eameses' iconic plywood elephant (13) from 1945.

71 🛴

Spherovelo, 2013
Andy Loveland (1971–)
Early Rider

Spurred on by his own three-year-old son, Andy Loveland founded the company Early Rider in 2006, to develop balance bicycles that help children learn to ride without the fear of falling off. The Spherovelo was added to the range to cater to the very youngest riders – children aged between seven months and two years old. Rather than wheels, the bike features two large spheres, which make balancing easier by allowing the bike to roll sideways instead of tipping over. For very young children, two small stabilizer wheels can be added to either side of the Spherovelo's middle section. The dip between the two spheres creates a seat with a low centre of gravity, which is only seven inches from the ground – further enhancing the bike's stability. The British-made design comes in four unisex colours, with a wipe-clean plastic shell, birch handlebars and polyurethane-covered wheels. Winner of the Red Dot Product Design Award in 2013, Spherovelo can be used both indoors and out.

Intreccio Sfera, 2015
Total Tool (est. 1999)
Play+

The soft and tactile Intreccio Sfera (Weave Sphere) was designed and produced as part of a project initiated by Play+, a company specializing in soft furnishings and environments for young children. Conceived by Milan-based studio Total Tool, the design comprises flat interlinking pieces that are assembled to create three-dimensional forms. The resulting enormous foam arcs come together to form a sphere that children can climb through, roll around in or burrow inside. The Play+ Soft line is designed to support children's self-learning through play, helping to stimulate logical thinking and motor-skill development, as well as honing their sensory perception. The two-toned colour of the Intreccio Sfera engages children's chromatic senses, while its surprisingly large-scale and pleasing proportions result in a flexible space that can accommodate an assortment of play activities.

Frisbee, 1948
Walter Morrison (1920–2010)
and Warren Franscioni (1917–74)
Pipco / currently Wham-O

Trained as a building inspector, Fred Morrison began his entrepreneurial journey selling cake tins to Santa Monica beach- and park-goers for them to play catch with. In 1948, he teamed up with Warren Franscioni, who owned a butane factory, to create a plastic version of the throwing disc, which they first sold as The Flyin' Saucer and, later, The Pluto Plate, through their company Partners in Plastic (Pipco). The term 'flying saucer' had been coined just a year earlier during the Roswell incident, and Morrison and Franscioni's product name capitalized on the era's fascination with Unidentified Flying Objects. In 1955, the Californian toy company Wham-O purchased the rights to the product, made modifications to the design and renamed it the Frisbee. The name is borrowed from Connecticut's Frisbie Pie Company, whose cake tins were thrown around for fun by Yale students. Since then, the Frisbee has been Wham-O's bestselling product and has led to the creation of several sports, including Ultimate Frisbee and disc golf.

74 ☾

Stacking Bed, 1966
Rolf Heide (1932–)
Müller Möbelwerkstätten

In 1966, the industrial designer Rolf Heide teamed up with Renate Herzog of the German women's magazine *Brigitte* to create a line of affordable modular furniture, suitable for the small living spaces of the era. The first glossy magazine to advertise furniture, *Brigitte* was instrumental in the home design revolution that would see a shift towards mobility and flexibility. 'I wanted to design a practical, affordable item of furniture that also expressed that generation's aspirations,'[1] Heide explained. Today a design classic, Heide's Stacking Bed is a modular day-bed system that is light, mobile, convenient and space-saving: there's always an extra bed if and when you require one. Available in adult and children's sizes, the bed responds to the need for adaptability that arose during Germany's post-war housing shortage. Its candy colours and rounded edges are perfect for children, while its clean lines also enable it to seamlessly transform into a couch during the day.

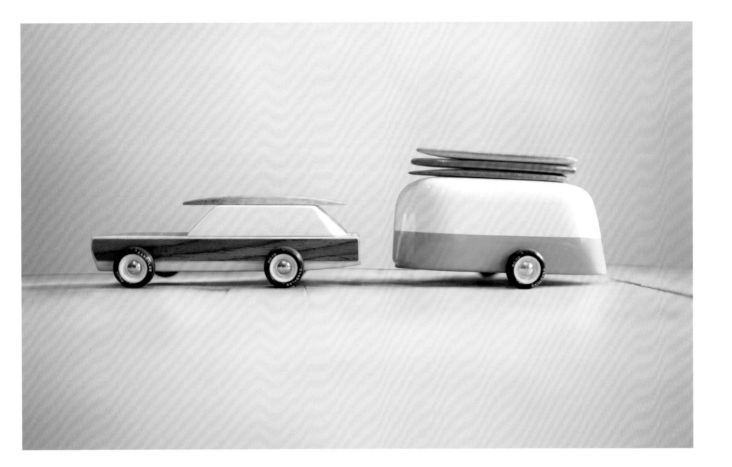

75

Woodie and Camper, 2013
Vlad Dragusin (1974–)
Candylab Toys

Stylish wooden cars from New York brand Candylab, like this Woodie-and-Camper combo, appeal to a nostalgic sensibility while still getting high marks for contemporary flair. Founded by architect Vlad Dragusin and product developer Florin Galliano, Candylab lovingly crafts vintage American autos in miniature beech form. 'For the most part, they are inspired by famous movie cars, so there is some pop culture mixed in with high design,' Dragusin explains.[1] The cars began as a side project for the duo in 2013, and immediately appealed to design-minded parents with a soft spot for classic cars. The Woodie estate car is especially charming, with a magnet on its roof for attaching the must-have surfboard accessory and another magnet under its trunk for hitching the two-tone camping trailer. It also features walnut veneer side-panelling and rubber tyres. Aside from the Woodie, Candylab produces an ever-increasing array of vehicles, including tow trucks, police cars and taxis.

Ortus, 2015
Pavla Boháčová (1988–)
Kutulu

Inspired by Modernist Czech toy designers, such as Libuše Niklová, Kutulu is a young company keeping the country's tradition of beautiful, thoughtfully crafted toys alive. Founded by Pavla Boháčová, who previously worked as an illustrator and pop-up book designer, the company designs and produces wooden toys that are infused with a sense of narrative and character. The Hipo series, created in 2015, comprises a set of beech horses are handmade and painted, and even have different names depending on their colour; the white horse is called Ortus and the black one Noxus. Like Kutulu's other designs, the Hipo collection is bright and geometric, their rounded bodies allowing children to comfortably grasp them and push the horses along. While Boháčová designed the company's first toys, each of Kutulu's products now represents a group effort, with the five-member team – including a woodcutter and technical production manager – working closely together to shape the final design.

Tio, 2009
Tim Holley (1985–)
Onzo

Sustainable living practices get personal with Tio, a spirited ghost-like character conceived by the British designer Tim Holley to playfully teach children about energy consumption. Honoured with the HSBC Award for Sustainability in 2009 and featured in the Museum of Modern Art's design exhibition *Talk to Me* in 2011, this child-centric light switch is designed to glow in one of three traffic-light colours. A smiling face and glowing green body indicates that the lights have been on for less than one hour. Tio glows yellow and its smile disappears when the lights have been on for more than four hours. After eight hours, red anger sets in and its expression grows similarly distraught. A web application connected to the device records children's long-term energy usage patterns, allowing them to observe their behaviour over time. The app also contextualizes energy consumption within the larger global environment, teaching kids both about the origins and impact of energy on other beings.

78 🍴

Knuddel Children's Cutlery, 1998
Ulrike Bögel (1954–)
WMF

Young children love to mimic their parents and the Knuddel cutlery set allows them to play along at mealtimes. With its safety features – a dull knife, short fork tines and rounded handles that fit snugly in the child's hand – the set (named after the word 'cuddle') is endearingly designed to help children to learn to eat both safely and independently. Created by Ulrike Bögel for WMF, the set is manufactured from the same 18/10 stainless steel that is used for the company's adult designs, making it rust-free and dishwasher-safe. WMF has a long history of producing fine tableware, having formed when two German metalworks merged in 1880 to become the Württembergische Metallwarenfabrik (WMF). Bögel is best-known for her work with porcelain companies, such as Arzberg and Royal Doulton. The Knuddel set is designed for children aged from three upwards and is available in a plain, polished finish, or embossed with illustrations of popular children's characters.

79 🐻

Family Figures, 1954
Antonio Vitali (1909–2008)
Creative Playthings

These smooth and undulating forms by Antonio Vitali represent a family and its pets, without ornament or surface embellishment. Their finely wrought curves have been scaled to a child's hand, inviting touch and celebrating the materiality of the wood grain. A Swiss sculptor, Vitali believed in the haptic value of play, opting to sculpt in wood for its warm, tactile quality. Inspired by the vernacular tradition of handcrafted wooden toys, Vitali initially produced playthings for his own children before creating a line for commercial sale. In 1954, Frank Caplan and Bernard Barenholtz of Creative Playthings asked him to adapt his hand-carved aesthetic into a series of wooden toys that could be mass-produced with a mechanical lathe. In accordance with the recommendations of psychologists and paediatricians of the time, Creative Playthings sought to create simplified, tactile toys that would free a child's imagination through abstraction. Vitali's figures were celebrated by art and design journals as a 'bold experiment in art education'.[1]

80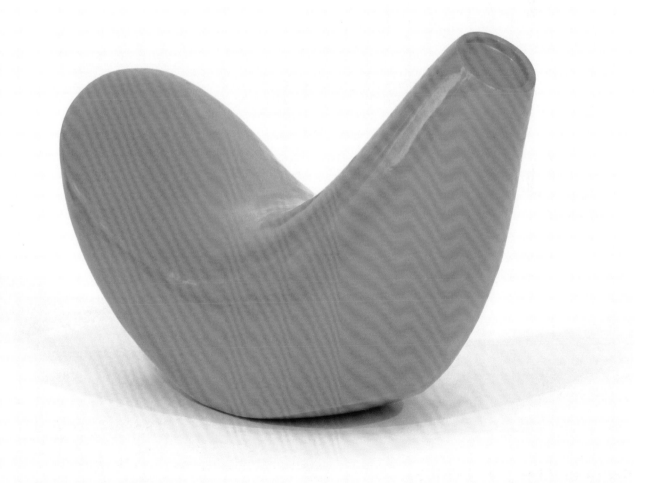

Duk Rocker, c. 1960s
Designer unknown
Manufacturer unknown

Durable, lightweight and easy to clean, it is perhaps little wonder that parents have been relying on plastic to simplify child-rearing for many years. While life without plastic may seem unimaginable today, it wasn't until the 1960s that the recently discovered material became affordable for daily use. In 1963, Kartell, an Italian company that had already been producing plastic for automobile manufacturing, launched Habitat, its furniture division. The following year, Marco Zanuso and Richard Sapper produced the K 1340 children's stacking chair (14), the first piece of furniture to be made entirely from injection-moulded plastic. Three years later, Marc Berthier collaborated with Roche Bobois to create France's first collection of furniture made entirely from fibreglass-reinforced polyester (419). The malleability of new plastics freed mid-century designers from the limitations of older materials and allowed for greater inventiveness in children's furniture. Most likely produced in France in the 1960s, this amorphic orange rocker is a fantastic example of how plastic had already begun to revolutionize both the world of product design and the modern interior.

Cabaninha Crib, 2011
Ana Ribeiro (1975–)
Murmur

Ana Ribeiro's Cabaninha Crib is immediately striking for its legs, which stand akimbo, making it appear as if it has been caught in the act of walking across the room. The lacquered white slats that make up the sides of the crib echo this effect, creating a playful sense of movement while adhering to all necessary safety standards. Made of sycamore wood, the crib is accompanied by a matching changing table that can be adapted to create a small storage unit or bookshelf once its primary function is outgrown. Ribeiro's multivalent design talents have led her to work in film, marketing, interior design and architecture. The Cabaninha collection was produced by Murmur, a furniture and product design company, which was headed up by Ribeiro from 2007–13. Her unusual take on nursery furniture feels fresh and dynamic, bringing a sense of unexpected whimsy while maintaining a modern, clean-lined feel.

82 🪑 🍴

Carota, 2005
Toshimitsu Sasaki (1949–2005)
SDI Fantasia

The legacy of the Japanese designer Toshimitsu Sasaki lives on in his furniture designs, several of which were revived for production in 2016. His award-winning pieces reflect the simplicity of Japanese design, while also displaying the designer's love of colour and bold shapes. The simple appearance of his Carota high chair belies the various ways in which it was designed to adapt to the growing child: the seat can be adjusted to four different heights, while the baby rail and leg guard can be removed as needed, accommodating children from the age of seven months to four years. A short-legged version of the maple and birch wood chair is also available. Sasaki, who achieved recognition as an award-winning furniture designer during his lifetime, founded the child-focused company Sasaki Design International in Tokyo in 2004, believing that children are as deserving of beautiful design as adults.

83 🍴

Infant's Fork and Spoon, 1986
Michael Wilson (1947–)
Tyke Corporation

With limited hand strength and gripping ability, young children have difficulty manipulating the fine, flat-handled utensils used by adults. With the creation of his fork and spoon for the Chicago-based Tyke Corporation, designer Michael Wilson cleverly proportions his utensils to suit a child's needs. Their rounded edges and easy-to-grip handles help children to cultivate a sense of independence and pride in their abilities. While diminutive and ergonomic, the lozenge-shaped handles and pleasing proportions of Wilson's design lend the fork and spoon a timeless elegance. A former advertising executive, Wilson was inspired to create the Tike-Hike booster seat for his then three-year-old daughter and went on to found the Tyke Corporation in 1981. Just a few years later, the Museum of Modern Art in New York celebrated the Infant's Fork and Spoon by including it in the 1988 exhibition, *Designs for Independent Living*. Speaking of their selection, the curators observed that 'nothing is extraneous',¹ praising the design for its economy and purity of form.

84 卤

Anyo Chair, 2006
Naoto Fukasawa (1956–)
Driade

With over fifty design awards to his name and work in several museum collections, the Japanese industrial designer Naoto Fukasawa is probably best known for the wall-mounted CD player that he created in 1999 for the beloved Japanese household and consumer goods company, Muji. Fukasawa's celebrated designs are often quiet, characterized by a humility, simplicity and timelessness that he refers to as 'Super Normal'. His Anyo Chair, a steel structure wrapped in foam and covered in fleece, demonstrates this ethos, as well as his interest in tactility. Fukasawa notes that he designed the children's chair with stuffed toys in mind, 'so that it gave you the feeling of being embraced by something dear to your heart'.[1] Its name references the colloquial Japanese term for an infant learning to walk.

85 🐻

Therapeutic Toys, 1969
Renate Müller (1945–)
H Josef Leven KG

It is almost as if the world conspired to bring Renate Müller to toy design. Born in Sonneberg, Germany – then the global epicentre of toy manufacturing – to parents who themselves owned a toy company, Müller attended Sonneberg's Polytechnic for Toy Design. There, she recalls that lessons about the Bauhaus and Friedrich Fröbel's pioneering ideas on childhood education taught her to 'always use very simple materials, and simple forms, for the best understanding of children'.[1] An assignment to create toys that could be used therapeutically by children with physical and mental disabilities prompted Müller to create the jute and leather toys for which she has become world-renowned. Ranging from handheld to ottoman-sized, Müller's multicoloured and mostly animal-themed toys are beloved by design connoisseurs and child psychologists alike. Originally produced by her family's company, Müller has continued to lovingly hand-produce a small quantity of her visually graphic, wonderfully tactile and exceptionally sturdy jute creatures since 1990.

86 🪑

Children's Chair, 1965
Baumann (est. 1901)
Baumann

Though names such as Thonet and J & J Kohn are best remembered as the pioneers of bentwood furniture production, they were rivalled in the early twentieth century by Baumann, a French company that developed a loyal following due to its range of home furnishings and café seating. The company was founded in 1901 by Emile Baumann, whose son, Walter, took over its management from 1903. This beech rocking chair, with its linked front and back legs, is a variation on the Scandinavian-inspired sled style that was popular during the 1960s. The chair showcases the company's bentwood mastery, which is particularly noticeable in the exaggerated curve of the backrest, the gentler arc of base and the curved sheet that forms the seat. Today, several versions of this children's rocking chair can be found; some have the vertical backrests lacquered in red, others feature a slightly different base. Baumann was sold in the 1990s and eventually closed in 2003.

87 ☾

Dog Lite, 2015
Pinar Yar Gövsa (1979–)
Lil'Gaea

Chances are, you once suffered from nyctophobia. Fear of darkness is one of the most prevalent childhood afflictions and has led to countless iterations of bedtime rituals; leaving the door ajar or sleeping with a night light, are just a couple of examples. Young nyctophobes may find some relief, however, in the steadfast companionship of the Dog Lite by Lil'Gaea, a child-focused spin-off brand from the Turkish company, GAEAforms. This little guardian is made from powder-coated sheet metal that has been bent into a simple graphic canine shape. The lamp's body is formed of three sections, two of which are indented at the base like tiny feet, while a single sheet bent along three edges forms a face and two floppy ears. An oval-shaped cutaway makes for a sweet, glowing nose when Dog Lite is illuminated, while the lamp's electric cord trails tail-like and adds a pop of colour to the otherwise subdued piece.

Caravan Crib, 2010
Johannes Pauwen (1976–)
and Michaele Simmering (1978–)
Kalon Studios

The Caravan Crib refines the high-sided silhouette of the archetypal circus cara-van, yet retains a sense of showmanship with its colourful lacquered rails. Most elements of the solid-wood crib, designed by husband-and-wife team Johannes Pauwen and Michaele Simmering of Kalon Studios, are handcrafted using locally sourced maple wood. In keeping with the Los Angeles-based studio's principle of local manufacturing, this means that cribs intended for European customers are made in Europe from European Maple, while pieces for American customers are made in New England using timber from sustainably managed local forests. The Caravan Crib features two mattress heights and can be converted to a child's bed, and eventually a divan, thereby making it designed to last a lifetime. Pauwen and Simmering were inspired to start their studio following the arrival of their first child, having found it challenging to obtain children's furniture that married design appeal with sustainable production practices.

89 🐻 🪑 ✏️

Skruvad, 2008
Maria Vång (1980–)
Prototype

Assembling a toy or piece of furniture from a box isn't typically considered a highlight of parent–child bonding. But what if it *could* be an activity that was fun and collaborative? Even better, what if it could also be educational? With her cheekily named Skruvad (Screw) series, the Swedish designer Maria Vång set out to create a design with both educational and creative value. Skruvad isn't just furniture – it's also a construction set. Arriving as an unassembled kit of parts, it encourages children to customize furniture into configurations of their choosing. A series of screw-on cubes and spheres, painted in white and jewel tones, allows for further customization and shape-coordination. In addition to boosting children's motor skills, Skruvad also fosters cognitive development through building, classification and play. An abacus component, which doubles as a chair back or other surface, adds a mathematical edge to the design.

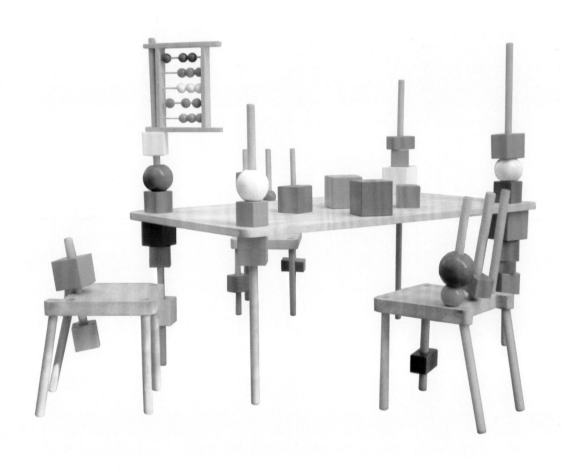

90

Qubis Haus, 2012
Amy Whitworth (1973–)
Qubis

As a mother, Amy Whitworth realized that the coffee table was a natural nexus for activity, as well as a convenient place to congregate and keep an eye on playtime. Seamlessly serving both of these purposes, Qubis Haus is so sleek and modern that it can easily blend in with the furniture. With its cantilevered structure and translucent panels, the design shares a clear alliance with the Bauhaus's preference for clean, geometric lines and marriage of form and function. The two-floor doll's house is made of birch plywood, which can be accented with sliding panels of coloured Perspex, allowing a child to configure the interior layout to their liking. An accompanying range of magnetic furniture and dolls can be assembled in a variety of ways. Qubis Haus is part of the permanent collection of the Victoria and Albert Museum of Childhood in London.

91 ☾

Vetro Crib, 2010
Daniel Fong (1958–)
Nursery Works

Clear acrylic can make a maximalist statement through minimal means, as demonstrated in iconic designs such as Philippe Starck's Ghost Chair or Ferruccio Laviani's Bourgie Lamp. Applied to a crib, however, the transparent plastic takes on an entirely new set of values by transforming the visible divide between a child and its environment. Designed by Daniel Fong for Nursery Works, this unusual and thoroughly contemporary crib is made from 100 per cent recyclable, non-toxic acrylic. A father of two, Fong's fascination with acrylic furniture and interest in pursuing an alternative to wooden cribs paved the way for the Vetro. Integrating completely with its environment, Vetro provides an unobstructed view between child and parent. Wong refers to his design as 'game-changing' due to its ability to ensure that babies feel safe and connected to their surroundings while inside it. Unsurprisingly, this statement crib has been a popular fixture in celebrity nurseries since its launch in 2010.

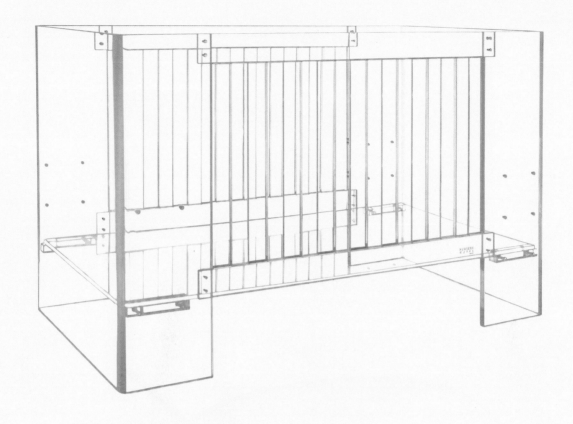

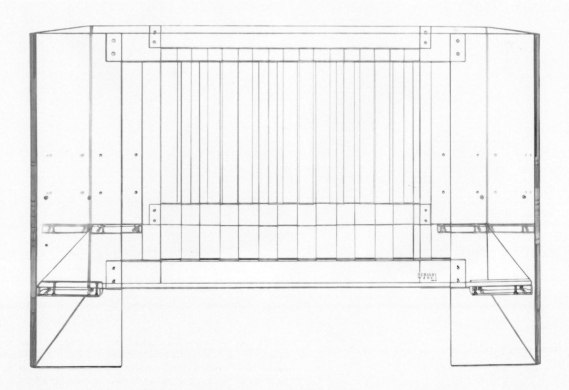

Moneyphant with Twins, 2011
Alfredo Häberli (1964–)
Georg Jensen

They say an elephant never forgets – so what better animal to help kids remember the importance of saving? This little family of elephants from Danish silver company Georg Jensen acts as a guardian of children's loose change, providing an attractive nesting form to decorate the top of a dresser or bedside table. The Moneyphants evolved from a beloved elephant-shaped bottle opener, which Jørgen Møller designed for Georg Jensen in 1987. The elephant's popularity among both adults and children led Møller to create a money box version in 2010, but following his death in 2011, Alfredo Häberli decided to put a new spin on the design. Best known for mixing contrasting materials in surprising ways, Häberli introduces wood into the classic silver design in the form of two tiny calves. Each twin is made from solid oak and nests perfectly under the larger Moneyphant's trunk.

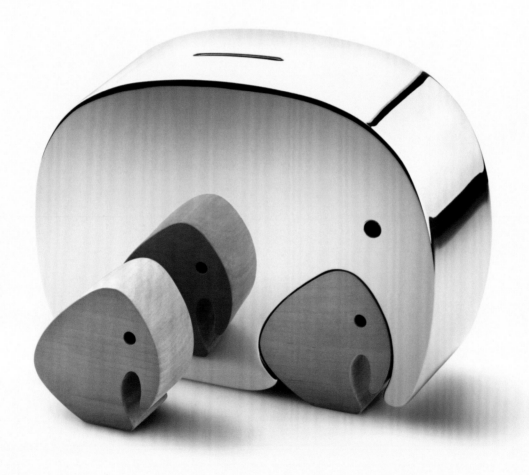

93 🐻

Hanno the Gorilla, Ursa the Bear
and Hattie the Elephant, 2008–10
David Weeks (1968–)
Areaware

Since founding his eponymous studio in 1996, David Weeks has successfully established himself as a favourite among architects and interior designers for his sculptural and modern lighting. A father of two, he found himself analyzing his children's toys as he played with them, an activity that led his studio into a number of toy design forays. His resulting collective of elastic-jointed, wooden animals for Areaware include Hanno the Gorilla, Ursa the Bear and Hattie the Elephant. 'I've wanted to imbue them with an energy that toys of this genre are usually missing [while] at the same time avoiding painting graphic, comic-book-style faces on them to make it easier to decipher their personality,'[1] Weeks explains. Public reception for his horde of wildlife (as well as for Cubebot, Weeks's primitive wooden robot, which folds into a perfect cube [181]) has been equally enthusiastic among both children and adults alike.

94 ☾

Lulu Cradle, 1963/2011
Nanna Ditzel (1923–2005)
Kold Savværk
/ currently Brdr. Krüger

Perhaps best known for her rounded, wicker Hanging Egg Chair of 1957, which quickly became a staple of 1960s' fashion shoots, the celebrated Danish designer Nanna Ditzel created the Lulu Cradle in 1963. Named after one of her daughters, the cradle has become a Ditzel family heirloom, which has been passed back and forth between relations for generations, with a small label attached to the crib each time it holds a celebrated newcomer. Made of Danish beech, its simple, elegant design has rendered it a highly collectible example of modern Danish craftsmanship. As with so many of her creations, Ditzel's training as a cabinetmaker is evident in her subtle design solutions and simple yet striking details. In 1998, the Danish Ministry of Culture suitably awarded Nanna Ditzel with a lifelong Artist's Grant. The Danish design company Brdr. Krüger relaunched a limited edition of 200 Lulu cradles in 2011, in close collaboration with Dennie Ditzel, Nanna's first daughter.

95 🪑

Little Nobody, 2007
Komplot (est. 1987)
Hay

For a design called Little Nobody, you might not expect much from it in the way of a personality. Yet, this mini chair from Hay has it in abundance. Designed by Komplot, the award-winning Danish design firm founded by Boris Berlin and Poul Christiansen, this seat first appeared in showrooms in an adult-sized version. When the Nobody hit the market in 2007, it was an industrial sensation. Using a manufacturing technique known as thermoforming, in which a plastic sheet is heated, formed in mould and trimmed to specification, Komplot's design was made from 100 per cent recycled plastic bottles. Sturdy, lightweight, environmentally friendly and tactile, this blanket-meets-chair was quickly scaled down to create the Little Nobody, a stackable seat that is ideal for children. Thanks to its high-tech construction, soft material and gently curving form, the Little Nobody can be safely clambered on, carried, pushed and toppled by intrepid little somebodies.

Rabbit Chair Baby, 2016
Stefano Giovannoni (1954–)
Qeeboo

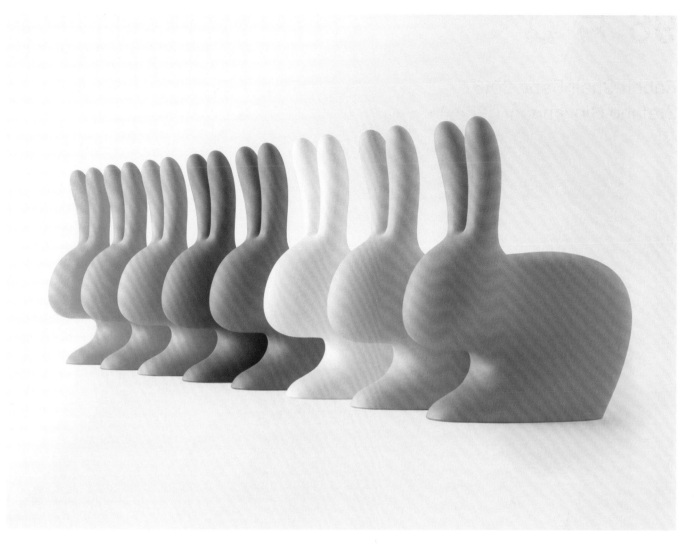

Stefano Giovannoni's characteristically innovative thinking and penchant for wit is on full display with his Rabbit Chair. The chair invites interaction in two ways: children can sit using the elongated ears as a back rest or sit astride the smooth, friendly form for more imaginative play. The polyethylene seat resembles the animal in silhouette, its simple, organic shape stripped of any embellishment. Having collaborated with illustrious companies such as Alessi, Moooi and Magis, Giovannoni's designs can be found in major museums throughout the world. Rabbit Chair, however, was created for Giovannoni's own brand, Qeeboo, which he launched in 2016. Qeeboo's debut collection included twenty-five, fun and functional plastic objects designed in partnership with Marcel Wanders, Nika Zupanc, Andrea Branzi, Richard Hutten and Front. The Rabbit Chair is also available as a lamp and comes in an adult version, too. 'Let's face it', Giovannoni says, 'we all want to go back to being kids again.'[1]

97 ♯

Mouse Chair, 2015
Nofred (est. 2014)
Nofred

Like many other designers focused on the children's market, Signe Holst and Sandra Kaas Greve were inspired to start their Scandinavian design company, Nofred, when they had children of their own. Driven to create durable, thoughtful, modern and sustainable homewares for children, Nofred draws on the natural world for both material and inspiration; a leaf-shaped quilt and animal-themed wallpapers being among the items in their collection. The Mouse Chair, conceived for children between the ages of two and five, is made from untreated oak and is defined by its two-part backrest, which is playfully shaped to resemble mouse ears. Similar to Takeshi Sawada's Bambi Chair (138), Nofred's design is refined enough to sit comfortably among adult furnishings, yet also playfully stimulates a child's imagination. Other versions of the design include a bench and a high chair, which are available in a range of colours.

Training Dresser, 2011
Peter Bristol (1982–)
Mountain View Cabinetry

As the head of industrial design at Oculus (developer of the Oculus Rift, the world's first consumer virtual-reality system), Peter Bristol is immersed in a high-tech world. But beyond being a creator of advanced experiential gadgets, Bristol is a designer of furniture, lighting and other goods. His training dresser, created to help children learn how to find and put away their clothes, cuts a clean-lined figure that appeals to parents, while the cartoonish shapes of its drawers give it a distinctly kid-friendly aesthetic. The dresser, made from maple plywood and finished with a clear catalyzed lacquer, is handcrafted in Bristol's home state of Washington. Each of the four drawers is shaped to identify the type of clothing it is meant to contain: tops, bottoms, undergarments and socks.

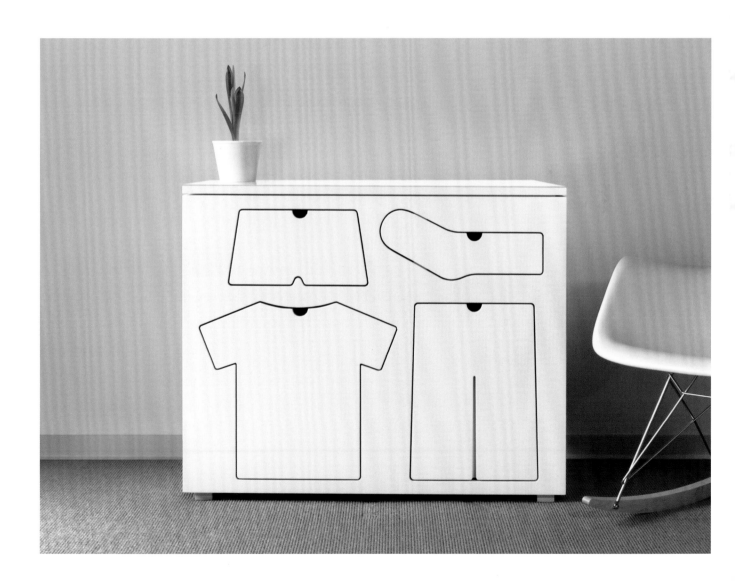

Doll's House with Suitcase, 2013
Anna Pfeiffer (1969–)
Hase Weiss

The Doll's House with Suitcase, designed by Berlin-based studio Hase Weiss (White Rabbit), gives the phrase 'living out of a suitcase' new meaning. The modular construction is made up of two small rooms, one large room, a parlour and set of stairs, all of which can be assembled in a multitude of configurations. When not in use, it is housed in a suitcase-like carrying case with a blackboard on the front. Hase Weiss was founded in 2002 by the architect Anna Pfeiffer and artist Ulrike Rumpenhorst, when Pfeiffer was unable to find children's furniture that she liked for her first child, Elise. What began out of need soon grew into a desire to create quality crafted wooden objects – specifically doll's houses and toy kitchens – that give children the opportunity to build their own worlds. Each object is handcrafted by studios that employ individuals with special needs. Inspired by toys of the past, Pfeiffer's multifunctional creations allow for open-ended play.

100 🐻

MetAnimals, 2014
Floris Hovers (1976–)
Prototype

'Growing up is one of the worst things that can happen to a human,' Floris Hovers exclaims. 'I would much rather have stayed a child.'[1] Trained at the prestigious Design Academy Eindhoven, Hovers sharpened his design skills in the studio of fellow-alumnus Piet Hein Eek, the Dutchman known for transforming wood scraps into high-style designs. Hovers boasts his own scrappy approach to the craft, applying the same childlike candour to all of his toys and furniture designs in order to achieve a quirky and charming simplicity. As with Archetoys (408) and CARtools (248), this ethos is equally apparent in MetAnimals, the designer's charming metal menagerie, which includes a flamingo, crocodile, lion, polar bear, pig and giraffe. The naive appearance of Hovers's work embodies his belief that a person should be able to determine how something was made simply by looking at it. 'The balance between reality and imagination – I think that's the art,' he affirms.[2]

101 🐻

Pingy, 2011
Eero Aarnio (1932–)
Magis

Eero Aarnio is a Finnish designer who distinguished himself from the Scandinavian aesthetic and natural materials championed by other Finnish Modernists, such as Alvar Aalto, by instead experimenting with plastics, vivid colours and organic forms. Aarnio's futuristic-feeling furniture came to define the 1960s: his Ball Chair (1963) transformed him into an international star and has since become one of the most famous chairs of modern design. Pingy is produced by Magis as part of its Me Too collection for children and recalls a beloved papier-mâché penguin that Aarnio created as a child. 'This little penguin has perhaps had a little too much to eat,' Aarnio remarks, noting that its 'rotund shape allows it to mimic the realistic waddling movement [of penguins], which makes it so lovable and cute.'[1] Made of a resilient polyethylene composition, Pingy is equally happy indoors and out.

Nevalyashka Roly-Poly Dolls, 1958
Igrushka Scientific Research Institute (est. 1915)
Tambov Powder Mill

During the Cold War, the drive to develop Soviet consumer items that embodied and supported communist ideals sparked an active period of Russian toy production. The Igrushka ('toy') Scientific Research Institute, one of hundreds of state enterprises, was dedicated to researching children's development and producing toy designs. Toy libraries, where children could borrow newly developed products, were also established. Conditioned by the era's ideological stand-off, capitalist countries were framed as manufacturing consumer goods according to frivolous whimsy, in contrast to the USSR's emphasis on scientific research as the basis for design. This Nevalyashka baby toy was one of the Igrushka Scientific Research Institute's most successful toys. Also known as a Vanka-Vstanka, the doll features a weighted mechanism that makes it roll back to a standing position, even when pushed over. A bell clinks as the doll wobbles, thereby developing babies' awareness of cause and effect, and hand–eye–ear coordination. The toy is now available in a huge variety of shapes, sizes, materials and designs.

Geometric Solids, c. 1910
Maria Montessori (1870–1952)
Alison's Montessori

Montessori is an approach to early childhood education that makes the most of children's innate curiosity. Developed by Maria Montessori, an Italian doctor and educator, it spread worldwide following the founding of her first school in Rome, the Casa dei Bambini, in 1907. She designed learning materials based on scientific observation and her experience of working with nursery children. These Geometric Solids belong to a range of 'sensorial materials' that were inspired by her belief that 'the senses, being explorers of the world, open the way to knowledge.'[1] Conceived to develop children's abilities to discern similarity and difference, the ten shapes are always painted cobalt blue, encouraging the user to focus on differences in form, and come with cards that feature outlines of each shape's base, to promote shape identification. Cultivating an understanding of form through touch, Geometric Solids help children to become more aware of the objects that make up their environment and lay the foundation for a future appreciation of form, shape and space.

104 🐻 ◐▲

Sculptural Building Blocks, 2015
Noah James Spencer (1979–)
Fort Makers

Founded by Nana Spears, Noah James Spencer, Naomi Clark and Elizabeth Whitcomb, the Brooklyn-based design and art studio Fort Makers views its shop as a Bauhaus-inspired gallery offering a range of items, including textiles, furniture, ceramics, jewellery and lighting. Often reflecting organic and natural forms, Fort Makers's work celebrates craft and individuality, with many pieces blurring the distinction between art and design. The studio's name stems from the childhood activity of building forts with blankets and embodies a sense of playfulness that is characteristic of the collective's work. For these Sculptural Building Blocks, Noah Spencer created a set of fifteen distinct pieces that recall Alma Siedhoff-Buscher's Bauhaus Bauspiel of 1923 (130). Equal parts toy and decorative object, the Sculptural Building Blocks appeal to both children and adults alike. Each carved walnut-wood piece is slightly imperfect, a testament to the handcrafted process involved in creating them.

105 🐻

Stuffed Chairs, 2015
Katie Stout (1989–)
Self-produced

Often playing with the motifs of suburban domestic life, Brooklyn-based designer Katie Stout characterizes her designs, which employ diverse media and techniques, and cover interior objects of all kinds, as 'naive pop'.[1] Her abiding interests in skewing traditional forms and reimagining the possibilities of various materials combine perfectly in her Stuffed Chairs. 'I just had this image of children holding stuffed furniture instead of stuffed animals,' Stout explains of her vision. 'You'd have these chairs that were just completely apathetic; they just gave up on being chairs and they're lying on the couch.'[2] In collaboration with her Rhode Island School of Design colleague and machine knitter, Zev Schwartz, Stout transforms various found textiles – corduroy, Mylar, a vintage sweater – into a range of squishable non-functional seats that struggle to stand upright. Together, they refer to their spirited stuffed seats as grumpy uncles and disgruntled kids.

106 🐻

Nido, 2005
Javier Mariscal (1950–)
Magis

Famed Spanish designer and illustrator Javier Mariscal is both prolific and versatile. His eponymous Barcelona-based studio heralds itself as 'the first multidisciplinary studio' formed in the country, bringing Mariscal's trademark bold approach to graphics, products, film and furniture. Created in 2005 for Magis's newly launched children's line, Nido (meaning 'nest') is a cosy cave in the shape of a cartoon-like insect. Both a toy and a piece of furniture, children can crawl in through the mouth of the plastic bug to hide, play or nap. Light and durable, Nido is equally useful indoors or out, depending on whatever adventure awaits. Magis' Me Too line prides itself on having 'big designers think little'.[1] One of several objects Mariscal has conceived for the line, Nido exemplifies how the brand thoughtfully enables children to experience the creativity, sensations and solutions envisioned by some of the most talented minds in contemporary design.

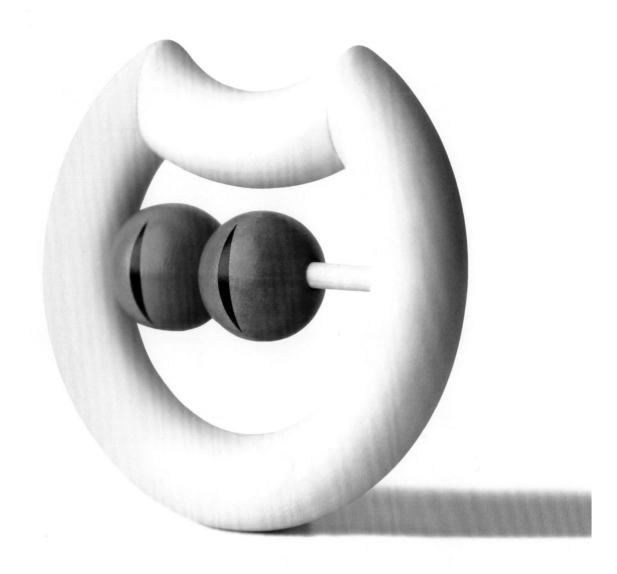

107 🐻

Miau, 2009
Heiko Hillig (1971–)
Naef

Two distinctive green eyes distinguish this rattle ring as a cat, despite the simplicity of the toy's abstract form. Made from untreated maple wood and finished with non-toxic paint, babies can safely use the Miau ring while teething. With sliding beads that rattle, Miau supports the development of sensory awareness and motor skills, such as grasping, and is accompanied by a matching pram string and dummy clip. The Miau ring was designed for babies by Heiko Hillig, who has been Naef's chief designer since 1995. Founded by Kurt Naef, the company has been producing wooden toys and puzzles since 1954, and thoroughly tests all of its baby products for safety and durability. Born in Saxony, Hillig now splits his time between Germany and Switzerland, and is responsible for many of Naef's award-winning designs.

108

Toy Guardian, 2010
Tsung-Yu Lu (1987–)
Prototype

You could call the Toy Guardian a monster on wheels, or an eater (or protector) of toys. The storage bin, which takes the form of a wild beast, was designed by Taiwanese graduate student Tsung-Yu Lu as a multipurpose didactic toy. Featuring wheels, an extendable handle and a large lid that can be easily opened and closed, the Toy Guardian brings a sense of playfulness to the act of tidying up. This friendly beast of a box turns a chore into a collaborative game and can double as a ride-on toy, with a base big enough for small children to straddle and a pull-out handle that enables parents to provide momentum. When not in use, the Toy Guardian can be stood on its end to save space. The toy box has won several design awards, including the iF Student Design Award and a Student Merit Award from the Industrial Designers Society of America (IDEA), both in 2011.

Hausschwein, 2016
Marcel Wanders (1963–)
Cybex

The Hausschwein or 'House Pig' was created with the belief that parents shouldn't have to sacrifice their good taste for their children's colourful plastic playthings. Part of the Parents Collection, a collaboration between the German child-mobility brand Cybex and Dutch design's notorious bad boy, Marcel Wanders, this endearing hog is part-sculpture, part-storage, part-toy. Winner of the 2016 Red Dot Design Concept Award, House Pig's soft, quilted rump is perfect for children to clamber over, while its tactile ears and tail can be gripped like reins. Its characterful snout doubles as a removable lid, revealing a hollow belly that is ideal for storing toys. Wanders first entered the spotlight with the Knotted Chair in 1996, a macramé-like design made of epoxy-soaked rope with a carbon-fibre core. With a giant rocking horse for adults to his name, as well as a brand logo that features his own face sporting a clown's nose, Wanders is adept at designing for kids of all ages.

Mostros, 2013
Oscar Nuñez (1975–)
Self-produced

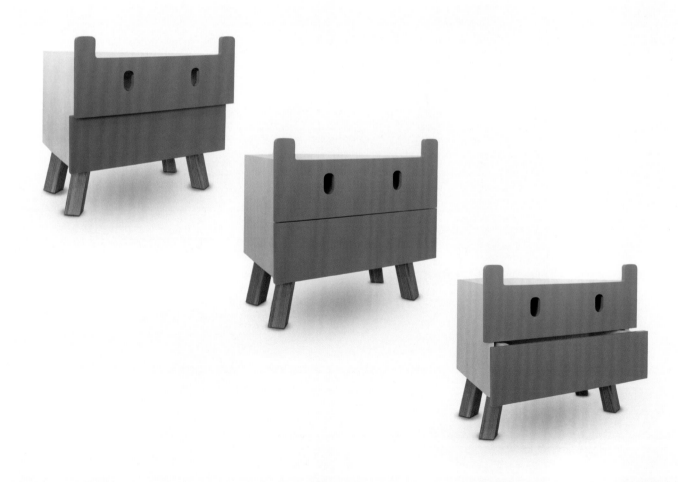

The Mostros (Monsters) collection, by Mexican designer Oscar Nuñez, brings childhood monsters out of the closet and into plain sight. Nuñez, who founded his eponymous studio in 2007, created his series of nightstands, dressers and toy chests to encourage children to develop a playful relationship with their furniture. The characterful pieces bring a subtle sense of fantasy to the home, with functional pull tabs that act as the eyes and ears of each monster. Made of lacquered MDF with ashwood legs, the collection comes in soft hues of blue and green, creating an aesthetic that is both tailored for children and refined enough to be at home in an adult environment. Following his studies at the Universidad Iberoamericana, Nuñez quickly gained acclaim for his furniture and interior design work. His finely crafted and often whimsical creations have been featured in publications such as *Wallpaper* and *Surface*.

111   🛴

Roo, 2011
Aldis Circenis (1965–)
Riga Chair Factory

Roo, a rocking kangaroo, is the Riga Chair Factory's take on the classic rocking horse. Based in Latvia's capital city, the manufacturer is led by Aldis Circenis, an interior and furniture designer best known for his award-winning Bloom Stool of 2011. Roo resulted from an ambition to design a rocker that could be produced out of a single piece of plywood. Drawing inspiration from traditional Japanese origami techniques, Circenis used industrial-moulding technology to 'fold' the wood into the form of a kangaroo – a playful alternative to the standard equestrian version. Available in several different woods and finishes, the spare, minimalist toy has the added benefit of being stackable, making it easier to store when not in use. Roo was awarded both the iF Product Design Award in 2013 and the German Design Award 'Special Mention' in 2014.

The Hesitant Car, c. 1920
Hermann Finsterlin (1887–1973)
Self-produced

Together with a group of German architects and artists, which included Bruno Taut, Walter Gropius and Wenzel Hablik, Hermann Finsterlin was a member of the Crystal Chain, a year-long cultural correspondence that began in the harsh post-war economic climate of 1919. Through letters, the group developed and shared ideas for imaginary, utopian architecture, signing their missives with pen names. Taut, the Crystal Chain's founder, established the group through an initial message that implored recipients to 'draw or write down at regular intervals those of his ideas that he wants to share with our circle, and [...] send a copy to each member.'[1] For both Taut and Finsterlin, architecture was a means of exploring ideas, much like child's play. Toys – like this car that goes two ways simultaneously – were another part of the architect's body of work. Similar to many of Finsterlin's architectural projects, this delightful object defies logic while playfully hinting at his exploratory approach.

113 🪑 🔺

Paper Chair, 2006
Charlotte Friis (1971–)
Self-produced

Children are encouraged to draw on the furniture with this unusual chair created by the Danish designer, Charlotte Friis. Following a postgraduate degree in Communication Design from the Royal College of Art in London, Friis created a collection of items that she calls 'storytelling furniture'. Among these, the Paper Chair from 2006 allows children to draw directly onto their seat, which is in fact a large roll of paper that feeds onto an easel-like backrest. The front spool provides stability, while enabling 500 metres (1,640 feet) of drawing paper to be slowly wound through a slot at the top of the chair and onto the rear spool as the child draws. Designed for children between the ages of two and seven, the height of the seat gradually changes as the paper is used. Once finished, the spool can be kept as an archive of the child's evolving creativity.

114 🪑 ▲●

Kenno S, 2011
Heikki Ruoho (1969–)
Showroom Finland

Part of a series that also includes an adult chair and stool, the Kenno S children's chair is made from recycled cardboard, which is then laminated with white paper. Scaled for children aged from three to six, Kenno S serves as both chair and canvas, encouraging kids to indulge in their creative – and mischievous – side by drawing on the furniture. Created by the award-winning Finnish designer Heikki Ruohu, the lightweight chair arrives flat and requires no screws or glue for assembly, making it easy to store when not in use and to recycle once outgrown. 'More than anything, I look at the life of the object: what is it used for and how?' Ruohu explains. 'What language does the object speak, how is it made, and how can it be made better? Form is only one part of the whole, of the object's DNA. The final product always has to be more than the sum of its parts.'[1]

115 ⊓

Seggiolina Pop, 2004
Enzo Mari (1932–)
Magis

Enzo Mari is no stranger to design for children. Three-time winner of the prestigious Compasso d'Oro prize in Italy, this prolific designer repeatedly turns his attention to the youngest members of society, creating objects that encourage children's imaginations and agency. Mari's interest in child psychology led him to create his first children's game, Sedici Animali (50), in 1956. The pared-down, universal shape of Seggiolina Pop reflects Mari's alignment with the ideals of the Arts and Crafts Movement of the early twentieth-century, and its push towards a more humanistic approach to design. First produced in 2004, the chair launched Magis's Me Too collection for children. Made from expanded polypropylene, its featherweight allows even the smallest child the freedom to move it around, and its durability enables use both indoors and out. Known for producing clear images and elementary forms, the artist and designer created many exceptional books, puzzles and objects for children during his prolific career.

116 🐻 ◼️

Zauber-Stempel-Spiel, 1970s
Designer unknown
Manufacturer unknown

The Zauber-Stempel-Spiel (Magic Stamp Game) is a strikingly presented set of geometric stamps, which was produced in Germany in the 1970s. Reminiscent of Bauhaus toys of the 1920s in its purity of form, geometry and colour, the game encourages children to create their own compositions using the various stamps and accompanying black ink-pad. The collection includes a rectangle, teardrop, crescent and a trapezoid, two lengths of wavy line, three lengths of straight line, and large and small versions of circles, triangles and squares. A set of sample compositions within the box depicting a cat, train, clown, flowers and more, demonstrates how only a small selection of tools can offer endless possibilities. The Zauber-Stempel-Spiel recalls the more broadly known Colorforms of the 1950s, which were toy kits of colourful vinyl shapes that could be stuck and re-stuck to laminated boards to produce endless compositions.

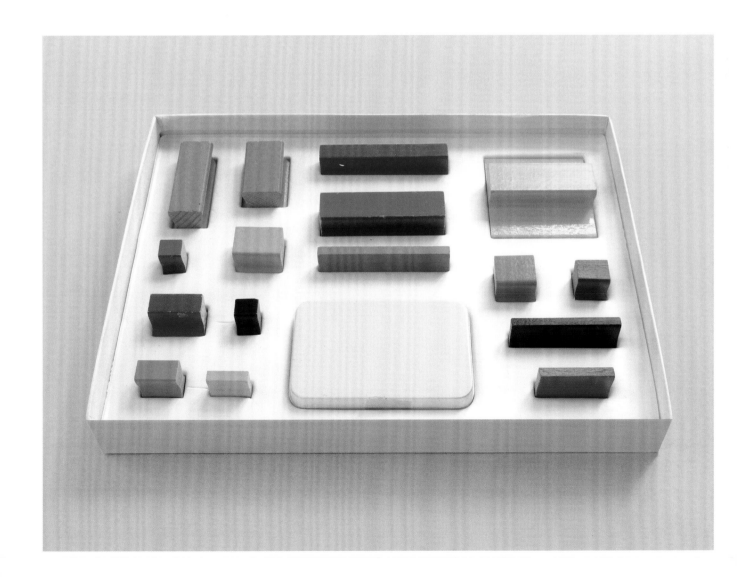

Tamago, 2009
Jānis Mercs (1977–)
and Indra Merca (1982–)
Merci Design

Going by the Japanese name for 'egg', Tamago is a set of children's play furniture made from the same 100 per cent recycled paper-pulp as egg cartons. Tamago includes seven different shapes that can be grouped together to make different letters and numbers, and with their softly rounded edges, the pieces also bear a passing resemblance to slices of a Japanese rolled-egg omelette! An interest in innovative and environmentally sustainable toys led Jānis Mercs and Indra Merca of the Latvian studio Merci Design to cook up the concept for Tamago. With its rearrangeable shapes, Tamago fosters the development of motor skills, while also providing children with an early introduction to their ABCs and 123s. Non-toxic, lightweight and versatile, Tamago's paper construction also allows children to personalize their set with drawings and paint.

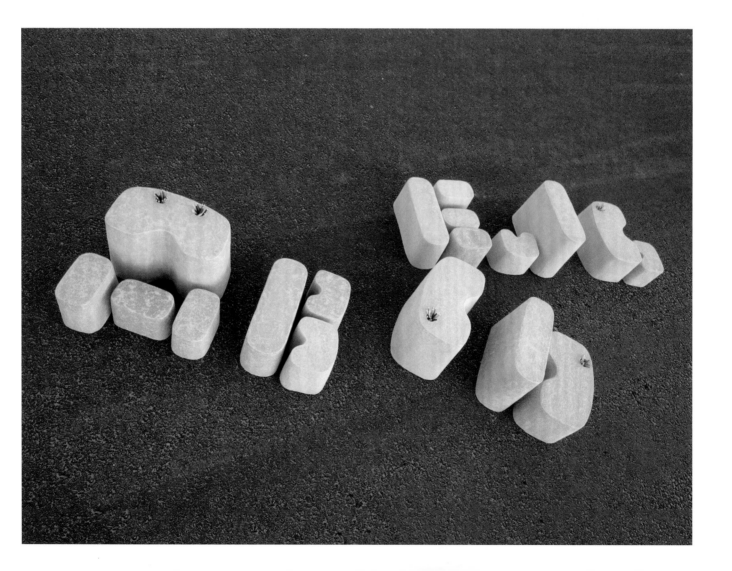

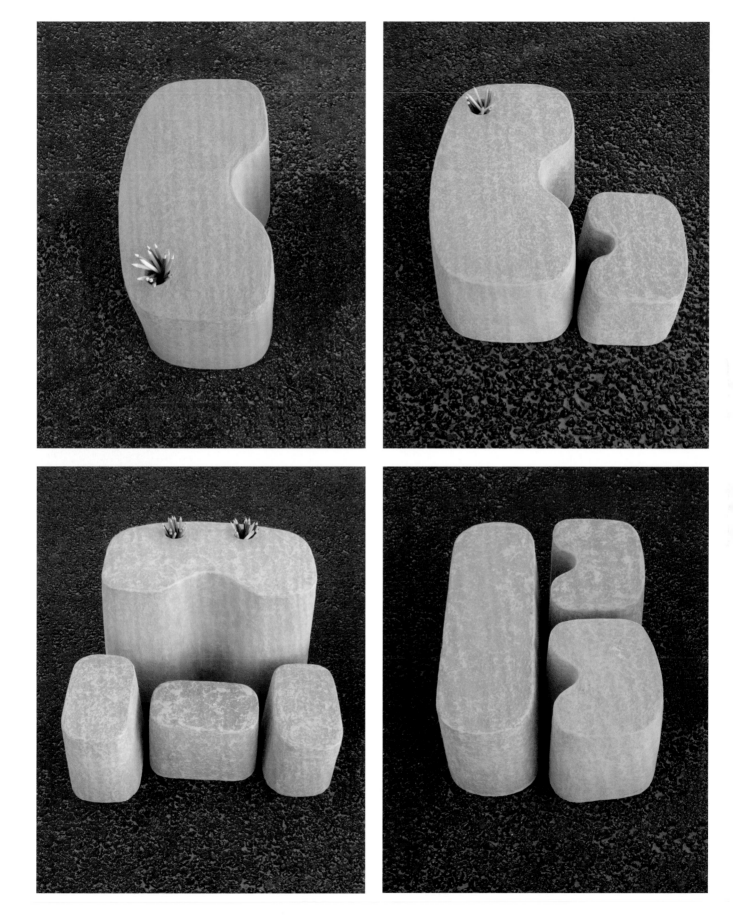

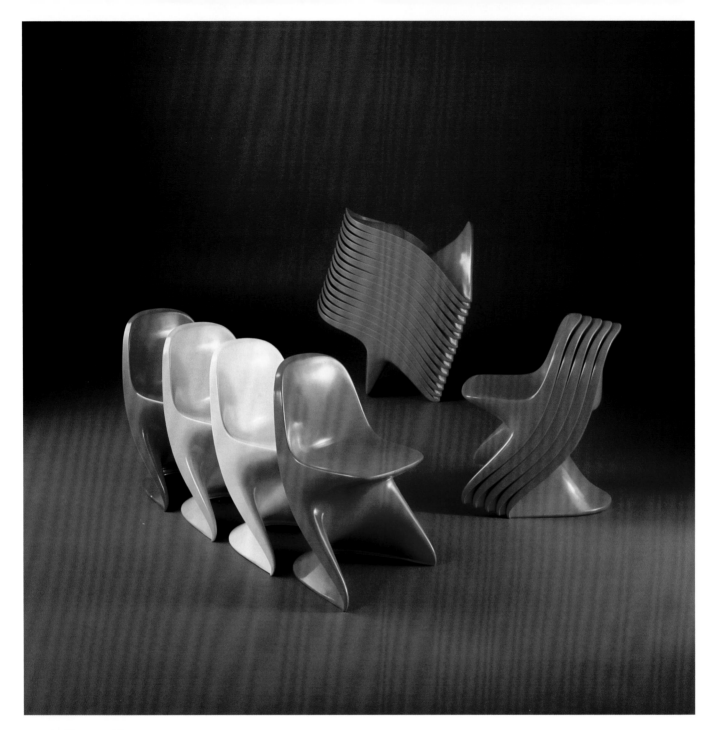

118 円

Casalino Jr, 1970
Alexander Begge (1941–)
Casala

With its dramatic, swooping form and cantilevered seat, the plastic-moulded Casalino Jr chair makes a unique design statement. Its creator, Alexander Begge, enjoyed a brief but brilliant design career, with the Casalino series being his only line of products. According to Begge, inspiration came from the line's futuristic form came from a 'wisp of fog'. This ephemeral vision informed both child- and adult-sized chairs, with the adult version also available as a stool and armchair. What makes the Casalino Jr so perfect for children, though – aside from its parent-pleasing aesthetic – is a host of convenient features: the chairs are stackable, boast soft, contoured edges and are easy to wipe down in the event of a spill. It's no wonder, then, that this seventies-era chair was revived in 2007, bringing its high-style design into the twenty-first century.

119 ♨ 🐻

Mico Chair, 2006
El Ultimo Grito (est. 1997)
Magis

Any orientation is the right way up when it comes to the Mico Chair. Its topsy-turvy limbs and abstract form encourage children's imaginations to run wild, allowing them to use the seat however they like. Named after the Mico monkey, the matte-red polyethylene chair was designed by the husband-and-wife team behind the Spanish studio El Ultimo Grito in 2006. Inspired by watching their daughter play, Roberto Feo and Rosario Hurtado realized that toys are often designed to educate children and slowly adjust them to the adult world. What might toys look like if they instead retained a child's sense of possibility and magical thinking, the designers asked? By not conforming to any specific typology or form, Mico encourages open-ended play. As the studio's first foray into challenging the idea of design and its predetermined guidelines, the Mico Chair launched El Ultimo Grito on its path of using design to explore the social, political and philosophical nature of human relationships.

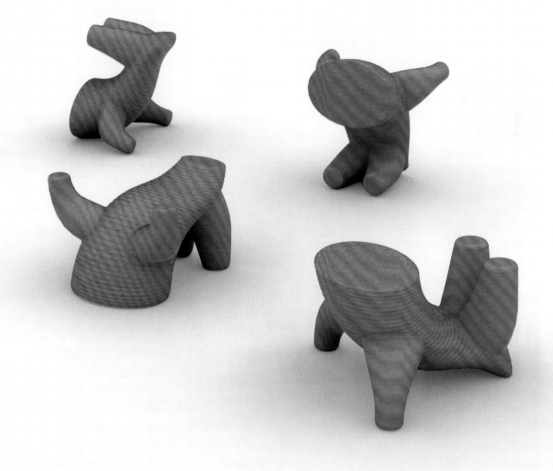

120 🐻

100% TobeUs, 2007
Various
TobeUs

For TobeUs, a line of quirkily shaped toy cars, simplicity is the key to creativity. Made of Lebanese cedar wood, the cars were formed as a response to the disappointing quality of children's playthings experienced by the Italian designer and architect, Matteo Ragni. Aspiring to something better, he founded TobeUs, crafting a line of durable little vehicles that emphasize simple design and conscious consumerism. Ragni took the line a step further with the creation of 100% TobeUs, a range of 100 cars by 100 distinguished designers. Enlisting the likes of Alessandro Mendini, the Campana brothers, Jaime Hayon, Marcel Wanders, Karim Rashid and Fabio Novembre, Ragni presented each designer with an identically sized block of wood and asked them to draw two lines: one longitudinal and one transversal. A carpenter then cut along these lines and carved spaces for the wheels. With this satisfyingly simple premise, 100% TobeUs playfully celebrates the childlike imaginings of today's leading designers.

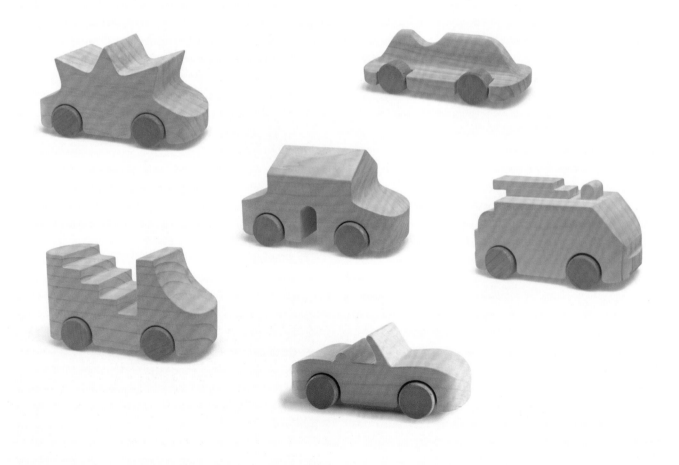

121 🛴

Rocky, 2008
PearsonLloyd (est. 1997)
Martínez Otero

Not your typical rocking horse, Rocky is also atypical of the kind of work produced by the award-winning British design studio PearsonLloyd. Having met in the 1990s as students at the Royal College of Art in London, Luke Pearson and Tom Lloyd quickly established a shared desire to bridge the gap between furniture and product design. Since founding their company in 1997, the duo have tackled a broad range of projects: cabin and seat design for the German airline Lufthansa; a modular, enclosed working environment for London-based office furniture manufacturer Bene; and a public wayfinding system for the city of Bath in England. Available in a variety of colours and alternating seating covers, Rocky combines two formed plywood parts to create a rocker in the abstracted shapes of a seal, whale or dog. Though not currently in production, Rocky was originally commissioned by leading Spanish manufacturer Martínez Otero.

122 🐻 🪑

MAXintheBOX, 1998
Thomas Maitz (1972–)
Perludi

With two boxy modules that can be assembled in a variety of formations, MAXintheBOX is more than just versatile children's furniture – it's more crucially a play set with endless possibilities. Designed for children aged from nine months to eight years old, the modules can be slotted, turned and nested to create tables, stools, shelves or armchairs of different heights. Thomas Maitz, the collection's designer, later founded the children's furniture company Perludi, which continues to produce MAXintheBOX in Austria, alongside other pieces that are often designed with input from Maitz's own children. In keeping with Perludi's design ethos, all materials used are organic and recyclable. MAXintheBOX is manufactured from sustainable birch plywood, with colours and finishes that can be mixed and matched. Once the cubic forms are assembled, the set becomes incredibly stable and robust. Like all of Perludi's offerings, MAXintheBOX is designed to encourage children's development through limitless discovery and imaginative play.

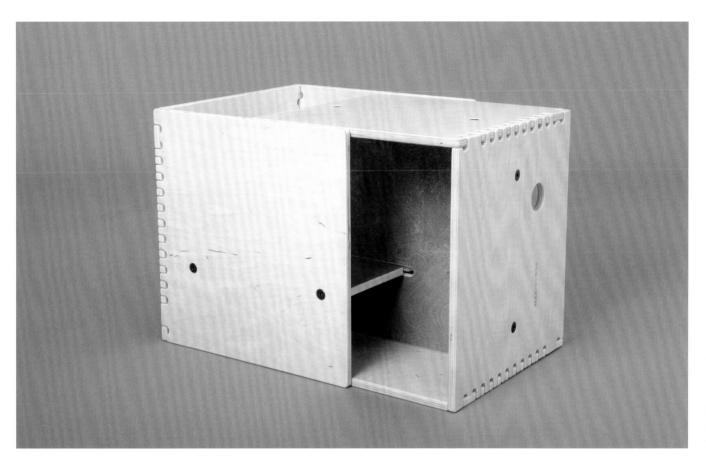

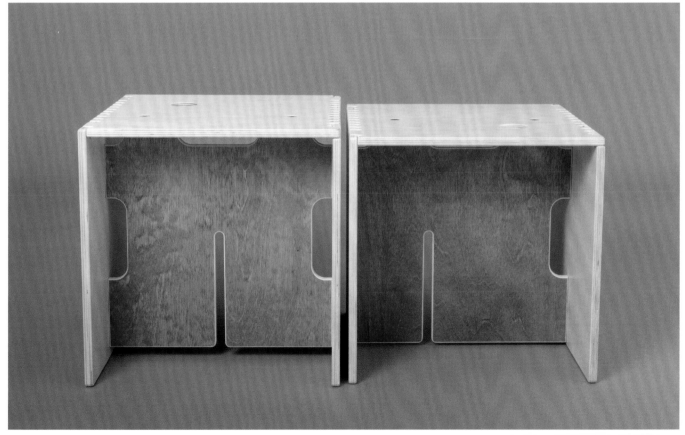

Trissen Stool, 1962
Nanna Ditzel (1923–2005)
Kolds Savværk / currently Snedkergaarden

Observing that a child's needs are different from those of an adult, the Danish designer Nanna Ditzel firmly believed that a child's chair need not be a copy of one made for adults. In 1962, inspired by the way that her children were in constant motion and loved stacking objects, she designed Trissen (Bobbin), a child's stool that could be rolled, stacked or used as a small table. Trissen's turned-wood design is at once elegant and robust. Intended for active use in play, it reflects a child's dynamic nature, and their desire to be free to build and modify their environment. Originally created in two sizes, its simple design proved so popular that it was quickly expanded to include adult-sized tables and bar stools. Nicknamed the 'First Lady of Danish Furniture Design', Nanna Ditzel's prolific and diverse body of work established her as one of the most imaginative, versatile and remarkable women of modern design.

124 🐻 ▲●◼

Naef Spiel, 1957
Kurt Naef (1926–2006)
Naef

Kurt Naef, founder of the eponymous Swiss toy company Naef, began his design business in 1954, following his training as a carpenter's apprentice and his studies in architecture. Naef initially set out to design interiors and furniture, however, this building set became one of his company's foundational and most iconic products. Each diagonally incised cube in the set of sixteen pieces features eight points that allow the units to stack and nest in surprising configurations. Due to the unique shape of the blocks, children can build vertical constructions that are wider at the top than they are at the base. Aside from designing his own toys, Naef would go on to make licensed reproductions of Bauhaus designs (see Alma Siedhoff-Buscher's Bauspiel construction set, 130), as well as to import toys from Japan and the United States. The company continues to produce high-quality, design-minded wooden toys today.

125 🐻 ◨

Clip Clap Table, 2016
Ferruccio Laviani (1960–)
Prototype

Ferruccio Laviani has served as Kartell's art director since 1991, designing countless stores, concessions, catalogues, advertising and exhibition stands around the world. In addition, he has also created several products, including Bourgie, his 2004 modern-day-meets-Baroque lamp, which has since become one of Kartell's bestsellers. As part of Kartell Kids, which was launched in 2016, Laviani created the Clip Clap Table, a piece that is part-furniture, part-toy. Transforming the traditional static play table into a building game, the Clip Clap has legs made from cubical, jewel-like blocks that can be clipped into each other like Lego pieces. The table's surface can thus be raised or lowered to the desired height, or taken apart entirely for block play on the floor. The Clip Clap Table's colourful translucence aligns with Kartell's innovative work in plastics, while also lending it an attractive playful aesthetic.

126 🐻 ▲▼◼

Jenga, 1983
Leslie Scott (1955–)
Leslie Scott Associates
/ currently Hasbro

A game of tumbling wooden blocks might seem timeless, but Jenga was actually conceived in the same era as computer games like Atari. To play Jenga, players take turns removing a wooden block from a stacked tower of fifty-four pieces until the structure collapses. Leslie Scott developed the game with her family during her teenage years in Ghana, making use of wooden blocks from the local sawmill. Her blocks proved to be a popular party game with Scott's British friends when she was in her twenties, so she put the game into production, naming it Jenga, which means 'to build' in Swahili. Jenga depends on each block being slightly unique in weight, size and texture, making certain pieces more difficult to remove than others, although these differences remain invisible to players. Hasbro, its manufacturer, attribute its popularity to the combination of skill, strategy and luck required to win the game. Following Jenga's phenomenal success, Scott has designed dozens of other games through her own company, Oxford Games.

127 🐻 🍴

Children's Stool HI 56, 1963
Stig Lönngren (1924–)
Lars Larsson

This striking conical high chair of birch plywood is the creation of little-known Swedish interior designer, Stig Lönngren. Its interconnected cylindrical base and circular tray incorporates wide cut-out openings for a child's legs and ample surface space for a child to play or eat. Lönngren was the founder of HI-Gruppen (HI-Group), an association of interior architects, furniture designers and craftsmen formed in 1957. During the mid-twentieth century, Sweden was experiencing an urban housing and industrial design boom. Lönngren's HI-Group instead sought to put craft back at the centre of the design process and ensure that architects, designers and craftsmen could continue to experiment without being beholden to the requirements of mass production. The group comprised sixteen members at its peak, and marked a seminal chapter in the history of Swedish design and interiors by sparking a renaissance in craft during a period more often associated with standardization and industrial manufacturing.

128 🍴

Co Zen Urushi Cutlery, 2009
Keisei Takekata (1975–)
Nushisa

For the Japanese studio Nushisa, the beauty of objects emerges through their use. Run by the designer Keisei Takekata, the studio intertwines design and utility in their fully functioning restaurant, which is furnished with their own products: wooden chairs, tables, ceramics and dining implements. Winner of a Good Design Award in 2009, the Co Zen children's cutlery set continues the tradition of *urushi* (Japanese wooden lacquerware) that dates back to the Jōmon period. The set's spoon, fork, knife, dessert spoon and chopsticks all fit neatly in a wooden case. The lid of the case can be turned over and used as a place setting, its rounded shape echoing a form commonly used for Japanese lacquer trays. Each set is individually handcrafted, mirroring the care and attention that goes into the preparation of organic vegetables and fresh fish at the Nushisa restaurant in Saitama, Japan.

129 🛴

Rocking Horse, 1936
Kay Bojesen (1886–1958)
Kay Bojesen Denmark

Trained as a silversmith under Georg Jensen, Kay Bojesen began carving wooden toys in the early 1930s. His wooden animals quickly became Danish national icons and he was appointed as a purveyor to the Royal Danish Court in 1952. Legend has it that when Bojesen sat down to draw a rocking horse in 1936, its form came so easily that it almost jumped off the page. While its shape simplified over time, this noble little horse has taken generations of Danish children on wondrous adventures and is perhaps the item most given as a present for toddlers in Denmark. Bojesen's craftsmanship and sense of design created toys that were both tactile and elegant, appealing to all ages. Along with stylish furniture, wooden toys were exported internationally in the post-war era, furthering the reputation of Scandinavian design and its quality. Still classics today, Bojesen's toys continue to be produced by his own company and enjoyed by children worldwide.

130 ◩ 🐻

Bauhaus Bauspiel, 1923
Alma Siedhoff-Buscher (1899–1944)
Bauhaus Workshops / currently Naef

In 1923, members of the Bauhaus collaborated to build the Haus am Horn in Weimar, Germany. The project was both an exhibition of Bauhaus design in the form of a fully furnished house and a prototype for affordable housing that could be mass produced. Alma Siedhoff-Buscher, one of the few female Bauhaus designers permitted to work outside of the school's weaving studio, was responsible for the house's nursery; this building set, carved from two pieces of wood, was among several of her designs for the room. Emphasizing flexibility, modularity and possibility through reconfiguration, the twenty-two-piece *Bauspiel* (construction set) represents Siedhoff-Buscher's efforts to design a toy that was attractive, economical and suitable for mass manufacture. The set encourages children's creative expression and experimentation, offering them opportunities to build imitatively or imaginatively, and embodies the Bauhaus belief in the pedagogical value of play. Siedhoff-Buscher's building blocks are still produced today.

Streamliner, 1984
Ulf Hanses (1949–)
Playsam

With its distinctive semicircular body and high-gloss finish, the Streamliner stands out among toy cars for its uniquely pared-down interpretation of form. Created in 1984 by Ulf Hanses, the Streamliner has become one of Playsam's signature products. Made of solid beech, the archetypal car is lovely to both hold and behold, with a design so simplified as to be little more than an idea on wheels. The shiny finish, smooth wheel mechanisms, weight and diminutive size all contribute to make the Streamliner a much-loved children's classic. Recognized in the top five Swedish designs of the past half-century, this iconic little car has even been illustrated on Swedish postage stamps. The Playsam Streamliner has since been expanded to include racing cars, convertibles, buses, aeroplanes and ships, and today also has matching attachable wooden-peg passengers.

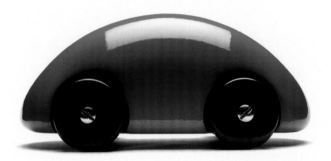

132 🛴

Jubilee Rocking Horse, 1977
Magnus Olesen (est. 1937)
Magnus Olesen

With its dramatic cantilevered legs, the Jubilee Rocking Horse moves with a gentle bounce rather than a traditional rocking motion. Made by the Danish furniture company Magnus Olesen in 1977, on the occasion of its fortieth anniversary, this graceful rocker was produced from laminated elm, along with a stool of a similar material and colour palette. The company is recognized for its collaborations with some of Denmark's most respected designers, and continues to produce durable, functional and Danish-made furniture that pays homage to its legacy as a purveyor of Scandinavian Modernist design. Magnus Olesen is perhaps best known for its 8000 Series Chair, which was designed by Rud Thygesen and Johnny Sørensen in 1981. Similarly to the 8000 Series, the Jubilee Rocking Horse employs a unique production technology to create joints without tenons, dowels or screws, resulting in a design that is lightweight, strong and supple.

Apetito Set, 2012
Helena Rohner (1968–)
Georg Jensen

Spanish jewellery designer Helena Rohner first stumbled upon her craft during her travels to Florence as a young woman. Since then, she has created items ranging from necklaces and cufflinks, to candleholders and housewares. Her aesthetic is marked by soft edges and delicate, refined materials, such as coral, porcelain and wood. In 2012, Rohner was invited to create a collection of polished stainless-steel items for Danish company Georg Jensen, which included tea sets and coffee presses. One of these designs is Apetito, a six-piece tablewear set for children, whose organic lines are characteristic of Rohner's award-winning work. The design's rounded forms, thoughtful details and reduced size have been elegantly adapted to suit small hands, while its material renders it both practical and dishwasher-safe. Conceived for toddlers who are just learning how to use cutlery, this sophisticated kitchenware will remain beloved long after its owner has outgrown it.

134 🪑

Cadeirinhas, 2014
Minúsculos (est. 2013)
Minúsculos

Children are naturally inclined to turn chairs into structures – draping sheets over them to form forts, or stacking them to create towers. These chairs, from Brazilian company Minúsculos, embrace that instinct, with each piece in the collection designed to look like a different type of building. Founded in 2013 by Julia Salles, Pedro Terra, Marko Brajovic and Teka Brajovic, Minúsculos specializes in creating objects for children that walk the line between utility and creative play, while making use of digital manufacturing techniques to optimize the design and distribution process. The Cadeirinhas (Little Chairs) are laser cut from sturdy laminated plywood, enabling them to be both flatpacked and easily slotted together using a minimum number of screws. As well as initially fabricating the chairs for sale through their own company, Minúsculos released the designs under a creative commons license – allowing users all over the world to download the digital plans and make the chairs directly themselves.

135 🪑 🐻 🌙

Rappelkiste, 1975
Luigi Colani (1928–)
Elbro

Luigi Colani's industrial design oeuvre is as prolific as it is diverse. Most widely known for his biomorphic cars, aircraft and boats, he also created numerous collections of furniture for both adults and children. Much like Bruno Munari's Abitacolo of 1971 (237), this all-inclusive creation by Colani incorporates the central components of a child's bedroom into one piece of furniture. The Rappelkiste (or 'rattling box', a colloquial German term for an old vehicle) cleverly incorporates a bunk bed, wardrobe, bench, desk and blackboard into a single structure, which is barely 2 square metres (21½ square feet) in size. The design is modular, enabling the elements to be separated, with the desk and bench an optional addition. Colani's decision to construct the Rappelkiste out of beech and plywood reflected a conscious return to traditional materials, a result of the growing petroleum shortages of the 1970s, which had directly impacted the price of plastic.

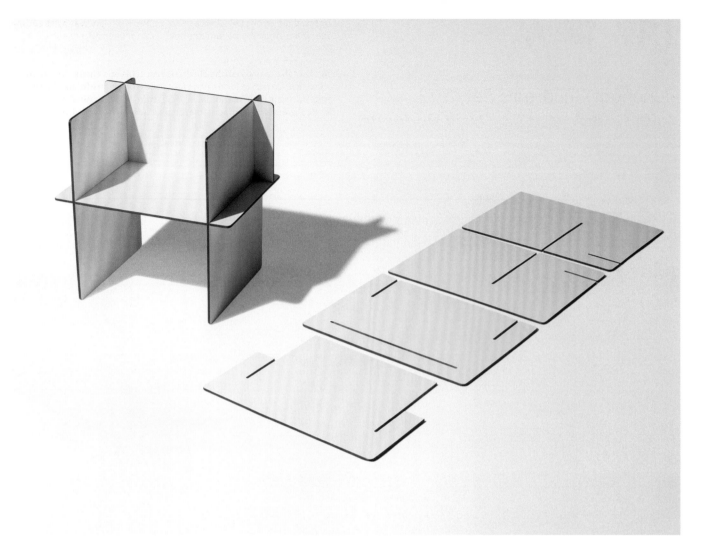

136 🪑 🔺⬛

Piccolo, 2005
Robin Carpenter (1977–)
Self-produced

Composed of just four pieces that slot together – no glue or screws required – the Piccolo chair is incredibly easy for even children to assemble and take apart. Its designer, Robin Carpenter, first trained as a cabinetmaker before studying design at the Berlin University of the Arts. The four boards are identically sized, meaning that they can be stacked efficiently for simple storage and transport. With each Piccolo being CNC-milled, this planar little piece reflects Carpenter's interest in applying digital tools to the practice of contemporary design. Produced in a variety of colours, with exposed plywood edges, the smooth durable surface of the Piccolo can easily be wiped clean and its wide-set legs render it extremely stable. The chair is available in two materials; a coated plywood for use indoors, and a water-resistant industrial hardboard that can be exposed to the elements.

137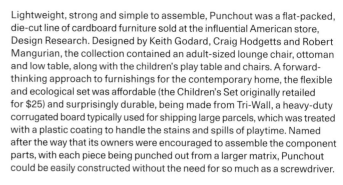

Punchout Children's Set, 1973
Keith Godard (1942–), Craig Hodgetts
(1937–) and Robert Mangurian (1944–)
Design Research

Lightweight, strong and simple to assemble, Punchout was a flat-packed, die-cut line of cardboard furniture sold at the influential American store, Design Research. Designed by Keith Godard, Craig Hodgetts and Robert Mangurian, the collection contained an adult-sized lounge chair, ottoman and low table, along with the children's play table and chairs. A forward-thinking approach to furnishings for the contemporary home, the flexible and ecological set was affordable (the Children's Set originally retailed for $25) and surprisingly durable, being made from Tri-Wall, a heavy-duty corrugated board typically used for shipping large parcels, which was treated with a plastic coating to handle the stains and spills of playtime. Named after the way that its owners were encouraged to assemble the component parts, with each piece being punched out from a larger matrix, Punchout could be easily constructed without the need for so much as a screwdriver.

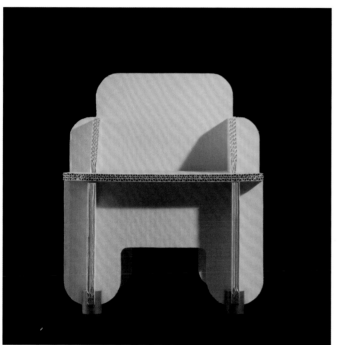

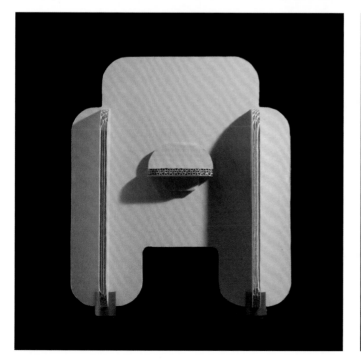

Cow, Bambi and Sheep Chairs, 2015–17
Takeshi Sawada (1977–)
Elements Optimal

Takeshi Sawada's Cow, Bambi and Sheep Chairs use faux fur, oak and walnut to distill the features of each animal into a diminutive and endearing stool with legs, a fuzzy body and protruding antlers. The combination of the chairs' proportions and materials will charm its young users, while making their parents happily nostalgic. A fashion designer by training, Sawada's work is characterized by a strong sense of playfulness and personality. Now the designer and director behind the Tokyo-based furniture brand kamina&C, Sawada translates his aesthetic inspirations into whimsical products that seek to create a connection with customers. 'When designing, it is the capacity of objects to evoke new feelings that I keep in mind,' he states.[1] The series is produced by Elements Optimal, a Copenhagen-based brand that endeavours to support the work of designers who share their dedication to remarkable Danish craftsmanship.

139

Rocking Sheep, 1981
Povl Kjer (1954–)
Self-produced

Danish product designer Povl Kjer specializes in wood furniture and toys, and his Rocking Sheep, first produced in 1981 and unchanged since, is his most famous work. Kjer grew up on a small farm and created the sheep for Julie, his brother's first-born child, to remind her of her rural heritage. 'In many of my works I go back to the magic of childhood,'[1] Kjer says. The rocking sheep's hand-carved face, and slender legs and rockers retain a Scandinavian design sensibility without sacrificing warmth, friendliness or durability. When outgrown, the sheep aptly functions as a handsome stool, footstool or decorative element within a room. Made of pine and lambskin, Kjer sources the pelts from Iceland, England, Ireland and New Zealand in order to obtain just the right colours and textures. Demand has continued to grow for his Rocking Sheep, yet Kjer continues to finish each toy himself, branding one leg with his signature stamp.

140 🪑 🔺⚫◻

Stacking Throne, 2011
Laurens van Wieringen (1974–)
Private commission

Dutch designer Laurens van Wieringen studied at the ArtEZ Institute of the Arts in Arnhem, the Netherlands, and London's Royal College of Art, before founding his own studio in Amsterdam in 2003. This somewhat quirky chair is the result of a private commission, for which the client was a one-year-old girl. In the early years of use, the foam booster seats that nestle in this bucket chair can be stacked within the wooden base to form a high chair. Then, as the child grows, the inserts can be removed one by one and used as colourful building blocks. As an oversized construction set, the inserts offer endless possibilities for building forts, walls and other hiding places. Stacking Throne was first shown at the Salone del Mobile, Milan, in 2011, as part of the Ventura Lambrate exhibition. In addition to furniture design, Van Wieringen specializes in interiors, exhibitions and food trucks.

Children's Furniture, 1926
Erich Dieckmann (1896–1944)
Staatliche Bauhochschule

This collection of children's cribs, tables and seating was designed by Erich Dieckmann while he was head of the carpentry workshop at the Staatliche Bauhochschule in Weimar, the school that succeeded the Bauhaus when it moved to Dessau in 1925. Dieckmann himself was a student of the Bauhaus and his designs reflect this influence, featuring the school's distinctive application of primary colours and simplified geometries. Like his peers, Dieckmann sought to produce designs suited to the standardized workers' residences being built in German cities during the 1920s. Collections such as these therefore comprised a uniform typology, with the intention that they could be efficiently and affordably manufactured for the masses. Like Dieckmann's designs for adult furniture, these pieces feature durable hardwoods, such as beech, oak and ash, which are then finished with coloured lacquers. The right-angled compositions and use of continuous lines that link armrests and legs are also typical of Dieckmann's work.

142 ◕◢◻

Frame Blocks, 2014
B6 Studio (est. 2010)
Protoype

Formed in 2010, B6 Studio is the brainchild of six Japanese Tama Art University design graduates. As these Frame Blocks show, their simple yet sophisticated work fuses smart and resourceful design with playfulness and colour. Taking a form similar to the typical steel truss, which has been used in all types of construction since the mid-nineteenth century, these red, yellow and white building blocks have a far more elegant industrial personality than your typical play set. Children can freely assemble the rectangular, square, octagonal and triangular pieces to create towers, buildings, playgrounds or even abstracted creatures from their imagination, while learning about basic construction and weight-bearing. Notably, the triangular ends enable blocks to fit flush together to form right-angle corners. Light and sculptural, these Frame Blocks also have an adult-friendly appeal, and could equally be at home on an architect's desk.

143

Villa, 2017
Fabio Novembre (1966–)
Kartell

Kartell is one of today's design brands to have recognized the value in creating children's products that equally appeal to a parent's contemporary aesthetic. Kartell Kids, launched in 2016, collaborates with celebrity designers, such as Nendo and Philippe Starck, to create ethereal, modern objects for children using the company's plastic moulding technology. For Villa, Kartell asked Italian designer Fabio Novembre to design a storage unit that could double as a doll's house – a challenge, but one to which Novembre took with ease after years of creating play architecture for his own daughters. The main body of the design consists of two floors, a pitched roof and cut-out doors and windows, making Villa instantly recognizable as a doll's house. However, with the addition of four legs, it gains further function as a piece of furniture. Open on one side, the 'rooms' of the house also act as compartments for a child's books and knick-knacks. Villa is cast in translucent plastic, bringing an airy, minimalist sensibility to the doll's house form.

144 🪑

Classroom Table and Chairs, 2007
Benjamin Cherner (1956–)
Cherner Chair Company

American industrial designer and architect Norman Cherner is perhaps best known for the moulded-plywood Cherner Chair, which at one point was so popular that it featured in a 1961 Norman Rockwell cover for the *Saturday Evening Post*. Cherner taught at New York's Columbia University and the Museum of Modern Art in the late 1940s. Then, in the 1950s, while working on pioneering developments for prefabricated housing in the US, Cherner was given the opportunity to advance his career in furniture design when George Nelson at Herman Miller encouraged the company Plycraft to hire him to develop a new plywood chair. The Cherner Chair proved incredibly successful, yet it fell out of production in the mid-1970s. In 1999, Cherner's sons, Benjamin and Thomas, founded the Cherner Chair Company to bring their father's iconic designs back into production. The new line is enhanced with items by Benjamin – also a trained architect – whose additions include the Cherner Classroom Table and Chairs, plywood creations that are scaled for children and perfectly suited for either school or home use.

145 ⌳

Beugel Child's Chair, 1927–30
Gerrit Rietveld (1888–1964)
Metz & Co

Informed by his experience as a father of six, Gerrit Rietveld's designs for children can be seen to marry the aesthetic explorations of the De Stijl movement with new experiments in tubular steel. Throughout the 1920s, an increased interest in children's health saw bent steel becoming a popular material for furniture – particularly school furniture – because of its sterile, utilitarian connotations. Rietveld's Beugel (Bow) children's chair, however, was among the first to embrace the sculptural potential of the material, while also representing a considered shift towards designs intended for mass production. Cleverly, its curving legs both enhance the structural stability of the chair and eliminate the need for bracing. The Beugel Chair was produced throughout the 1930s by the Dutch furniture store Metz & Co, a retailer with a particular interest in pedagogical toys and furnishings for children.

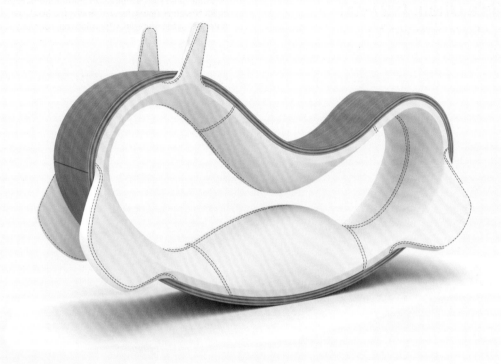

146 🛴

Enzoo, 2015
Mathieu Douadi (1982–)
and Nicolas Laghetti (1984–)
Enko Creatio

The Enzoo rocker takes a distinctly contemporary and abstract approach to the traditional equine toy. Its hollow kidney-bean shape highlights a set of four little feet, a belly and a pair of ears or antennae on its head. Just like a conventional rocking horse, this playful toy is meant to sway back and forth over its curved belly. Whether it is insect or animal is up to its rider to determine. Sculpted by Mathieu Douadi and Nicolas Laghetti for the French creative studio Enko Creatio, Enzoo comes in two versions, Classic and Limited. The Classic version, moulded out of BPA-free plastic, can live happily indoors or out, while the Limited is more luxurious, with its wooden exterior and leather-accented interior, and is available in more than twenty colours. Enzoo maintains the playful animated look that kids love, just as its sculpted, ergonomic aesthetic makes it equally appealing to parents by blending in with the decor of modern homes.

147 🐻

Expeditie Toy Truck, 1930s
Ko Verzuu (1901–71)
ADO

Beloved by design enthusiasts for their Modernist sense of colour, proportion and shape, these post-war Dutch toys have become collector's items. Yet, as their name, ADO – an acronym for *Arbeid Door Onvolwaardigen* (Work by the Incapacitated) – suggests, there is more to them than first meets the eye. In 1925, when Ko Verzuu, then a construction supervisor in the city of Utrecht, was hired to oversee the recently established physical therapy programme at the Berg en Bosch tuberculosis sanatorium, he quickly transformed it into a vibrant studio for the creation of children's toys and furniture. A father of eleven children, Verzuu immersed himself in the artistic and educational ideas of the Modernist avant-garde, shaping ADO designs to reflect Bauhaus and De Stijl ideologies, as well as the influence of furniture designer, Gerrit Rietveld. One of the first designers to focus on children's toys, Verzuu believed that ADO products should both feed children's imaginations and inform them about the beauty of life.

148 🐨

Child's Wheelbarrow, 1923
Gerrit Rietveld (1888–1964)
Gerard A van de Groenekan

Composed of elemental geometric forms, primary colours and inexpensive wood, this wheelbarrow exemplifies the stylistic characteristics of the Dutch artistic movement, De Stijl. As one of its leading figures, Gerrit Rietveld sought to achieve harmony and equilibrium by distilling things down to their most basic shapes and hues. While best known for his Red and Blue armchair of 1918, Rietveld, a father of six, also designed some of the twentieth century's most iconic and influential pieces of children's furniture. Originally produced for family and friends, Rietveld's designs for children gained wider recognition with the help of the *De Stijl* journal, which published several of his pieces. This wheelbarrow, made for the son of Dutch architect and fellow De Stijl advocate Jacobus Oud, proved so striking as to later be commercially produced by his furniture factory. With their combination of design-forward function, strong geometric forms and bold colours, Rietveld's designs were deemed visionary during the child-centric and design-obsessed mid-century years.

149 🐻

Humming Top, 1880
Lorenz Bolz (1856–1906)
Lorenz Bolz / currently Simm Spielwaren

Printed with colourful patterns and illustrations, Bolz spinning tops mesmerize children with their swirling designs and soothing sound. The first hand-pressed zinc spinning tops were produced in 1880 by Lorenz Bolz for his eponymous company in Zirndorf, Germany. Bolz altered the classic wooden children's toy, producing it first in zinc and then in tin plate, and added both a pull-cord that launched the spinning top from a swivelling handle, and small incisions to the metal body, which reacted to airflow to create a humming effect. The company's major innovation was the 1913 drill top, which could be set spinning by pushing and pulling a threaded rod up and down through the top's round body. Musical tops followed and by the mid-century, Bolz was one of the world's leading producers of spinning tops. The Bolz Humming Top is still popular today, and continues to be produced in tin and plastic versions by the Czech–German company, Simm Spielwaren.

150 🐼

Mécanimaux Elephant, 1984
Raoul Philip (1947–)
Vilac

In 1984, the toy manufacturer Vilac produced the first five Mécanimaux, a series of wheeled, wooden animals inspired by the machine aesthetic. As they roll, each animal exhibits a characteristic movement, from the horizontal wobble of the elephant's head to the bob of the rabbit's ears. Devised by the French architect and designer Raoul Philip, the Mécanimaux collection began with a red elephant, turtle, rabbit, anteater and a Native American on a horse; before later expanding to include a host of other spirited animals, each one inspired by the streamlined, mechanical qualities of industry. Founded by Narcisse Villet in the heart of the mountainous Jura region of France in 1911, Vilac has maintained the region's tradition for producing lacquered wooden toys for over a century. While no longer in production, the Mécanimaux series is in the collection of the Musée des Arts Décoratifs in Paris.

151 🐻 ✏

Lola Doll's House and Desk, 2014
Atelier Sans Souci (est. 2013)
Atelier Sans Souci

The Lola Doll's House and Desk straddles function and play. Its open design lends to the stowing of knick-knacks or books, but it might just as easily be populated by miniature domestic scenes that a child has created. Made of oak and lacquered beech, Lola comes with a set of mustard-coloured stairs and a small green box, both of which can be integrated into narrative play. The members of Atelier Sans Souci are united by a common desire to bridge the fields of both industrial and graphic design, bringing elements of poetry and craftsmanship to all of their work. In its design, the Lola draws attention to the nature of play itself, in which the 'ordinary becomes theatrical'.[1] Children's furniture should inspire, and this piece does exactly that. As stated on their website, the Atelier's aim is to create 'small universes that tell stories'.[2]

152 🪑

Cube Collection, 2012
Small-Design (est. 2005)
Small-Design

Eglantine Charrier and Anja Lykke founded Small-Design while Charrier was on maternity leave. 'When you're pregnant, you really get to see what kind of [children's] furniture exists,' Charrier explains. 'We wanted to make furniture that's durable and that kids could use for many years, with many different functions – as a table but also as a chair, or to put books on.'[1] The clean lines of Small-Design's colourful furniture collections echo those of mid-century designers, such as Gerrit Rietveld, while also drawing on their own Scandinavian design heritage. In the Cube collection, squares and rectangles are used structurally to create boxy tables, benches and armchairs, while cut-out circles contribute a sense of visual levity and act as built-in handles. This makes it easy for children to relocate and reconfigure the pieces according to their own whims. Composed of laminated-birch plywood, each piece is made in Denmark and many of the company's designs can be flat-packed.

153 🐻

Devil Box, 1920
Václav Špála (1885–1946)
Artel Cooperative
/ currently Modernista

Designed by the Czech painter and illustrator Václav Špála, this spirited wooden box reflects the bold, emotional style of Špála's early paintings, which were influenced by the Fauvist movement. During the 1920s, he collaborated with the Artel Cooperative, producing (among other things) this design for the Prague Christmas markets. The cooperative was an influential craft workshop based in Prague that sought to impart everyday life and environments with greater beauty, drawing inspiration from folk traditions. With its melding of handicraft and modern influences, this character-filled box is typical of the cooperative's avant-garde products: the painted figure's 'stomach' slides open to reveal a small compartment, perfect for the storing of sweets and other treasures. The original is held in the Museum of Decorative Arts in Prague and reproductions of the design are today produced by the Czech design company Modernista. Špála was awarded the title of National Artist in 1946, and the Václav Špála Gallery in Prague has carried his name since 1959.

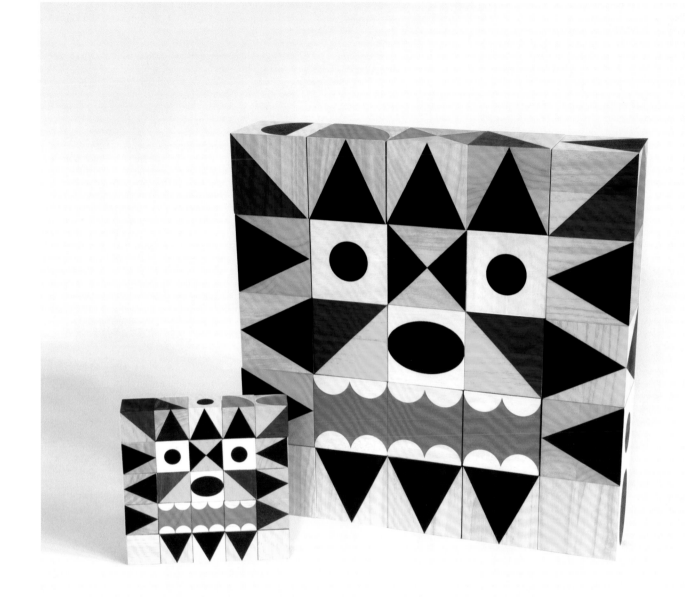

154 ▲●▼

ShapeMaker, 2008
Zoe Miller (1968–)
and David Goodman (1969–)
MillerGoodman

Taken individually, each of the twenty-five hand-printed rubberwood blocks within ShapeMaker is a graphic cube of swirls, arcs, dots and simple, geometric shapes. In concert, however, each block's beauty magnifies into an enchanting patchwork, be it a face, an animal, a flower, a boat or a storm. Blocks can be stacked into small constructions, or lined up for a flat, graphic look. The surface patterns selected by its designers, Zoe Miller and David Goodman, are generous in their interpretive power, lending their shapes to teeth, eyeballs or whatever else a young imagination dreams up. Conceived as an 'endless jigsaw puzzle without a solution',[1] each set comes with some suggested pattern ideas as prompts, but the ShapeMaker's form is ultimately up to the child to engineer. Since its release, the design has become an award-winning classic, appealing to parents and children alike due to its timeless, imagination-probing approach to play.

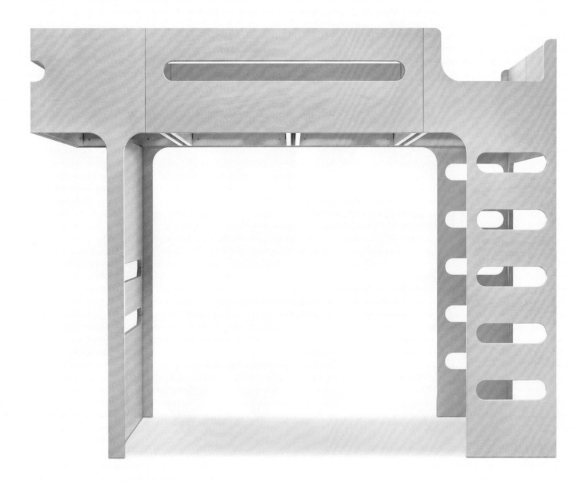

155 🌙

F Bunk Bed, 2012
Agata Seredyn (1976–)
and Arek Seredyn (1976–)
Rafa-kids

The children's furniture line Rafa-kids is the brainchild of two Polish architects, Agata and Arek Seredyn, who were inspired by the birth of their sons, Robert and Frank. Their aim was to create a company that offered quality, affordable design for children, with Agata handling aesthetics and Arek managing the technical components. The F Bunk Bed, recommended for children aged six and upwards, was designed with an eye on versatility and safety as much as for its clean-lined, contemporary styling. Ladders on both sides of the top bunk enable the bed to be placed freely within a room and a supporting leg, perched beneath the slightly cantilevered upper level, provides space for kids to pin up photos, drawings or posters. Another notable feature are the 45-degree mitre joints used on the bed's corners, contributing to the unit's seamless, uber-sleek look.

156 🪑 🐻

Chica Modular Children's Chair, 1972
Jonathan De Pas (1932–91),
Giorgio Decurso (1927–),
Donato D'Urbino (1935–)
and Paolo Lomazzi (1936–)
BBB Bonacina

The Chica, also known as 'The Junior', is a modular children's chair produced by Jonathan De Pas, Giorgio Decurso, Donato D'Urbino and Paolo Lomazzi, a group of Milanese designers who trained as architects and embraced the optimism of the post-war years to create fun and flexible pieces of modern design. Despite being less well known than some of their design contemporaries, De Pas, D'Urbino and Lomazzi created Blow, the first mass-produced inflatable chair, in 1967, which has since become a pillar of Italian design history. Following the trend towards modularity and multi-use pieces, Chica is both an item of furniture and a game. Its different components, made in the three bright colours, are lightweight in construction, encouraging children to reconfigure the chairs and tables into screens, dens, and any other playspace creation that they might dare to imagine.

157 🪑

Little Triple Chair, 2012
Frederik Roijé (1978–)
Studio Frederik Roijé

The Dutch designer Frederik Roijé studied at the prestigious Design Academy of Eindhoven before moving on to hone his skills in the studios of both Piero Lissoni and Marcel Wanders. Now with his own eponymous agency, Roijé produces collections of furniture and lighting, as well as doing bespoke interior design work. The Little Triple Chair, as its name suggests, is a diminutive version of Roijé's popular Triple Chair, intended for adults. Unlike its larger counterpart, the children's version is covered in a polyamide fibre coating, which provides a durable yet soft surface for playing and drawing. By combining a chair, table and lamp into one piece of furniture, Roijé says that the 'Little Triple Chair emphasizes the value and enrichment of reading for children'.[1] Suitable for children aged from two to six, this all-in-one piece is ideal for a range of settings, from homes and schools, to libraries and nurseries.

158 🛴

Adada Rocking Horse, 2016
Fermob (est. 1900s)
Fermob

Since the early 1900s, the French company Fermob has been producing quality outdoor furniture that can be found around the world, in places including the High Line and the Whitney Museum of American Art in New York, the Science Museum in London and the Rijksmuseum in Amsterdam. This friendly little quadruped, made from existing parts of other items of Fermob furniture, happily joined the company's children's line in 2016. Light and lean, the rocker's style echoes the aesthetics of Fermob's iconic Luxembourg collection, designed by Frédéric Sofia to reinterpret the legendary chairs of the Jardin du Luxembourg, which it has manufactured for the Parisian public garden since 1923. Recognized for their inimitable colour variety, Fermob offers Adada in an astounding range of twenty-four fade-resistant hues. Suitable for children aged ten months and older, the versatile rocking horse is weatherproof and comes with rocker pads to protect interior floors. Weighing just 2.5 kg (5.5 lbs), Adada can be easily transported from outdoor to indoor pastures.

159 🪑 ✏️

Asilo Sant'Elia School Chairs, 1936
Giuseppe Terragni (1904–43)
Palini di Pisogne

Charged with designing the Asilo Sant'Elia kindergarten in his hometown of Como, Italy, the architect Giuseppe Terragni set to work conceiving both the building and its interior. The resulting light-filled structure garnered praise as 'the prototype of the new Italian school'.[1] For its furnishings, Terragni turned to Palini di Pisogne, with whom he created three chairs whose tubular-steel construction clearly reveals the influence of Marcel Breuer. The Lariana, perhaps the most notable of Terragni's three designs, distinctive for its elegantly curving back support, was originally conceived for another of his buildings, the Casa del Fascio. It is still produced today by Zanotta as the Sant'Elia Armchair. An architect at the forefront of Italian Rationalism, Terragni produced a small collection of remarkable structures, mostly within Como, in a brief career that would last for only thirteen years. The Asilo Sant'Elia furniture was temporarily reproduced by Atelier in the 1980s, although the company is no longer in operation.

Rocking Item, 2009
Markus Gamsjäger (1983–)
Hausna

Markus Gamsjäger, who began his career working with the Dutch design luminary Maarten Baas, founded his studio, Hausna, in 2004. Nestled in the rural alpine town of Hallstatt, Austria, Gamsjäger focuses on small quantities of products at a time, making each one by hand. This Rocking Item – not quite a horse, or a sheep, or any other recognizable creature – received attention in 2009 at 100% Design Tokyo, where it was included in the *Spot on Wien – Flashing Austrian Design and Music* exhibition. At once quirky and minimalistic, Rocking Item abstracts the form of an animal into two blocks of wood perched jauntily on four, splayed, Bambi-on-the-ice legs. Even without a mane, tail, reins, or a saddle, the Rocking Item still prompts the child to ride through its accessible seat height, large red or green rocking base and handles that jut out like ears.

161 🪑

Alma, 2006
Javier Mariscal (1950–)
Magis

Since establishing Estudio Mariscal in 1989, the Spanish designer Javier Mariscal has consistently produced imaginative, whimsical work, bringing his distinctive style and playful approach to each of his projects. Known for his illustration, Mariscal imbues his furniture with the same emotion and personality that enliven his cartoon characters. Created as an accompaniment to the Linus table, the stackable Alma chair is a poetic plastic seat, its ribbed backrest adorned with tree branches to suggest its structural support. The injection-moulded polypropylene is designed to reflect the four seasons in its colourways; green (spring), orange (summer), brown (autumn) and white (winter). Mariscal took his inspiration for this hard-wearing yet delicate seat from the mystical forests found in fairytales, delivering a design to tickle the imaginations of people of all ages. Alma can be used indoors or, better still, outside among the flora that it favours.

162 🛴

Cavalcade, 2015
Luca Boscardin (1983–)
Studio Bluc

Following the success of Archiville, a cardboard kit of parts that invites children to create their dream city, illustrator and toy designer Luca Boscardin launched his own toy design studio, Bluc, in 2016. Its inaugural collection, Cavalcade, is a band of merry, rocking animals. Constructed from a single piece of wood, each creation is then painted to reflect its species: horse, zebra, deer, crocodile or giraffe. Their intuitive shapes echo the naive spirit of children's drawings, providing a fresh take on the familiar rocking horse. 'My toys are the good old toys – the same ones I used when I was a child,'[1] Boscardin explains. The designer always seeks to keep things simple and abstract, in order to engage a child's imagination and encourage creativity. With the help of a small set of wheels that can be engaged to allow their riders to propel them forward, these endearing creatures are ready to rock and roll.

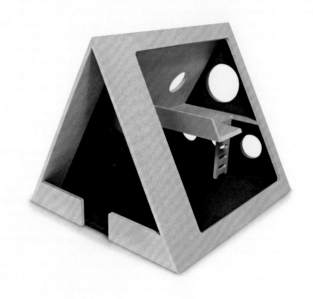

163 🐻

A-Frame Doll's House, 2009
Our Children's Gorilla (est. 2002)
Our Children's Gorilla

Put away the Barbie Dreamhouse! This innovative doll's house, by Swedish toy company Our Children's Gorilla caters to the architecturally minded parent. Designed as a mid-century-modern A-frame, its form is based on the Reese House, designed in 1957 by Andrew Geller in Long Island, New York. Geller was a popular architect of what he called 'summer-use playhouses', feeding the post-war appetite for affordable holiday homes. These simple and experimental beachfront houses were geometric gems, and designed to be both low-cost and low-maintenance. Just like the house that Geller designed for his friend, Elizabeth Reese, this miniature wooden fibreboard version features sloping eaves and a lofted mezzanine. Claiming that his coastal houses were 'for play, so you can do fun things with them',[1] there are perhaps few Modernist architects whose work is better suited to be reinterpreted as a toy than Geller's.

164 ♨ 🐻 🍴🍷

Unfold Table, 2014
Thomas Laurens (1977–)
Self-produced

Across industrial design and architecture of the twenty-first century, sustainability is an omnipresent theme, influencing research, material development and manufacturing methods. With his Unfold Table, the industrial designer Thomas Laurens investigates another important aspect of the sustainability debate: the capacity for a product to endure over time. By fashioning two tiny seats into either end of an elongated table, he creates a dual-purpose piece of furniture. For children, it's a worktable for two; for adults or older children, the surface is a handy, attractive coffee table. By creating a unit that isn't sent to the dump or charity shop as soon as a child has outgrown it, Laurens has helped to avoid the wasteful practices and inbuilt obsolescence commonly associated with children's products. For Laurens, 'the best tool of the designer is his grit to strive for design that is so good it will become timeless.'[1]

165

Lego, 1958
Gotfred Christiansen (1920–95)
The Lego Group

The Lego brick stands as forceful proof that a well-conceived design can transcend age, gender and even culture. Ole Christiansen began manufacturing wooden toys in Billund, Denmark, in 1932, naming his company 'Lego', after the Danish *leg godt* (play well), two years later. Little did he know that the Latin translation of his chosen name, 'I put together', would prove so apt. One of the first Danish companies to invest in injection-moulded plastics, Lego began using the material to produce its Automatic Binding Bricks in 1949. It would be another nine years before the stud-and-tube version, with which we are so familiar today, would be created by Ole's son, Godtfred Christiansen. The Lego brick proved an immediate success, and was celebrated for its enormous potential for imaginative play and stimulation, as well as for its bright colours, durability and easy storage. More than 600 billion Lego parts later, the toy has been universally adopted, inspiring an entire subculture of competitions, films, games and theme parks.

166 🐻

Mozartkugel Music Box, 2006
Adam + Harborth (est. 1998)
Siebensachen

The Berlin-based duo of Jörg Adam and Dominik Harborth, working under the moniker Siebensachen (Seven Things), have developed a unique type of music box based on the appearance of a popular Austrian confection by the same name. Adam + Harborth co-opted the spherical shape of the Mozartkugel, traditionally a liquor-filled chocolate truffle, to produce an object that emits Mozart's melodies with the help of an eighteen-note mechanism. Manufactured in a village bordering Germany's Black Forest, the tennis-ball-sized orb can be wound by a silver key to play the composer's popular aria, 'Voi che sapete', from *The Marriage of Figaro* (1786). The key can be removed to allow the beech ball to roll freely, or alternately can be left in and kept stationary with the help of a small metal ring that serves as a base. The minimal music box now comes in an array of shapes and finishes, including a diamond, a cube and a special-edition lacquered white sphere, aptly named Snowball.

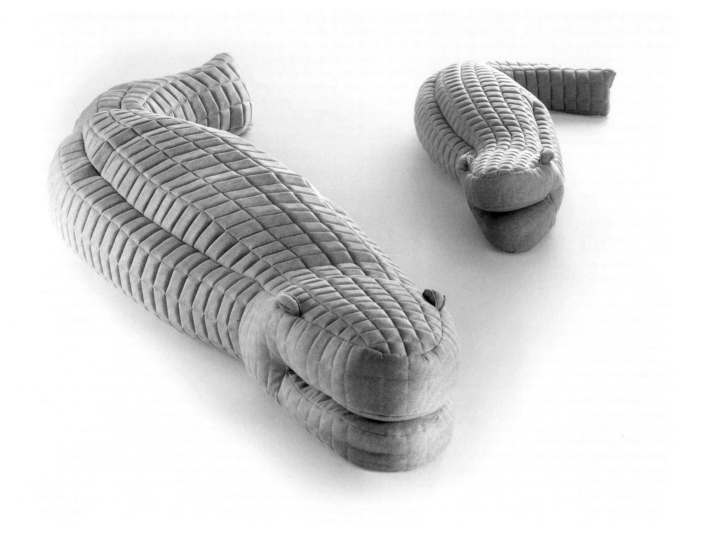

167   🪑   🐻

Crocodile Bean Bag, 2010
Sarit Shani Hay (1964–)
Self-produced

After spending several years in New York, London and Africa, the Israeli designer Sarit Shani Hay returned to her homeland in 1997 to launch her eponymous design studio in Tel Aviv. 'Through the birth of my daughter, I finally discovered my professional and creative calling,'[1] the designer explains. Hay seeks to celebrate childhood, believing that a child's environment plays an essential part in the shaping and nurturing of young sensibilities. By approaching design both rationally and emotionally, her aim is to create objects that also appeal to a child's senses and inspire imaginative thinking. As her Crocodile Bean Bag demonstrates, Hay's work often combines function and wit to transform a child's surroundings into a place of fantastical exploration. Her eclectic portfolio ranges from interior design and pedagogical environments, to custom-made furniture for children and adults.

168 ✎ �🪑

Kloss Modules, 2016
Friis & Moltke (est. 1954)
Kloss

Created by the Norwegian architecture and design firm Friis & Moltke, the Kloss Modules are part of a comprehensive collection of children's furniture conceived to incite curiosity and stimulate motor skills through exploration. Founded in 1954, the firm became known for introducing the strong rectilinear forms of Brutalist architecture to Norway. Today, Friis & Moltke's portfolio of work comprises architecture, furniture, lighting and products – all designed with sustainability and the user in mind. The Kloss Modules are characteristic of this approach: the multicoloured, stackable units are inspired by children's natural tendency to build their own universe from the objects around them. Made from plywood that has been coated with environmentally friendly laminate and linoleum, they are designed to be long-lasting. At once storage, seating and shelving, the modules are both functional and aesthetically pleasing.

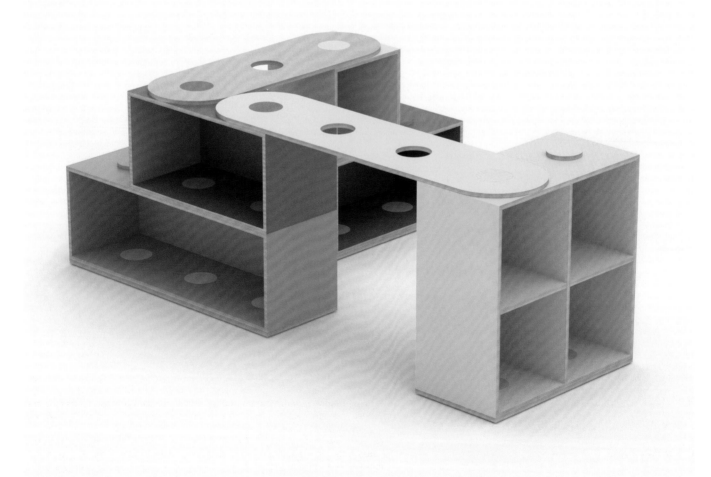

169 🪑

Wood-Stock, 2010
Alberto Fabbian (1981–)
Prototype

While waterproof, wipeable plastic can be a handy material when it comes to cleaning up after kids, its negative environmental impact is well-known. Alberto Fabbian's Wood-Stock furniture concept offers a clever response to this problem. When it debuted at Milan's Salone del Mobile in 2010, it presented a noble idea: to reduce the use of plastic by creating a modular, multi-use design. By producing a single, flexible piece of plastic through rotational moulding, Fabbian devised a basic structure that can be outfitted with different wooden attachments in order to alter its form and purpose: with short wooden legs, the unit functions as a footrest or play horse; with long ones, it transforms into a stool; in between, it's a dinky child-sized chair. The collection's name is a play on 'rootstock', a horticultural term, which describes a plant or stem onto which another variety is grafted. Like the plant's rootstock, the Wood-Stock lets users combine different parts of the piece together to create something new, allowing the furniture to grow and adapt to the changing needs of the family.

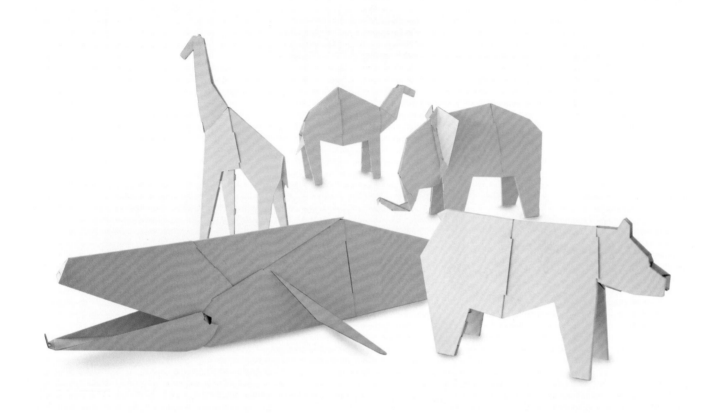

170

My Zoo, 2012
Martí Guixé (1964–)
Magis

The Catalonian designer Martí Guixé prides himself on work that is unconventional and unexpected, so it seems only fitting that his collaboration with the child-centric Me Too collection created for Magis would result in a happy cohort of giant origami animals. Each cardboard creature, be it an elephant, bear, giraffe, camel or whale, comes flat-packed, with folding assembly instructions. Available in small or (impressively) large sizes – the large whale is 7.3 metres (24 feet) long – the animals' unadorned surfaces invite personalization through colouring or drawing. 'All the animals are good; they do not bite, they are not heavy and they can be recycled,'[1] Guixé quips. Trained in Barcelona and Milan as an interior and industrial designer, Guixé is known for his brilliantly simple ideas and imaginative inventions in food design. He has also collaborated with many of the industry's best-known companies, such as Camper, Desigual, Droog, Danese and Alessi.

171 🐴

Rocky Rocking Horse, 2012
Marc Newson (1963–)
Magis

With Rocky, the traditional rocking horse gets an arresting makeover. Taking inspiration from medieval jousting horses, the internationally acclaimed Australian designer Marc Newson created a thoroughly modern-day interpretation of this children's design mainstay. Like the Bunky bed (257), Newson's first foray into the kids market, Rocky is made from rotational-moulded polyethylene, chosen for its durable qualities. The material allows the body of the horse to be shaped from a single piece, producing a seamless form with no sharp edges or exposed moving parts. As with other objects in the designer's considerable body of work, Rocky represents a cartoon-like reinterpretation of a familiar form. Here, its rocking mechanism is hidden: instead of the usual curved wooden rockers, two steel bars are covered in silicone tubing to dampen noise and produce a gliding motion. Designed for children between the ages of two and six, Rocky's chic silhouette and sisal reins lend his rider an air of effortless panache.

School Desk, 1946
Jean Prouvé (1901–84)
Ateliers Jean Prouvé

In the post-war years, devastation in Europe, rising birth rates and a shortage of materials called for greater creativity and collaboration in the building of new schools. This desk, made for two pupils aged eight to fourteen, displays the eminent French designer Jean Prouvé's keen interest in materials and avant-garde techniques. With its attached chairs and use of enamelled steel, the desk demonstrates both an economical use of space and an innovative application of industrial metal-processing practices to increase its durability. Through his material experimentation, Prouvé introduced both the Machine Age and the streamlined aesthetic to European interiors. Trained as a metalworker, Prouvé considered himself an engineer, rather than a designer, and was hugely knowlegeable of production processes. Over the course of his career, he turned his hand to industrial, architectural, structural and furniture design.

173 🛴

Hippomobil Rocker, 1998
Tone Fink (1944–)
Tischlerei Künzler

While the Austrian artist Tone Fink is best recognized for his fanciful, darkly humourous drawings and paintings of everyday objects, he is also known to occasionally turn his hand to product design. Hippomobil, created in 1998 from a variety of materials and in different scales, stands as angular (and rocking) proof of this. The modern abstracted form of this functional sculpture maintains a whimsical playfulness due to its rocking-horse form and quirky anthropomorphics. Hippomobil was produced in a stout and slim version, in both a natural oak and white-lacquer finish, by the Austrian furniture makers Tischlerei Künzler in 2007. Easily doubling as a bookcase or side table due to its sharp vertical ends and horizontal surfaces, Hippomobil has been widely celebrated, appearing in Austrian design exhibitions and collections, including the Werkraum Bregenzerwald handicraft museum in Andelsbuch, and at Galerie Walker at Schloss Ebenau.

174 🛴

Cavallo Soft, 2015
ZPZ Partners (est. 1998)
Play+

Supportive enough to straddle but flexible enough to accommodate a playful gallop, this foam horse is equal parts seat, cushion and toy. Like the other furnishings in the Play+Soft range, Cavallo Soft is made of foam with a removable fabric covering, making it easy for children to move the horse themselves, as well as simple to clean. Play+Soft is a collaboration between the play furnishings company Play+ and Italian architectural firm ZPZ Partners, and is based on the Reggio Emilia approach to childhood education. Developed in the post-war years by psychologist Loris Malaguzzi, and parents of the villages surrounding Reggio Emilia, the philosophy considers the physical environment of early childhood learning to be fundamentally important, referring to it as the 'third teacher' (after adults and children). The Play+Soft range is designed to introduce a variety of sensory stimuli to children's play environments, including a rich chromatic spectrum, seen here in the Cavallo Soft's striking combination of orange and yellow.

175 🍴

Dydinnela Dinner Set, 2013
Doiy Design (est. 2008)
Doiy Design

In 2008, Elodie Deviras, a self-styled entrepreneur and trendspotter, teamed up with her engineer–designer husband, Jaime Monfort, to create a brand that offered cool lifestyle objects at affordable prices. The Barcelona-based company Doiy Design, creates contemporary homewares and lifestyle accessories that bring order to life with a sense of playfulness. This Dydinnela Dinner Set embodies their clean, witty aesthetic. Made from melamine, it features individual slots – each shaped like an element of a sunny, domestic landscape – for a fork, knife, spoon, plate, bowl and cup. When designing the set, Doiy thought about children's cognitive growth: fitting the variously shaped cutlery and plastic crockery into its respective places helps children to develop a sense of precision. The dishwasher and microwave-safe dining set also helps to teach children how to set the table and, with any luck, keeps cutlery from sliding onto the floor.

176 🪑 🍴

Onni High Chair, 2010
Hannes Vähäsöyrinki (1978–)
Puusepänliike Hannes Oy

Finnish furniture making company Puusepänliike Hannes Oy (Hannes Oy Carpentry) is a small family business dedicated to making quality hand-crafted wood products – so much so that the Onni High Chair, its most popular and widely produced piece, took many years and several variations to perfect. Designed in 2010 by company founder Hannes Vähäsöyrinki, the birch chair embodies the simple elegance and functionality of Scandinavian design. Made using a combination of manual woodworking and CNC technology in a series of twenty-five meticulous steps, each part is hand-crafted in a former sleigh building factory in Tuulos, Finland. For easy maintenance and increased durability, the upper ring and seat are reinforced with the highest quality cross-laminated birch plywood, highlighting the beautiful natural pattern of the material. Recommended for toddlers who are able to sit upright by themselves, the Onni affords minimal interference between child and parent, helping to build an inclusive, non-hierarchical atmosphere in the home.

177 ✎

Ladrillos, 2005
Javier Mariscal (1950–)
Magis

When the pioneering Italian furniture company, Magis, launched its Me Too line for children, it challenged designers to not only scale down adult-oriented furniture, but rather to 'view the world and the objects in it through the eyes of a child'.[1] Created by Javier Mariscal, Spain's polymath designer best known for creating the graphic identity of the 1992 Summer Olympics in Barcelona, Ladrillos demonstrates how effectively he is able to adopt a child-like perspective with his bookshelf system. Reflecting Mariscal's early career in comics and a strong graphic sensibility, this piece features shelves of laminated wood supported by colourful moulded-plastic *ladrillos* (bricks) shaped like various cartoon characters. Each supportive figure comes with its own name and can be mixed and matched according to a child's taste. Whimsical and playful, Ladrillos enables children to establish both a functional and emotional relationship with the objects that surround them.

178 ⌗ 🐻

Welcome to the Jungle, 2010
Rui Alves (1977–)
Self-produced

Born in Paços de Ferreira, an area of Portugal famed for its furniture production, Rui Alves grew into the trade observing his grandfather at work in his small carpentry shop and his father working in an industrial furniture factory. Alves's own studio, Rui Alves Design Office, was established in 2001. Welcome to the Jungle is a character-driven collection of nesting and interlocking furniture pieces that can be arranged in various configurations to serve as tables and stools, or even stack to become shelves. 'Like many children his age, my son loves to play with his growing collection of toy animals', Alves explains. 'I came up with the idea of creating a group of small pieces that might make children and adults feel the same about items of furniture.'[1] Their playful colours, proportions and names, from Jerry the giraffe and John the hippopotamus to Joe the crocodile, are the perfect source of motivation for the next generation of Alves furniture makers.

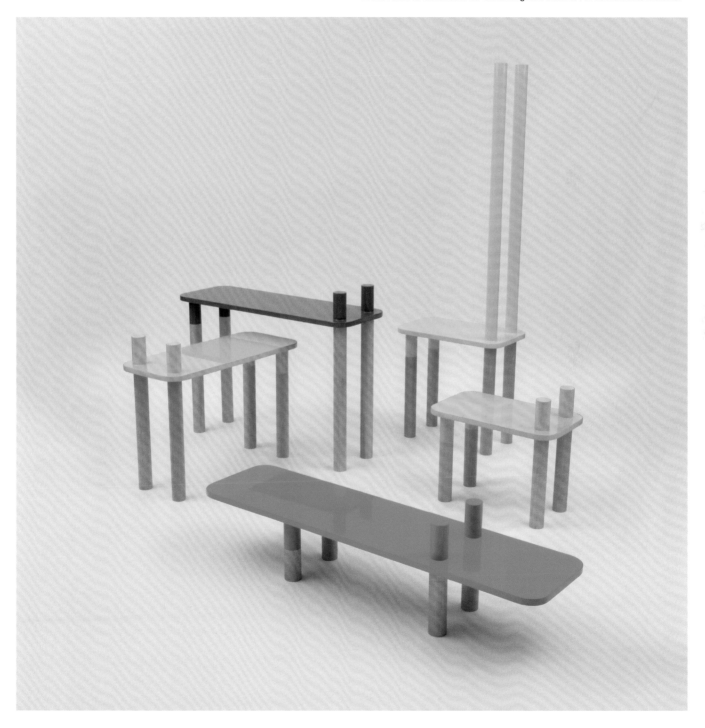

179 🐻 🪑

Tobifant Child's Writing Desk and Chair, 1977
Luigi Colani (1928–)
Kinderlübke

Luigi Colani's visionary design has a look all of its own. At once biomorphic and futuristic, his forward-thinking creations have ranged from supersonic aeroplanes to racing cars, furniture and watches. While best known for his pioneering work in plastic, Colani also produced a number of wooden designs over the course of his career, including this unusual children's desk and chair. Each planar surface of the set serves as its own unit, fastened to the others with a small wooden wedge. Tiered notches on the chair's legs and back, as well as on the table, enable the user to adjust the size of the set to best fit their needs. Colani's design was originally sold with an optional toolset. With a quick knock, the mallet in the set could hammer out the fastening wedges and collapse the furniture entirely.

180 ♯

Plytek Chair, c. 1965
Ken Garland & Associates (est. 1962)
Prototype

The English studio Ken Garland & Associates produced many designs for children during the 1960s, led by its namesake graphic designer, who was also a prolific writer and activist. Over the course of the decade, they designed both graphics and toys for Galt Toys, one of the studio's biggest clients. Along with other London-based designers, such as Roger Limbrick, Patrick Rylands and Fredun Shapur, Ken Garland & Associates were part of a movement that applied late-Modernist approaches to children's play objects and environments. Their belief that stimulating open-ended play is conducive to a child's development is reflected in the Plytek Chair's bright primary colours and the modular function of its interlocking pieces. The chair – an unrealized prototype – was exhibited at the London Festival of Architecture in 2015, as part of a show organized by the British design practice Systems Studio, which brought together lesser-known toy designs from the 1960s.

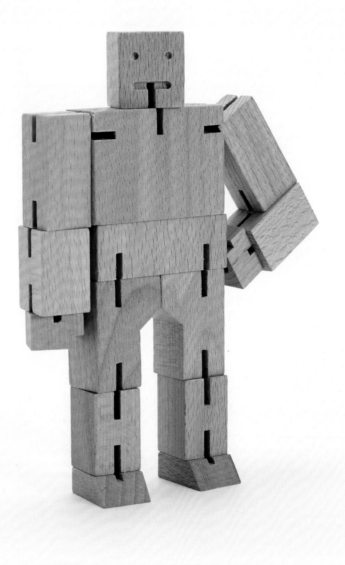

181 🐻

Cubebot, 2010
David Weeks (1968–)
Areaware

This sprightly wooden robot, whose elastic joints and simple configurable form allows for dozens of unique, dynamic poses, is the creation of New York-based furniture and lighting designer David Weeks. Inspired by three-dimensional wooden puzzles called *kumiki* (a word which itself means 'to join wood together'), Cubebot can also be folded away into a perfect cube. The toy was the result of a design challenge in Weeks's studio and can be produced entirely using simple workshop tools. Cubebot quickly became much beloved by children and adults alike and, while the original design remains the same, it is now manufactured by Areaware in micro, small, medium and large sizes, as well as in several painted colours, each with its own facial expression. 'I think the reason for his popularity is the simplicity, the benevolence, the asex-uality,' Weeks explains. 'He's not threatening, he doesn't have an action-figure attitude, and I think the wood really adds that element of quality.'[1]

Go Car, 2013
Lisa Mahar (1965–)
Kid O

As a disciple of the thoroughly modern belief that children learn best through play, the American company Kid O creates toys that engage children with a host of shapes, colours and moving parts. Lisa Mahar, a mother of three, founded Kid O with the idea of infusing Montessori ideals – namely, that simple design stimulates the imagination – within all of her toys. The Go Car's pared-down form is the result of careful observation into the way that young children play. Its rounded body and cut-out handle allow small hands to securely grip the car, while its rubber-coated wheels make for a satisfyingly free-wheeling play experience. Like most of Kid O's products, Go Car is made using PVC- and BPA-free plastic. Deliberately gender-neutral, Go Car puts both girls and boys in the driver's seat, providing an appealing way to develop their hand-eye coordination skills.

183 🐼

Contraband Cork Cargo Ship, 2013
Daniel Michalik (1972–)
DMFD

Any parent of a young child knows how difficult it is to stave off the onslaught of plastic toys. This challenge is only heightened at bath time, for which this Cork Cargo Ship provides an environmentally responsible alternative. Shipshape for the tub, pool or tabletop, this toy from DMFD, the studio of Brooklyn-based designer Daniel Michalik, is lightweight, pleasantly tactile and as elegant as it is playful. The designer has been working with cork for over a decade, initially drawn to its affordability while a student at the prestigious Rhode Island School of Design. His Cortiça chaise longue, made entirely out of cork discarded by the bottle stopper industry, caught the design world's attention in 2006. The designer has continued to experiment with the material over the past decade, celebrating both its sustainability and traditional uses, while continuing to discover its new capabilities.

184 ♯

Children's Chair, 1961
Walter Papst (1924–2008)
Wilkahn

The German industrial designer Walter Papst designed this convertible child's chair in 1961 for the office furniture company, Wilkahn. Its fibreglass-shell seat can be reconfigured into a rocker, high chair or swing with only a few additional components. Responding to the baby boom and housing shortage of the post-war years, manufacturers like Wilkahn looked to appeal to parents with affordable, multipurpose and space-saving designs. Papst conceived this versatile single-seat construction following in the footsteps of Charles and Ray Eames, whose iconic PAW Shell Chair of 1950 was the first design to use the preform method of reinforced-plastic moulding. Papst received several prominent awards for his avant-garde designs, including at the Musée des Arts Décoratifs in Paris, iF Design Award in Hanover and the Triennale in Milan. His Rocking Sculpture (221) further exemplifies his pared-down futuristic style.

185 ☾

Grand Berceau Crib, 1969
Olivier Marc (1930–)
Prototype

This unusual cradle's high sides create a comforting cocoon-like space, reflecting Olivier Marc's interest in rounded forms as spatial expressions of a mother's womb. As both an analyst in the traditions of Freud and Jung, and an architect, Marc sought to understand architecture as a reflection of our inner selves. His book, *Psychology of the House* (1972), even opened with a chapter analyzing womb-like structures around the world, informed by Marc's own extensive travels. This cradle was produced by Mobilier National, a French state agency dedicated to preserving and restoring collections of palace furniture. In 1964, André Malraux, the French writer and Minister of Cultural Affairs, initiated a contemporary design workshop within the agency. His ambition was to cultivate a contemporary French style to rival the courts of Louis XIV and Louis XV. The workshop ARC has collaborated with hundreds of designers to produce over 600 prototypes since it was founded. As such, this fibreglass-reinforced polyester cradle was most likely a prototype that was only produced in limited numbers.

186

Charly Balance Bicycle, 2014
Wolfgang Sirch (1964–)
and Christoph Bitzer (1964–)
Sirch

With its slim design, the Charly Balance Bicycle looks fit for the velodrome. Made by Sirch, which specializes in steam-bent wood designs, honed through years of sled production, the body of the bicycle is made from solid ash wood that is cut to form after being shaped, stored and dried, yielding an extremely strong frame that has a simple finish of clear lacquer. The Charly bike helps children learn how to balance and features an adjustable steering control that prevents extreme handlebar movements. Its thin rubber tyres allow for a smooth and comfortable ride, while eliminating the need for inflation. The saddle, made of grey lacquered birch, is adjustable to two heights, enabling children of different ages to ride it. Designed by Wolfgang Sirch and Christoph Bitzer, every detail of the Charly bike is made in Germany, right down to the tyres. The winner of several awards, Sirch is known for producing minimalist, heirloom-quality toys that are rugged enough to last generations.

187 ◱

StratFlex Rhino, 2013
Al Stratford (1949–)
Wintec Innovation

Al Stratford has served as the president of the South African Institute of Architects, but he is best known for his industrial design work and development of innovative building technologies. One of these is StratFlex, a wooden, flat-pack technology that combines plywood with specialized rubbers, enabling products to be shipped flat then folded into shape upon delivery. Demonstrating the qualities that led this patented material to win Design Indaba Expo's Innovation Award in 2013, the StratFlex Rhino draws inspiration from Charles and Ray Eames's iconic, plywood elephant of 1945 (13). Unlike the Eames Elephant, however, Stratford's creation can be flexed to express different stances, or even unfolded completely. Refining the pattern with computer and paper models over a period of months, Stratford finally brought the spirited animal to life, and in so doing, desiring to call attention to the plight of the endangered South African rhino.

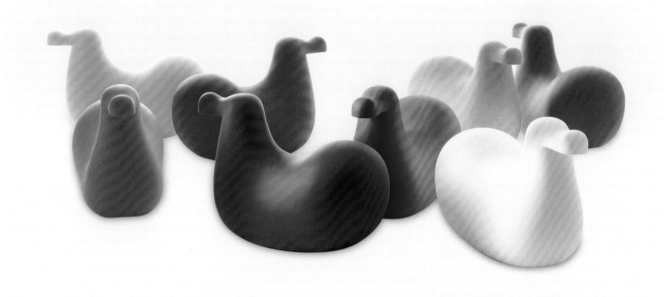

188

Dodo, 2009
Oiva Toikka (1931–)
Magis

Oiva Toikka is perhaps best known for his glassware, notably the collection of birds he created for Finnish design company, Iittala. Toikka has also worked as a costume designer for Marimekko, Finland's celebrated home furnishings, textiles and fashion company. Reminiscent of his bright and playful glass sculptures, Toikka's rocking chair of 2009 translates his avian theme into a different scale and material. With Dodo, Toikka's polyethylene interpretation of the extinct flightless bird, once native to the island of Mauritius in the Indian Ocean, echoes the life-size scale of the bird, which stood at 1 metre (3 feet) tall. Here, Dodo's characterful beak is complemented by its smooth, inviting form. At home both indoors and out, this child-centric 'feathered' friend arrives in red, blue, white and yellow, and is sure to bring joy to any environment.

189 🛎 ⬛ 🐻

Fun(k)tion Object, 2001
El Ultimo Grito (est. 1997)
Nola Industrier

Like the Spanish studio's multi-limbed Mico Chair (119), El Ultimo Grito's Fun(k)tion Object is a multifunctional stool that encourages children to sit or play in a variety of ways. In addition to functioning as a seat, the K-shaped block can act as a side table, footstool or magazine holder – merely by changing its orientation. Stacked in multiples, it can transform into large building blocks to create a wall or any structure of a child's imagining. Husband-and-wife team Roberto Feo and Rosario Hurtado originally met in Madrid, before founding their studio, El Ultimo Grito, in 1997. With combined backgrounds in economics, sociology and social anthropology, Feo and Hurtado create work that playfully probes the role of design. Widely exhibited, their designs have been included in the permanent collections of the Victoria and Albert Museum, London, the Stedelijk Museum, Amsterdam, and the Museum of Modern Art and Museum of Arts and Design, both in New York.

Piccola Via Lattea, 2009
Mario Bellini (1935–)
Meritalia

Designer and architect Mario Bellini is a celebrated figure of late twentieth-
and early twenty-first-century design. His career has taken him from the
storied offices of Olivetti to the editorial ranks of *Domus* and the galleries of
New York's Museum of Modern Art. Piccola Via Lattea (Little Milky Way),
Bellini's super-lightweight range for Meritalia, makes a stellar addition to the
world of children's design. Its modular units are made from low-cost materials that are infrequently seen in the children's furniture market – stainless-
steel mesh from industrial filters, and recycled fibres used in construction
and transportation. Each piece is filled with pockets of air, using a concept
borrowed from packaging design. Able to be easily moved around and even
lifted overhead by youngsters, the series is also durable enough for both
indoor and external use. Lest you feel left out of the fun, Bellini experimented
with a similar collection for adults, including a version that glows in the dark.

191 🐻 ◧

Free Universal Construction Kit, 2012
Golan Levin (1972–)
and Shawn Sims (1986–)
F.A.T. Lab and Sy-Lab

When artist and engineer Golan Levin observed his son trying to fit pieces from different construction sets together, he decided to put his professional skills to work in a new way. With the help of a 3D printer, Golan created the Free Universal Construction Kit, a set of nearly eighty connectors and adaptors that allow pieces from ten different construction toys – from Lincoln Logs to Lego – to interface with one another. Golan's so-called 'meta-mashup system' opens the door to new creative worlds, encouraging radically constructive play and enabling children to create entirely different forms. Produced with the help of fellow artist and designer Shawn Sims of Synaptic Lab (Sy-Lab), the Free Universal Construction Kit is not for sale. Rather, the design of all of its adaptors can be downloaded from Thingiverse.com as a set of 3D models in .STL format, suitable for reproduction by open-source 3D printers such as Makerbot.

192 🐻

Jacks, 1850s
Designer unknown
Various

Jacks is one of humanity's most abiding games, with variations that criss-cross the globe and date back millennia. The most familiar version, with ball and metal pieces, dates from the 1850s, although the jacks – with their four rounded and two spiky points – are a modern version of the sheep knucklebones that were used in games as far back as Ancient Egypt. While versions have varied over time, the essential gist of the skill-based game remains the same: once the jacks have been tossed on the ground, the player bounces the ball and must pick up one jack before catching the ball with the same hand, before it falls to the ground a second time. Each subsequent round requires the player to pick up an additional jack, with the winner being the person who manages to go the most rounds. Jacks and its variations can be played alone or with others, and can assist in the development of children's hand-eye coordination.

Pippocampus, 2004
Gianpietro Gai (1972–)
and Luca Nichetto (1976–)
Disguincio

The name of this 'postmodern ode to a rocking horse'[1] alludes to the fact that it is indeed a rocking seahorse (or *hippocampus*, in Latin). The idea for the curvaceous creature emerged when Gianpietro Gai made a wooden rocking horse for his friend's first child. Realizing that he wanted to design a modern take on the traditional toy, Gai and Luca Nichetto, both members of the Italian design studio, Disguincio, quickly turned to rotational-moulded plastic for its durability and cost effectiveness. The pair's interpretation mimics the organic surface and deep fold of the seahorse's tail, creating a form that has been rigorously tested to ensure that it cannot overturn. Suitable for children aged one to three, the durable plastic body of Pippo-campus makes it well suited to rough play and outdoor living. However, its sleek, sculptural frame was conceived so that it would be equally at home indoors and not a fish out of water amongst adult furniture.

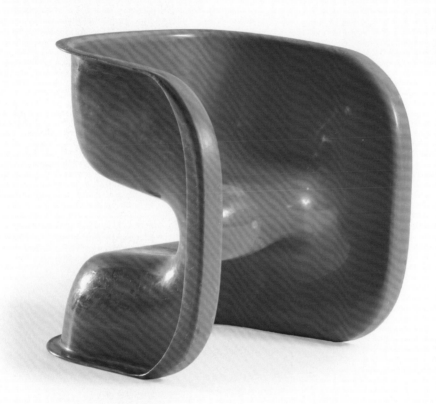

194 🪑 🛴

Space Chair, 1970
Johannes Foersom (1947–)
and Peter Hiort-Lorenzen (1943–)
Cado-France

The Space Chair, also known as the Cantilever Chair, by eminent Danish design duo Johannes Foersom and Peter Hiort-Lorenzen, typifies a modern design sensibility with its swooping lines, use of moulded plastic and clear reference to the space obsession of the post-war era. Yet its simplistic-seeming form belies its double functionality: the chair is reversible and can also be inverted for a child to ride like a rocking horse. For Hiort-Lorenzen, the 1970s were a time of significant advancement in materials and manufacturing technology, signalling a critical point in children's design. 'My inspiration was partly to work with a design that inspired children's motor skills, and partly to realize the type of 3D forms possible with injection-moulded plastic.'[1] The chair was manufactured by Cado-France, led by Poul Cadovius, a Danish pioneer in designer plastic furniture. With its sculptural suggestion of constant movement, this undulating chair has a futuristic feel – befitting of the dynamic activities that it is sure to host.

195 🪑

Piedras, 2006
Javier Mariscal (1950–)
Magis

The apparently monumental and rough-hewn Piedras (Stones) collection might appear to have emerged from a quarry, yet it is actually made from plastic. Crafted and sized for children, the sofa, armchair and low table playfully evoke a primitive caveman style, with the natural tones, organic textures and abstract forms that make them equally at home in an adult environment. Suitable for use both indoors and out, the Piedras trio is part of an extensive collection that Javier Mariscal created for Magis's Me Too children's line. Prolific, playful and irreverent, Mariscal established his own Barcelona-based studio in 1989, and has since applied himself to everything from furniture, painting and sculpture, to graphic design, illustration and interior design. His design for Barcelona's Summer Olympic Games mascot in 1992 saw him heralded a national design star.

196

Bronto Children's Chair, 1997
Richard Hutten (1967–)
Droog / currently Gispen

Best recognized for his 'No Sign of Design', clean, anti-design aesthetic, Dutch designer Richard Hutten gained world acclaim shortly after graduating from the renowned Design Academy Eindhoven in 1991. Always interested in the process of making, Hutten's Bronto Children's Chair emerged in 1997 from his desire to create a piece of furniture that was not constructed. Using a self-made rotational moulding machine, Hutten injected it with two plastics of different consistencies and colours. The harder plastic was used on the load-bearing sections of the chair, while the more rubber-like plastic was used on corners, making it ideal for children. The surface pattern of each chair varied according to the result of the mixture of the two materials in the rotating mould. Named after the long-necked Brontosaurus, Bronto was originally produced by the conceptual Dutch studio Droog, which Hutten has been involved with since its inception in 1993. The chair was later adapted and produced by Gispen.

Happy Bird, 2015
Eero Aarnio (1932–)
Magis

Four decades after Eero Aarnio broke onto the scene with his Ball Chair in 1963, he made a triumphant return with several pieces for Me Too, the children's line of Italian furniture brand, Magis. Known for creating playful work that invokes a sense of endearment, Aarnio drew inspiration for Happy Bird from an experience close to his heart. 'For a long time, we have been feeding birds which don't migrate south before the winter,' Aarnio explains, 'and they have become like well-loved friends.'[1] Available in two sizes and three colours, Happy Bird provides a spirited perch for children, who can straddle the bird's body like a horse. Alongside Pony (229) and Puppy (01), Happy Bird is the latest in Aarnio's growing stable of sculptural seats that can double as beloved pets, showcasing Aarnio's ability to see things from a youthful perspective.

198 🍴

Snack Rabbit Nesting Utensils, 2015
Winnif Pang (1962–)
Fred & Friends

A bunny rabbit clings to a carrot, forming a tidy cutlery set that brings a touch of whimsy to children's mealtimes. The diminutive set features soft, ergonomic handles made from BPA-free virgin silicone, making them comfortable for little hands to grip, while the fork and spoon are stainless steel. As an everyday item with a playful twist, the Snack Rabbit utensil set encapsulates the fun and functional spirit typical of both its designer, Winnif Pang, and manufacturer, Fred & Friends. Based in Hong Kong, the prolific designer produces some 100 designs a year, having built a global reputation for inexpensive products that appeal to the inner child in everyone. His novelty ice trays and tea infusers have been widely imitated. Pang's own studio, Hoobee, designs numerous household items for Fred & Friends, seizing on a gap in the market for fun and useful but also affordable products.

199 ♨

Children's Highchair, 2003
Maartje Steenkamp (1973–)
Droog

As a young mother, Maartje Steenkamp observed that her children liked to be held up at her height so that they could observe the world from the same level. A designer by training, she decided to take matters into her own hands, creating a chair that could elevate infants to new heights; as the child grew taller the chair would get smaller. Steenkamp's simple beech design displays notches on the legs to indicate each possible stage of the chair. Sold with a saw and instructions printed on sandpaper, the chair enables parents to adapt its height in line with the changing needs of their growing child. Part of the collection of the esteemed conceptual Dutch design company Droog, Steenkamp's Highchair debuted at the Salone del Mobile, Milan, in 2003, and went on to win the prestigious international Red Dot Award for product design in 2006.

200 ♯

Truss Collection, 2004
Scott Klinker (1965–)
Context Furniture

The Truss Collection, developed by Scott Klinker and produced by Context Furniture in Royal Oak, Michigan, bases its form on architectural frameworks, specifically the truss. Klinker, an alumnus of Cranbrook Academy of Art, and now head of its graduate 3D design programme, primarily developed Truss as a line for adults, but also created a child-sized chair that pairs perfectly with the coordinating, scaled-down occasional table. Each piece is made from CNC-milled birch plywood topped with a laminate surface. Items pack flat and can be assembled without fuss. Created in 2004, the Truss Collection reflects Klinker's interest in 'router aesthetics', or forms that explore the sensibility brought about by CNC technology. The result, says Klinker, is 'a no-nonsense functionalist aesthetic with some exaggerated proportions, which read as cute, without being "cutesy."'[1] Neither whimsical nor clichéd, Klinker describes the Truss children's furniture as being 'for "modern" kids, who can appreciate clean lines'.[2]

201 🛴 🪑

Smile Rocking Chair, 2000
Luis Ramírez (1968–)
Estudio Dekuba

With its joyful swinging movement and curving red back, this aptly named children's rocking chair feels almost as sculptural as it is functional. Created by the Cuban designer Luis Ramírez, the Smile Rocking Chair borrows some of its visual cues from his other adult seating designs and is made of wood, with hand-embroidered fabric and stainless-steel fixtures. Ramírez studied industrial design in his hometown of Havana, where he continues to live and work today, specializing in furniture, ceramics and interior design. A prolific designer, Ramírez founded Estudio Dekuba with fellow designer Miguel Garcés in 2005 and has gone on to receive Cuba's National Industrial Design Award multiple times. Driven to raise awareness about the value of design, he also serves as the vice president of the Caguayo Foundation for Monumental and Applied Arts, whose mission is to promote Cuban art and design both locally and around the world.

202

Bauhaus Hampelmann, 1926
Margaretha Reichardt (1907–84)
Naef

As one of the female progeny of the Bauhaus, Margaretha Reichardt is remembered for her weaving and textile designs, which included upholstery for Marcel Breuer's tubular-steel chairs. The wooden toys that she designed as a first-year student at the legendary design school have proved to be equally enduring, however, and her Hampelmann (jumping jack) continues to be produced by the Swiss wooden toy company, Naef, today. Similar to conventional jumping jack toys, Reichardt's is a painted wooden figure with limbs that dance when the string is pulled. By pinning hers to a wooden frame, Reichardt showcases the puppet's bright geometry, with careful attention paid to rhythm and contrast, qualities shared by her later weavings. Created for a preliminary design class run by Josef Albers and László Moholy-Nagy, the toy represents the playful side of the Bauhaus, which cultivated a joyful, childlike student culture in its exploration of new educational approaches.

203 🐻 ◼️▲●

Birds-on-a-Tree, 1964
Creative Playthings (est. 1951)
Creative Playthings

Founded by Frank and Theresa Caplan in 1945, Creative Playthings was among the post-war era's greatest toymakers, collaborating with the likes of Isamu Noguchi, Louis Kahn, Antonio Vitali and the Museum of Modern Art, New York, to create simple, beautifully designed toys that stimulated a child's creativity and imagination. The couple, both scholars and educators, maintained that abstract forms that emphasized shape, colour and texture over lifelike details were better for a child's development. As with Enzo Mari's Sedici Animali (16 Animals) of 1957 (50), Birds-on-a-Tree uses clean incisions to transform a single block of wood into a tree with eleven birds, leaving no unused space. The puzzle also doubles as a do-it-yourself sculpture kit, as the birds can be made to perch on the branches in any variety of ways. The design's simplified palette and abstracted shapes are a perfect reflection of Creative Playthings' modern design proclivities.

204 ◭

Build-a-Wall, 2008
Christian Lessing (1960–)
Lessing Produktgestaltung

Humans have used dry stone walls to demarcate territory and enclose livestock for thousands of years. Their construction embodies a fascinating, ad-hoc design ethic: held together without mortar or any other binding agent and composed of found materials from the surrounding landscape, dry stone walls rely on wedging stones together into a supportive patchwork. The nimble construction of such walls allows them to withstand fluctuating temperatures and precipitation, with well-formed versions standing for a century or more. German designer Christian Lessing turned to dry stone walling for Build-a-Wall, his unusual, award-winning, building-toy-cum-puzzle. Drawing inspiration from their overlooked engineering marvel, Lessing designed forty individually shaped blocks, carved out of maple, beech, elm and walnut wood to emulate the natural tonal variation of rocks. Although Build-a-Wall requires precision and patience, each builder has the satisfaction of knowing that their creation is entirely unique. In 2010, Lessing extended his Build-a-Wall concept into the construction of a sofa, a modular seating design consisting of nine foam 'stones'.

205

Joupii, 1970
Patrick Rylands (1942–)
Il Leccio

British designer Patrick Rylands has been creating children's toys since the 1960s. As the chief designer for Ambi Toys for over thirty years, he is responsible for some of the most iconic objects designed for play. His pared-down, sophisticated designs, exemplified in his Bird and Fish (39) and Duck (341) bath toys, effortlessly combine simplicity and movement, encouraging children to use their imaginations to bring the characters to life. Joupii was created in 1970, when Rylands became the youngest person to win the Duke of Edinburgh's Prize for Elegant Design (now known as the Prince Philip Designers Prize), at the age of twenty-seven. Carved from wood, Joupii's limbs attach to its body with elastic cord, allowing the little figure to strike any number of poses. 'The main purpose of a toy is to enable children to enter the world of make-believe,' Rylands explains, 'as it is in this way that children relate to reality.'[1]

206

Nesting Dolls, 2011
Ingela P Arrhenius (1967–)
Omm Design

Drawing inspiration from the graphic design of matchboxes, vinyl and magazines from the 1950s and 1960s, the Swedish illustrator Ingela P Arrhenius describes her style as 'naive'. Her book, textile and children's designs are often characterized by endearing renditions of people, animals and everyday objects, as well as by an exuberant use of colour, promoting both visual stimulation and tactile engagement. This is exemplified by her popular series of lift-the-flap children's books, which encourage toddlers to peel back pieces of felt in order to uncover successive parts of the book's story. These nesting dolls, illustrated by Arrhenius, which come in a variety of characters from robots and circus figures to animals, incorporate the same storybook aesthetic. Unlike traditional versions, they are fabricated from moulded plastic, making them more durable, and easier for kids to take apart and reassemble. Produced for Scandinavian toy company Omm Design, Arrhenius's striking graphic sensibility makes these toys as decorative as they are playful.

207 ꕥꕥ

Mono Petit Cutlery, 1959
Peter Raacke (1928–)
Mono

This diminutive knife, fork and spoon set was designed by Peter Raacke as the children's version of Mono-a, the iconic German cutlery that brought flatware into the modern era. Developed in 1959, Mono-a presented a simplicity and affordability that differed radically from the ornate table silver typical of the time. Produced from a single piece of metal, each item rejected decorative detail, streamlining cutlery to its most elemental aesthetic. The design was considered so unorthodox that the company's president, Heinrich Seibel, requested that his son, Herbert, develop the project with Raacke in secret. Its launch marked the birth of Mono, a design-forward tableware company that has since produced wares ranging from teapots to pepper mills. Mono-a became the bestselling flatware set of the post-war era, and is now considered an icon of modern design. Made of stainless steel, Mono Petit has been scaled for small hands. Unlike its big brother, each utensil features a small ornamental fish, bird or snail.

208 🐻

Maison Rive Gauche, 2012
Wolfgang Sirch (1964–)
and Christoph Bitzer (1964–)
Sirch

With its sleek flat roof and transparent acrylic walls, the Maison Rive Gauche by Sirch is a far cry from the traditional gabled-roof doll's houses of yester-year. Part of the Swiss company's award-winning Sibi line of toys, the house is a smaller version of Sirch's similarly contemporary Villa Sibi of 2004. Accessible from all four sides, the birch plywood Maison comes furnished with four stools, a sofa, two beds, a kitchen counter and an aluminium shower. The acrylic walls can also be moved to create different interior layouts. Created by Wolfgang Sirch and Christoph Bitzer, the two designers behind the Sibi children's range, Maison Rive Gauche is named after the Left Bank in Paris, the post-World War I home of artists, writers and philosophers, and the current location of the city's largest development project, Paris Rive Gauche. Sirch and Bitzer's doll's house nods to the contemporary glass buildings that now define the area.

209 🪑

Family Furniture, 2012
Frederik Roijé (1978–)
Studio Frederik Roijé

Family Furniture exhibits the simplicity and functionality for which Dutch designer Frederik Roijé is known. Whether through furniture, lighting, interior or product design, Rojié's Amsterdam-based design agency maintains a quiet, linear tone. Family Furniture's trim profile is characteristic of Roijé's inter-connecting designs, such as his Little Triple Chair, which incorporates a built-in table and standing lamp (157); and Guidelines, a wall fixture that serves as a magazine rack. Made to encourage more intergenerational family time, Family Furniture underlines Roijé's concern for the practical over the conceptual. 'I think the relation between product and user is very important,' he affirms.[1] Fashioned from powder-coated aluminium cut into a ribbon-like strip, Roijé's design gently folds to delineate a taller chair for an adult and a smaller children's version. Two back rests, sized accordingly, curve upwards. Light wood strips at its base complete this minimalist white piece.

210 🪑 🍴

Zig-Zag High Chair, 1940
Gerrit Rietveld (1888–1964)
Metz & Co

The story of this unusual Zig-Zag design by Gerrit Rietveld begins in 1934, when the goal was to make a chair that could be constructed by folding a single piece of material. Initially experimenting in fibre, steel tube, sheet steel and plywood, Rietveld later abandoned his single-sheet idea in favour of four pinewood cupboard shelves, which could better support a person's weight. In order to produce a stable seat, each zig-zag fold is fastened with screws and dovetail joints, and reinforced with triangular wooden wedges. The high chair version of this unorthodox design adds vertical supports and a horizontal dining surface. This was not Rietveld's first dalliance in highly sculptural high chairs; in 1915, he created a De Stijl-like construction reminiscent of his iconic Red and Blue armchair (270). Almost two decades later, Danish designer Verner Panton would revisit the zig-zag form with the help of new material advancements, resulting in the Panton chair (400).

Marionettes for *König Hirsch*, 1918
Sophie Taeuber-Arp (1889–1943)
IC Design

Marionette shows were a popular cultural form in the early twentieth century – even among avant-garde artists, who conceived of the puppets as sculptures in their own right. In 1918, the Swiss artist Sophie Taeuber-Arp created seventeen marionettes for a richly embellished Dada staging of Carlo Gozzi's fairy tale *König Hirsch* (*The Stag King*) in Zürich. Her abstracted wooden figurines marked a departure from the construction of traditional marionettes. Turned on a lathe, rather than carved, and with their mechanics exposed, their limber, ringbolt-jointed movements reflect Taeuber-Arp's experience as a trained dancer who had performed in Dada soirées at Zürich's Cabaret Voltaire. The director of the puppet theatre closed *The Stag King* after just three performances, claiming that Taeuber-Arp's creations were too modern and daring; yet, their euphoric reception by the avant-garde made the production an icon of Dadaism. In 2016, Ameico collaborated with the Museum of Design in Zürich to reproduce three of the marionette designs, each one handcrafted by a professional woodworker in Germany's Black Forest.

Walkee Tricycle, 1945
William B Fageol (1880–1955)
Fageol Motor Company

In contrast to the familiar pedal-propelled tricycle, William Fageol's aptly named Walkee Tricycle of 1945 was designed with walking in mind. In his patent application, Fageol described the 'simple but rugged' tubular-steel construction as 'affording an unimpeded movement of the legs'.[1] Thanks to the wide, open stance of its front wheels, riders propelled themselves in a walking movement without bumping or scuffing their feet. The top cross-bar further supported the user, while also serving as a steering device. Rubber discs above each wheel served as 'bumper collars', softening impact for a careering youngster. While the Walkee was not Fageol's first vehicle design, it was certainly his smallest. As a teenager, William and his brother, Frank, built an eight-passenger self-propelled vehicle that they claimed was Iowa's first car. The Fageol brothers went on to earn a sizeable reputation from the creation of vehicles of all kinds, from luxury cars and racing cars, to trucks, marine engines and tractors.

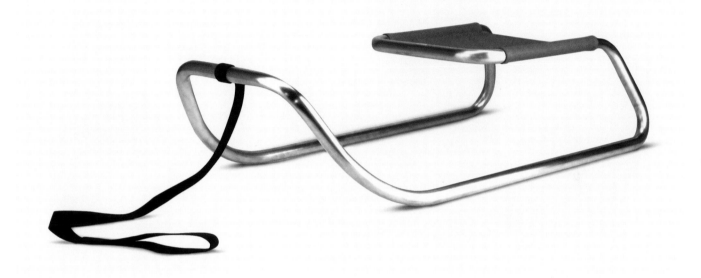

213 🛷

S 333 Sled, 2006
Holger Lange (1967–)
Thonet

If Marcel Breuer had designed a sled, this would have been it. Produced in 2006, the sleek profile and bent metal frame of the S 333 Sled is a nod to the form-follows-function principles of the eponymous Bauhaus school. Streamlined and shiny, the lightweight aluminium sled was designed by the celebrated German industrial designer, Holger Lange. In addition to its formal elegance, the cantilever of the seat both echoes Thonet's S 33, the first cantilevered chair of 1926, and acts as a shock absorber to aid smooth, speedy descents. When it was founded in nineteenth-century Vienna, Gebrüder Thonet introduced the world to bentwood furniture. Its Chair No. 14 of 1859 was a breakthrough in industrial production and launched Thonet onto the global scene. Inspired by the designs of Breuer, Ludwig Mies van der Rohe, Le Corbusier and Mart Stam, the company expanded its production line to include tubular steel in the 1920s.

214 ✏️

Drumbo Elephant Money Box, 1972
Bernd Diefenbach (n.d.)
Dresdner Bank
/ currently Commerzbank

Today a collectible item, these elephantine money boxes were originally given to children opening bank accounts or making a deposit at Germany's Dresdner Bank. Drumbo – the elephant's name – was chosen from 1,600 employee suggestions and combines the words Dresden, Dumbo (Disney's 1941 cartoon protagonist) and Jumbo (a famous nineteenth-century African elephant). Created in 1972, the original elephant was green, although it has since been produced in several colours and three different sizes. To encourage children to accumulate change for their savings accounts, some versions required a key to open them, or even featured a plastic flap that had to be broken in order to open the bank. Happily, Commerzbank, which acquired Dresdner Bank in 2008, still distributes yellow Drumbo piggy banks today. Drumbo is the work of Bernd Diefenbach, yet it is often misattributed to the famed German designer Luigi Colani, who designed an elephant mascot for the paint company Caparol, in 1984.

215 🐻

Duck and Duckling, 1959
Hans Bølling (1931–)
Architectmade

A family of ducks made history in 1959 when they stopped rush-hour traffic in Copenhagen. One by one, the mother duck and her ducklings waddled out into the road in the Frederiksberg neighbourhood, safeguarded by a quick-thinking policeman, who brought cars and pedestrians to a halt. The story made headlines and was turned into an iconic poster by the artist Viggo Vagnby. That poster, 'Wonderful Copenhagen', is now one of the city's most famous images. Hans Bølling was also struck by the charming tale and created this group of teak ducks to capture the whimsy and charm of this memorable moment in Copenhagen city life. Now considered classic Danish toys, Bølling's duck and ducklings are among a series of wooden creatures made by the designer, whose collection also includes a mermaid, his humorous Strit figurines, and Oscar the dog. Bølling's career, however, expanded beyond product design: trained as an architect, he also designed town halls and domestic complexes.

216 ☾

Cradle from the Children's Hospital in Faenza, Italy, c. 1930s
Designer unknown
Manufacturer unknown

Similar to Prouvé's cradle (opposite), this interwar Italian crib is defined by its linearity and striking metal ribs. Used in the children's hospital of Faenza, the northern Italian town, famous for its fine enamelled ceramics called Majolica, the red iron cradle is very much a product of its time and origins. Its pared-down geometry speaks to the influence of the Bauhaus aesthetic and the rise of Rationalism (see Giuseppe Terragni's Asilo Sant'Elia School Chairs, 159). With the country in the firm grip of Fascism, Benito Mussolini was intent on defining a style of design and architecture that befitted the new Italy. He favoured the Rationalists, who sought to strip the classical forms of ancient Greece and Rome of their adornment, and instead translate them into modern materials. For Mussolini, who understood the importance of winning over the nation's youth to ensure the perpetuation of Fascist ideology, design was put to service as a powerful propaganda tool. This cradle appears at once poised and austere.

217 ☾

Cradle, 1936
Jean Prouvé (1901–84)
Private commission

Known for his innovative use of industrial engineering techniques, French designer, architect and engineer Jean Prouvé is one of the most influential figures of early modern design. Trained as a metalsmith, Prouvé's intimate knowledge of the practice remained the foundation of his career and work, his furniture often displaying novel approaches to both materials and construction. Striving for the most efficient design, Prouvé drew inspiration from the new technologies of the day, namely within the automotive and aeronautical industries, often imbuing his objects with a futuristic look. This interwar cradle was a commission for the baby daughter of Prouvé's collaborator and friend, Marcel Lods. His signature use of metal is here displayed like a rib cage, providing structure and safety to the exterior base of the bed. The mobile bassinet borrows the look of early aviation design, with its rubber wheels resembling an aeroplane's landing gear.

218 🛴

Hobbel, 1967
Piet Hein Stulemeijer (1941–2009)
Placo Esmi

With its Modernist look and smiling profile, the Hobbel, by Dutch designer Piet Hein Stulemeijer, is as sculptural as it is functional. Made of solid beech with lacquered beech spindles in either red or blue, the designer's training as an architect is visible in the rocker's strong three-dimensionality. Stulemeijer designed the Hobbel when he was just twenty-six years old – its multifunctional features reminiscent of the Schaukelwagen of 1950 (438), another rocking toy designed to be ridden both upside down and right side up. Manufactured by Dutch furniture company Placo Esmi, Hobbel is part of the furniture collection of the Stedelijk Museum in Amsterdam, as is Stulemeijer's High Chair (268), which was produced the following year. A multi-talented designer, he would go on to produce large-scale sculptures for public institutions, later becoming known for his work with glass.

219 ☽

Cradle, 1957
Frank Rohloff (n.d.)
Self-produced

An early work of the Californian designer Frank Rohloff, this walnut-wood cradle features a sculptural form and solid wooden construction, which is typical of the American Studio Craft movement. Characterized by its bold, abstract forms, the post-war movement is known for its interest in non-traditional materials and new techniques, and its rejection of mass production. Rohloff produced both one-off pieces and prototypes during his career, later becoming known for combining woodwork with new materials like plastic resin, which he treated as if it were a decorative wooden inlay. The higher manufacturing costs of his small production runs were buoyed by post-war prosperity. Rohloff was later appointed to oversee manufacturing at Metropolitan Furniture in San Francisco, a company which, like Rohloff, was active in defining the mid-century design spirit that came to be known as California Modern. This cradle was exhibited in New York at the Museum of Contemporary Crafts (now the Museum of Arts and Design) in 1957.

220 ♯

Cut-Out Chair, 1990s
Isku (est. 1928)
Isku

Finished in primary-hued acrylics of yellow, red and blue, this plywood chair was designed and produced by the Finnish company Isku in the 1990s. Despite its apparent minimalism, the chair is memorable for its circular, punched-out, decorative peek-a-boo detail and distinctive folded form. Moulded from maple-veneer plywood, the Cut Out is one of many designs that Isku has produced for children, with schools and learning environments continuing to be a key focus area for the company. Founded in 1928 by Eino Vikström, the Finnish family-owned company continues to manufacture all of its designs at its factory in the city of Lahti. Committed to ecologically sustainable production, Isku sources its timber from sustainably managed forests and is unique among Finnish furniture manufacturers in adopting the PEFC Chain of Custody certification system to track the origin of all its raw materials.

221 🛴

Rocking Sculpture, 1958
Walter Papst (1924–2008)
Wilkhahn

With a knack for eye-catching, sculptural furniture, the German designer Walter Papst produced a number of memorable fibreglass works in the 1950s and 1960s. One of them was this cardinal-red child's rocker, created for Wilkhahn, which received accolades at the Milan Triennale in 1960. Referring to its original horse-form with only a few wiry 'tail hairs', this rocker exchanges naturalistic representation for formal grace. Notably, it is made from moulded fibreglass – still a novel material for furniture and toys at the time of its design in 1958. In its simple form and avoidance of the usual 'rocking horse' classification, Papst's plaything reflects the era's pedagogical preference for encouraging imagination and interpretation through abstraction. In 2007, Wilkhahn reissued the Rocking Sculpture in a limited edition run of 1,500, in celebration of their one hundreth anniversary.

222

Creatures, 2003
Donna Wilson (1977–)
Self-produced

Like children's doodles brought into three dimensions, Donna Wilson's idiosyncratic knitted creatures positively overflow with personality. The Scottish designer began producing animals that 'weren't too pretty and cute, or ugly and scary'¹ when she was a student at the Royal College of Art in London. She traces her passion for colour and texture to a childhood spent on a farm in Banff, Aberdeenshire, and cites among her influences her grandmother, who taught her to draw and paint, the colourful, pattern-filled designs of Alexander Girard and Stig Lindberg's quirky Scandinavian creations. Today, Wilson's repertoire extends to textiles, clothing, homewares, furniture and even a confectionary collection. However, production of her beloved plush toys continues – as does her commitment to handicraft. Each of Wilson's wild and wacky creations is made by hand in her East London studio, before being named and given a set of amusing traits, such as Fee, the cat who is said to enjoy 'the finer things in life'. We can relate.

Milky Desk, 2015
Pinar Yar Gövsa (1979–)
Lil'Gaea

Sparked by the birth of their first child, Lila, Turkish designer Pinar Yar Gövsa and her husband, Tugrul Gövsa, founded Lil'Gaea, a child-friendly offshoot of their furniture brand, GAEAforms. The Milky Desk, part of the brand's inaugural collection in 2015, is a child-centric, adjustable series that adapts to the needs of a growing child. Comprising a desk, bench, chair and series of storage cubes, the Milky line is made from birch plywood with a range of natural finishes. The seating and desk can be tailored, by virtue of their extendable legs, to suit children of varying ages, thereby also extending the life of the pieces. Lil'Gaea's commitment to clean-lined, ecological and practical creations for kids has produced a number of attractive objects, from furniture and lighting, to carpets and toys, including the Dogbox (238) and Dog Lite (87).

224 🐻 ✎ 🔺

Rigamajig Junior, 2016
Cas Holman (1974–)
Heroes Will Rise

'If we always give children toys that have the story built into it, we rob them of the opportunity to … make up the story themselves,'[1] says Cas Holman, a toymaker and Associate Professor of Industrial Design at the Rhode Island School of Design. To counter this tendency of offering children a prescribed narrative within play, Holman created Rigamajig, a large-scale building kit of wooden planks, wheels, pulleys, nuts, bolts and rope that comes with no instructions. In Holman's view, giving children less leaves room for them to contribute more, and thereby 'develop habits of agency, independence and self-determination'.[2] Launched in 2011, Rigamajig accommodates between two to twenty children playing under supervision. Widely seen as a tool to encourage creativity, unstructured play and process over outcome, the kit has been adopted by museums, classrooms and parks. In 2016, Holman introduced Rigamajig Junior, a smaller kit of 160 parts, designed for home use. 'When children have agency in their play,' she states, 'they learn to have agency in their lives.'[3]

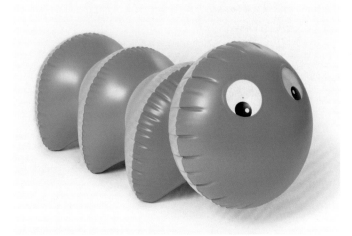

225 🐻 🛴

Inflatable Animals, 1969
Libuše Niklová (1934–81)
Fatra / currently Maammo

Libuše Niklová, one of the Czech Republic's most important designers, created a range of extraordinary plastic toys that are still collected today. Believing that children should play as actively and creatively as possible, Niklová sought to design toys that appealed to all of the senses. The designer's most lively creations were her inflatables, which included characters from a variety of cultures, animals, aeroplanes and astronauts, and ranged in size from small enough to hold in one hand to large enough to sit on. Conceived in the mid-1960s, the inflatable giraffe, horse, pig, caterpillar and elephant (among others) were intended for children to ride. Their flexible nature meant that the toys would begin to walk as a child moved. Cutting-edge in their use of rubber sheets and heat-welded joints, the collection became familiar fixtures in many Czech households. Originally produced for Fatra, Niklová's animals are now made by Maammo.

226 🪑

Zorro Chair, c. 1972
Meurop (est. 1947)
Meurop

In the early 1960s, the Belgian furniture company Meurop abandoned its use of typical materials, such as metal and wood, in favour of plastics and other synthetics – embracing the space-age aesthetic that was to define the coming decade. The company's artistic director, Pierre Guariche (1926–95), is credited with Meruop's shift in direction and this children's chair represents the company's new focus on producing modern, family-friendly furniture at an affordable price. Made of fibreglass-reinforced polyester, Zorro is durable, lightweight and easy to clean. Its bubble-like form is an exaggeration of the smooth curves found in Guariche's adult designs from the same period. Comprised of two interlocking halves, the chair's hollow interior can serve as a toy box, or the two pieces can be separated to become two low seats. Today, some of the designer's work for Meurop has been brought back into production by companies such as France's Maison du Monde.

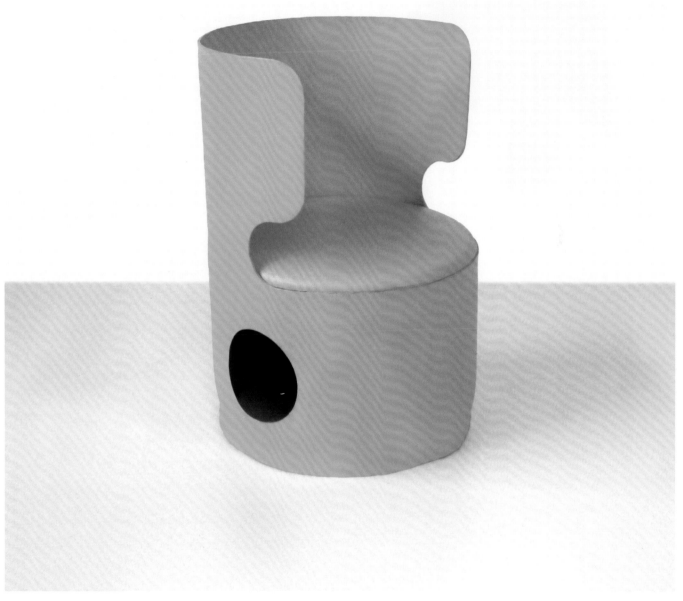

227 🪑

Elephant Chair, 1967
Jean-Louis Avril (1935–)
Marty LAC

Many architects and designers experimented with inexpensive and unconventional materials in the 1960s, seeking to democratize modern design. Influenced by the utopian aspirations of his Parisian milieu, Jean-Louis Avril became a leading figure with his sculptural cardboard furniture, which was manufactured by Marty LAC from 1967–73. Avril began experimenting with cardboard thanks to his father-in-law, who worked at a factory that produced the material. His designs combine volumetric forms with cutout details to create furniture that sings with harmony and proportion. The Elephant Chair (so-called because of the shape of its backrest) is part of a children's line that was lacquered in bright jewel tones of yellow, red or blue. Lightweight enough for a child to move around, the chair is fashioned from celloderm, a high-density fibreboard often used for archival boxes. Avril's work earned him widespread recognition and led to his inclusion in the French Pavilion at the World's Fair in Montreal in 1967, and in the Milan Triennale of 1968.

228 🪑

Efebino Stool, 1970
Stacy Dukes (n.d.)
Artemide

These stools represent a unique hybrid of American design and Italian production. Designed by Californian interior designer Stacy Dukes, the Ebefino Stool was produced by Italian manufacturer Artemide in 1970. With their bright colours and injection-moulded ABS plastic construction, the stools reflect the era's enthusiasm for everything 'plastic fantastic', buoyed by European manufacturers such as Artemide and Kartell. The stackable stool was designed for the Los Angeles Public Library and was accompanied by the Efebo Stool – a wider, double-height sibling, which accommodated adults. With their four-legged designs, the stools are both durable and stable. Dukes went on to found Stacy Dukes Design in 1983 and works as a designer in Orange County. Artemide continues to work with contemporary designers, today specializing in producing lighting for the home. Their designs have been collected by major institutions around the world, including the Efebo, which is held in the collection of New York's Brooklyn Museum.

229 🛴 🪑

Mini Pony, 1973/2011
Eero Aarnio (1932–)
Melaja

The late 1960s saw Scandinavian designers Eero Aarnio and Verner Panton using newly available materials to push the formal and functional boundaries of furniture. Since 1962, Aarnio has built a reputation for his space-age flair, sculptural know-how and pioneering use of materials. While his pudgy Pony appears to be designed for a child, it was originally scaled for adults. Its playful Pop sensibility transforms the traditional hobby horse into a chair, toying with our expectations of what adult furniture should be. First sculpted from polyurethane and metal in 1973, Pony takes its place alongside the Ball Chair (1963), the Pastil Chair (1968) and the Tomato Chair (1971) as an instantly recognizable Aarnio creation. In 2011, Aarnio produced a scaled-down version in soft plastic, the Mini Pony. At its lower height, this design is easier for young riders to mount and its durable material means that it could safely spend time in the pasture – or even just in the garden.

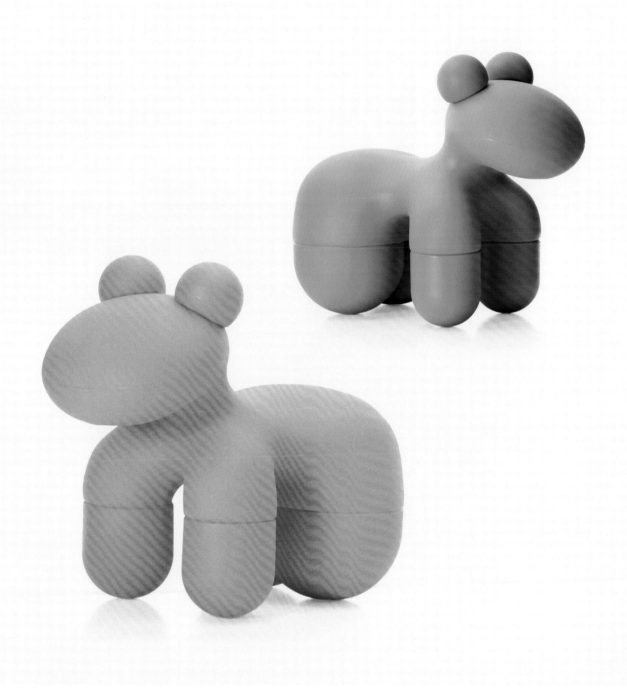

230 🐻

Play Kitchen, 2014
Mia Dela (1975–)
Sebra Interior

When designer Mia Dela gave birth to her first son Gustav in 2002, she found herself surrounded by a world of unappealing pastel and plastic. Wanting more aesthetic and ecologically conscious options, she took matters into her own capable hands, founding Sebra Interior in 2004. Her textiles, lighting, furniture and toys are made from natural materials, such as wood, wool and organic cotton, and feature a subtle colour palette. Dela's Play Kitchen, made of birch with metal detailing, has a refined, curved design that makes it appear more like a piece of contemporary furniture than a toy. Happily at home in an adult environment, its oven, two dials for hotplates and a removable sink invite active play cooking, cake baking – and easy cleaning! The play kitchen, best suited to toddlers aged from one to three, comes in both grey and rose gold.

231 🛴

Plywood Car, 2006
Hideo Yamamoto (1957–)
Muji

No flashy colours, no logos, no bells nor whistles: this ride-on car, made of plywood and produced by Muji in 2006, embodies the humble, sensible design ethos of its Japanese manufacturer. Muji first opened its doors in 1980 with forty household and food products, under the name Mujirushi (no-brand) Ryōhin (quality goods). Nearly thirty years later, the company has ballooned as an enterprise, with 7,000 products for sale and 400 stores in Japan alone. Focusing on simple, well-designed items, the company has become much-loved for its clean-lined products, which range from kitchen-ware to electronics, and even ride-on toys. As a brand, Muji tends not to identify individual designers behind a product, however this particular one was conceived by Hideo Yamamoto. Material selection is of key importance to the company's design process, and this wee wheelie puts it on full display with its unpainted plywood body and minimal hardware.

232

Bird Whistle, c. 1920s
Jožka Baruch (1892–1966)
Modernista

Jožka Baruch trained as a woodworker before going on to study painting and printmaking at the Academy of Applied Arts in Prague. While best known for his advertisements, posters and books, Baruch also produced a number of wooden toys during his career, items which frequently reveal the influence of Czech folk art and craft traditions. By combining geometric forms with painted folk motifs, toys like this Bird Whistle can be seen as a response to Art Deco's embrace of a rustic folk aesthetic. Baruch's work is admired for its childlike perspective and literary influences, informed by his extensive work in book illustration and cover designs. Today, replicas of his wooden figures are produced by Tilia Studio, a Czech arts and crafts workshop that employs and supports socially vulnerable people.

233 🪑 ✏️

Munkegård Desk and 3105 Chair, c. 1952–5
Arne Jacobsen (1902–71)
Fritz Hansen

The lucky children of the Munkegård School spent their days in a world designed entirely by the iconic Danish designer and architect, Arne Jacobsen. Situated north of Copenhagen, the school embodied the popular belief that children feel most at home in intimate environments scaled to a child's body. The single-storey school, designed to house a thousand students between the ages of seven and fifteen, retained a sense of intimacy through classrooms that functioned as self-contained units, with ample lighting and easy access to specially landscaped gardens. Jacobsen designed the school furniture in three different sizes to accommodate children at various ages. Manufactured by Fritz Hansen for the school, this plywood and tubular-steel desk, with its green Formica writing surface, had a hook for a satchel and was lightweight enough to be moved easily according to the classroom's needs. Both Jacobsen's desk and stackable beech chair exhibit the thermo-form technology that permeated Scandinavian design in the 1950s.

234 🌙

Milky Sleeper, 2015
Sarah Simone Jørgensen (1981–)
Ollie|s|Out

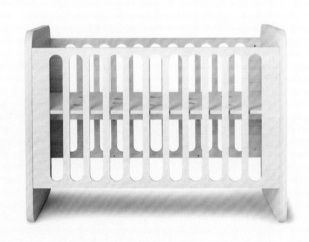

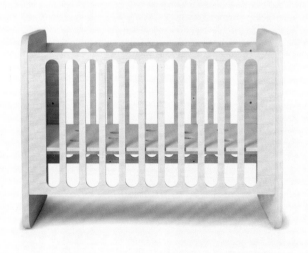

Sarah Simone Jørgensen founded Scandinavian interior design company OllieIsIOut in 2015 with a mother's concerns in mind. Rooted in the language of Scandinavian design, Jørgensen's crib is streamlined, timeless, subtle and unisex in appearance. Each OllieIsIout piece incorporates natural materials to create an object of enduring quality and Milky Sleeper, which features an oak veneer that has been painted with an organic water-based paint, is no exception. Designed to fit a standard baby mattress, the crib can adjust to three different height settings to accommodate the child's growth from newborn to toddler. Small bed rails provide an additional precautionary measure for children old enough to climb in and out of bed on their own. Milky Sleeper's rounded corners, clean lines and subdued hue will bring a sense of calm to any child's nursery.

235 🍴

Rebel Dining Set, 2005
Johan Verde (1964–)
Stelton

As his celebrated Spir range of porcelain demonstrates, Norwegian designer Johan Verde is a master at devising innovative ceramics. His elegant and ergonomic Rebel line, produced for Stelton of Denmark, shows this skill. As a father of three, it is not surprising, perhaps, that the shape of the mug, dish and spoon are inspired by close observation of a child's actions at the dinner table. The plate, designed as a bowl within a bowl, has a concave edge that easily catches spilt food. Its pleasing porcelain shape is made practical by a rubber base, which helps to keep it stationary. Similarly, the porcelain mug has a rounded top to facilitate drinking and a broader base that stabilizes it. The shape of its easy-to-grasp handle is echoed in the stainless-steel spoon. The Rebel trio won an iF Design Award for exceptional product design in 2006.

Ducky, 2014
Dor Carmon (1977–)
Normann Copenhagen

The first Ducky that Israeli designer Dor Carmon created was a treasured gift to his baby daughter. Drawing inspiration from the timeless charm of wooden toys, Carmon sought to design something 'emotive and irreplaceable that [his daughter] could have with her throughout her adult life'.[1] Known for employing a variety of techniques in the design development process, including ceramic casting and metalwork, Carmon used injection-moulded plastic to test and perfect Ducky's form for mass production. Available in black, grey or a natural oak finish, the subtle application of rubber on Ducky's wheels makes for pleasingly smooth movement. Filled with nostalgia and character, this sophisticated toy showcases Carmon's characteristically careful attention to proportion and creation of fluid curves. Ducky is produced by Normann Copenhagen, a multi-award-winning Danish furniture, lighting and accessories company.

237 ☾ 🐻

Abitacolo Bed, 1971
Bruno Munari (1907–98)
Rexite

While Bruno Munari is best known for his inventive children's books, the Italian artist, designer and inventor created remarkable designs for children in a variety of scales and mediums. Conceived in 1971, the Abitacolo Bed is a multifunctional and customizable piece of furniture that makes a child the master of their own micro-universe. Recalling high-tech industrial equipment, Abitacolo ('cockpit' in Italian) eschews typical childish motifs and loud colours for a pared-down, sophisticated and yet playful approach to children's design. Munari drew on his own childhood desire for an imaginative and contemplative space as the impetus for Abitacolo, writing of the resulting design, 'It's a habitat … it's the minimum but gives the maximum… at every moment transformable.'[1] The coated-steel structure is open in both form and concept, inviting children to personalize the unit to suit their own tastes and storage needs.

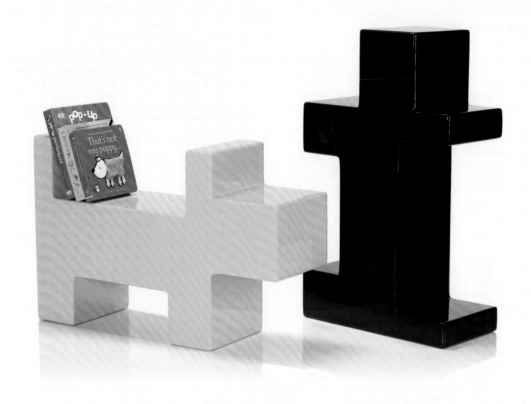

238 🪑 ✎

Dogbox, 2015
Pinar Yar Gövsa (1979–)
Lil'Gaea

When Turkish design duo Pinar Yar Gövsa and Tugrul Gövsa had their first child, Lila, they decided it was time for their studio, GAEAforms, to expand as well. The result was Lil'Gaea, a design label devoted to creating clean-lined, ecological creations for little people. Part of their inaugural collection in 2015, the aptly named Dogbox is a sculpturally angular canine made of painted wood, which readily adapts to a number of uses. When positioned horizontally, it can serve as a seat, desk or easily accessible shelf for a child's most beloved books. Amusingly, when stood vertically, it resembles a fire hydrant. Coated in a glossy, non-toxic paint, Dogbox is weatherproof, child-safe and sure to be a beloved member of the family.

239 ⚘

Mokuba Rocking Horse, 2003
O&M Design (est. 1973)
Brdr. Krüger

The work of Takashi Okamura and Erik Marquardsen, co-founders of Copenhagen-based furniture studio O&M Design, is inspired by each partner's cultural heritage: Japanese design philosophies meet the traditions of Danish craftsmanship and *hygge*, the notion of creating cosy and convivial atmospheres to nurture well-being. This refined sense of artisanry and warmth is visible in their limited-edition Mokuba ('rocking horse' in Japanese), which was designed for the 125th anniversary of Brdr. Krüger, a company known for its contemporary interpretations of the Danish Modern aesthetic. Mokuba's elegant, simple and honest features give it a friendly appeal; its smooth surface and robust frame invite children to engage. Made from lacquered Danish beech and with a tail of vegetable-tanned leather, the horse's familiar, lighthearted design and natural materials give it a comforting presence.

240 🪑

Mammut Children's Chair, 1993
Morten Kjelstrup (1959–)
and Allan Østgaard (1959–)
IKEA

Since its launch in 1993, the Mammut series of chairs, stools and tables has been IKEA's most popular and enduring children's collection. Architect Morten Kjelstrup and fashion designer Allan Østgaard recognized that children's furniture must respond to different proportions and functional requirements than those of adult's furniture. Mammut, with its cartoon-inspired stubby proportions, was designed to cater to a children's world of fantasy rather than to their parents' aesthetic preferences. The robust furniture is hollow, making it lightweight and easy to manoeuvre; however, it is also very stable, thanks to the bottom-heavy shape of the legs. Consulting their own children to determine the range of soft, sherbet-colour tones, Kjelstrup and Østgaard chose to use a non-toxic, durable plastic that can be used indoors or out, and can easily be wiped clean. The chair was selected as Sweden's Furniture of the Year in 1994.

241

Ziggurat, 2009
Enzo Mari (1932–)
Danese Milano

The Italian designer Enzo Mari is known for his sensitivity to form and colour, as well as his belief that design should be not only functional but also beautiful – an ethos informed by his communist convictions. Ziggurat was designed for Mari's grandson and features wooden sticks in a range of lengths and colours, which can be assembled into an endless array of forms, such as buildings and cars, or abstract compositions. The simplicity of these wooden blocks exemplifies Mari's belief that the true spirit of Italian design comes from its artisanal roots, which values the humanism of craftspeople over their capacity as industrial workers. The painted birch blocks are solvent-free and were produced by the Italian design company Danese Milano, with whom Enzo Mari has been a long-term collaborator. The company, which was founded in 1957, is known for its design-driven play objects, which they claim work to 'recover the dimension of play as a cognitive tool'.[1]

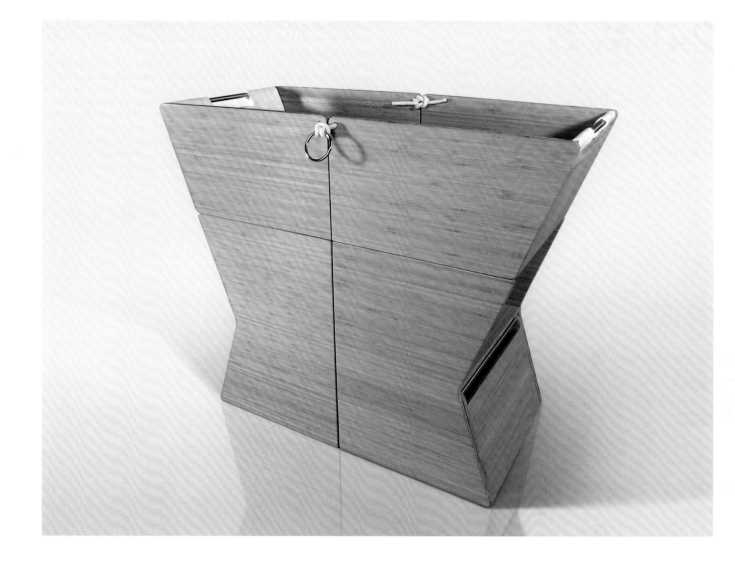

242 🌙

YiAhn Bassinet, 2007
Min Kang (1973–)
Self-produced

While preparing for the arrival of his first son, YiAhn, Korean designer Min Kang discovered a problem with much of the children's design on the market: it quickly falls into obsolescence as the child outgrows its initial function. Significant in size and investment, bassinets are among the worst offenders, frequently out-living their purpose within months of purchase. Kang's response was the YiAhn Bassinet (pronounced 'e-ahn'), which is designed to evolve with the child through primary school. Starting with the form of a bassinet that can cradle the tiniest of babies, its units may be separated, and reconfigured into a bookshelf and a container for toys, providing a storage solution to the child's accumulating collection of playthings. With the growth of the toddler, YiAhn can be trans-formed into a child-sized play table and chair. The bassinet's adaptability, clean lines and environmentally friendly materials led to it being awarded the prestigious Red Dot Design Award in 2007.

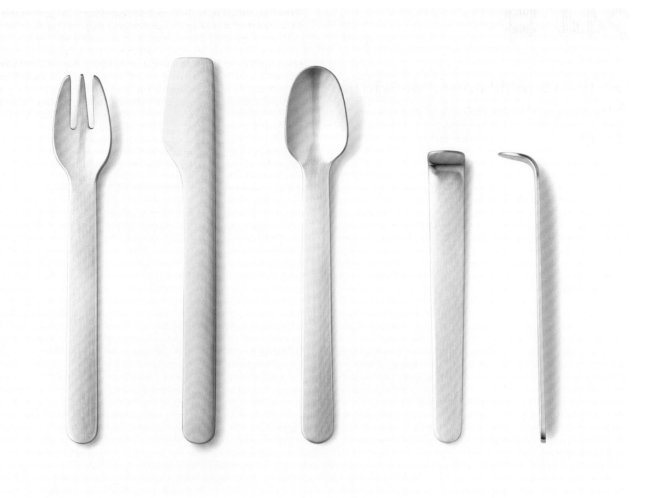

243 🍴

Children's Cutlery, 2014
Louise Campbell (1970–)
Georg Jensen

Louise Campbell's work has been honoured with numerous awards and is collected by museums throughout the world. One of the leading figures in contemporary Danish design, she has collaborated with a long list of respected companies, from Louis Poulson, Hay and Royal Copenhagen, to Muuto and Zanotta. When Georg Jensen, the renowned Danish design brand, approached Campbell to create a set of children's cutlery, she dived headlong into research, making hundreds of cutlery models in a wide variety of materials. 'I felt it important that such an intimate tool as cutlery [that is intended to] be used by hands, should also be formed by hand,'[1] she explains. Far from the garish plastic children's sets that have become ubiquitous, Campbell's stainless-steel cutlery is utterly simple and discreet, with logical, gently rounded forms that feel timeless. 'Cutlery should be a trustworthy aid,' she notes. 'I hope users of all ages take this cutlery for granted, but with pleasure. Like springtime. Or tea.'[2]

244 🪑

Children's Table and Chairs, 1970s
Patrick Gingembre (n.d.)
Selap

Most likely conceived by the French designer Patrick Gingembre, this children's furniture set reflects design trends that were shaping adult furniture in the 1960s and early 1970s. The era's penchant for plastic also represented the dawn of a new era in designs for children, to which the qualities of the material – smooth child-safe edges, lightweight construction, durability and ease of cleaning – were uniquely suited. These stackable chairs are each made from a single piece of plastic, while the table can be disassembled into three pieces for storage. Plastics enabled the designers of children's furniture to embrace a new spirit of imagination and experimentation. With the moon landing in 1969, the Space Race reached its climax and Space Age fantasies abounded in pop culture (see Space Chair, 194). As with this Selap-produced set, the possibility of space travel provided fertile imaginative ground for designers, who seized the opportunity to produce bold futuristic forms in vivid colours.

245 🪑

Low Hideaway Chair, 2014
Think + Shift (est. 2012)
Starex

The low-slung Hideaway Chair positively invites children to clamber into its cosy wool-upholstered interior. Designed by New Zealand studio Think + Shift, the chair is the product of their collaboration with New Shoots, an organization which operates a number of childcare centres. Observing that children love to sit in a range of different positions, they set about designing a chair that enables little ones to curl up, lie upside down, sit with friends or 'hide away' from the noise of their surrounding environment. Hard-bent plywood panels form the nautilus-like shell of the chair, which is manufactured from local, sustainable materials by the New Zealand company Starex. Longer legs can be installed as children grow. The panels can easily be taken apart for cleaning or replacement, while crumbs and dirt can simply fall through the gaps between the panels, making this low-maintenance chair as appealing to adults as it is to children.

246 🛴

Wishbone Bike 3in1, 2008
Richard Latham (1969–)
Wishbone Design Studio

Richard Latham knew he was onto something when other parents asked him where they could buy a balance bike like the one he built his son Noah, created in 2005 to help him explore New York's Central Park. Latham founded Wishbone Design Studio three years later with his wife, Jennifer McIver, to service growing demand. The Wishbone Bike's attractive three-in-one design accommodates children from twelve months to five years by converting from a three-wheeled tricycle to a two-wheeled balance bicycle. The curved frame can also be flipped to raise the seat for older children – making it one of the largest balance bikes on the market. The Wishbone studio chooses its materials with sustainability in mind: the bikes feature a preservative-free birch frame in a natural finish, accented with inflated rubber tyres for a smooth ride. Children can then customize their bikes using a variety of sticker packs, seat covers and handlebar grips. The studio also produces limited-edition versions featuring specially-commissioned artwork.

247

Build the Town, 1943
Ladislav Sutnar (1897–1976)
Self-produced

Czech toys have gained international renown, largely because of the strong tradition of beautiful wooden playthings established by Artel, the innovative applied-arts cooperative that existed between 1908–24. One of the cooperative's leading designers of modern toys, Ladislav Sutnar, started developing his building-block sets in the early 1920s: some years later, he began work on the Build the Town construction set after his exile to the United States in 1939. Sutnar believed that his creation would be a popular alternative to the American construction sets of the time, which he deemed too neutral in shape. Conceived as a modular city of industrial infrastructure, Sutnar's aim was to instead enable children to construct modern building types. However, Build the Town was rejected by American manufacturers, in both 1941 and 1943. Sutnar went on to produce several samples at his own expense, yet sadly this elegantly proportioned toy never made it on to the market.

CARtools, 2015
Floris Hovers (1976–)
Magis

Released by Magis in 2015, these classic miniature vehicles are reminiscent of a bygone era. The set of twenty-six birch pieces comprises simple geometric shapes in an assortment of hues that recall the bold yet unsaturated palette of vintage comic books. CARtools, which can be mixed, flipped and stacked to form different interpretations of vehicles, are a follow-up to the assemblage of steel model cars, ArcheToys (408), created by the Dutch designer Floris Hovers in 2013. But whereas ArcheToys is a set of individual units, CARtools is a kit of parts. At once abstract yet familiar, these 'design tools', as Hovers calls them, allow users to explore their collective memory to construct and deconstruct archetypal vehicular forms. As with all of Hovers's work, which includes miniature cities and full-scale furniture, CARtools is the product of stringent reductionism and a longing for craft. For both children and adults, this timeless puzzle of sorts is built to last.

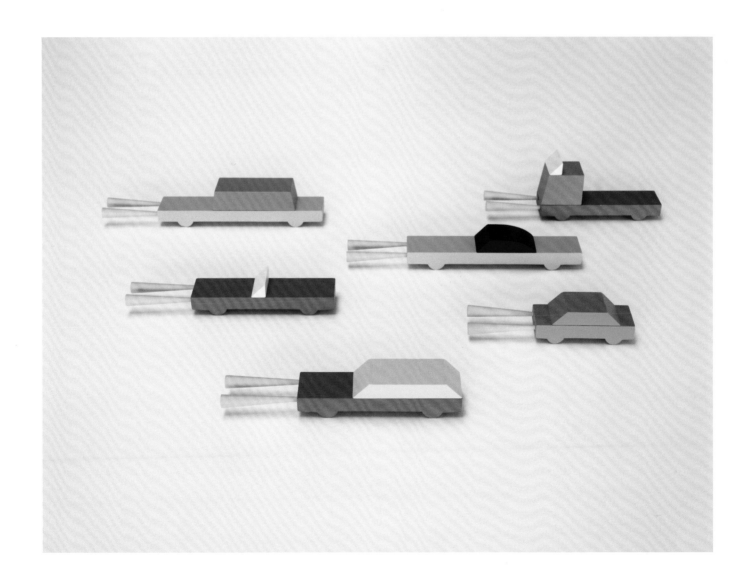

249 ☾

Hagia Bassinet, 2008
Argington (est. 2002)
ODA

This clean-lined bassinet represented the initial foray into children's furniture by the acclaimed New York-based architecture firm ODA (Office for Design and Architecture). The Hagia Bassinet is a versatile, mobile crib that can be converted into a co-sleeper and, later, a toddler's rocking horse. To help in the realization of the design, ODA teamed up with Argington, an eco-conscious children's furniture company, which was founded in 2002 by husband-and-wife team, Andrew Thornton and Jennie Argie. Hagia's simple, natural materials and clean structural form combine to create an elegant piece of furniture, which is at once sculptural and functional. Made of wood veneer in either walnut or white oak, Hagia comes with wheels for easy transport and an overhanging canopy-like frame, which is perfect for suspending a mobile from. As the child gets older, the bassinet's base can be removed, turned over and converted into a children's rocker. Endearing without being cutesy, the Hagia provides a refreshing take on the contemporary crib.

250 🛴

Nanook of the North Seat, 2015
Matteo Cibic (1983–)
Scarlet Splendour

This crescent-shaped rocker forms part of the Vanilla Noir collection of Scarlet Splendour, one of India's first internationally recognized luxury furniture brands. Created by Matteo Cibic, recipient of the Elle Décor International Design Award for Young Talent in 2017, the design is a nod to the masterpieces of his native Italy, and the traditional bone and horn inlay techniques of India. Rather than bone, however, the rocker uses a resin compound developed by Cibic and lacquered by skilled Indian craftspeople. Balancing whimsy with a sense of over-the-top luxury, Nanook of the North is a playful reference to the eponymous silent documentary film made about an Inuk man in the Canadian Arctic, of 1922. Part of Scarlet Splendour's inaugural collection of intricately decorated objects that debuted at Milan Design Week in 2015, this rocker is as much a purely aesthetic object as it is an element of play.

251 🪑

Plain Collection, 2009
Ole Petter Wullum (1965–)
Kloss / currently Plain Production

The Plain Collection was designed by Ole Petter Wullum, an industrial and architectural designer who teaches at the Norwegian University of Science and Technology. Each item in the set can be assembled from a few flat-packed pieces, with the thin, exposed profiles of the plywood lending the designs their striking angular silhouettes. Featuring birch-plywood finishes and a Formica laminate in a range of rich tones, the pieces in the collection can be mixed and matched according to preference. While production of the series was recently taken over by Wullum's own company, it was originally released by Kloss, a Norwegian manufacturer that aims to produce furniture that facilitates play, thereby enabling children to shape their own environments using the functional objects around them.

Vodo Masko, 2014
Ambroise Maggiar (1978–)
TOG

This playful table and stool is part of a collection of children's furniture that French designer Ambroise Maggiar created for the Brazilian design brand, TOG (All Creators Together). Vodo Masko leads an impressive double life: its gently sculpted form lends it a hand-carved quality when functioning as a table and seat, but if tipped on its side, each object's underbelly reveals a design akin to an African tribal mask. A small hole in the rotational-moulded plastic enables the final transformation from furniture into decorative wall-hanging. Maggiar's penchant for twin-functioning design is further evident in Castable, another table and stool creation, with legs that become the towers of a medieval fortress when inverted. Maggiar's playful approach clearly reveals the influence of Philippe Starck, with whom he worked for several years.

253 🐻 ◗

Optischer Farbmischer, 1924
Ludwig Hirschfeld-Mack (1893–1965)
Bauhaus Workshops / currently Naef

With a spindle centre and interchangeable slide-on discs, this wooden spinning toy offers its users seven different lessons in colour theory. Its designer, Ludwig Hirschfeld-Mack, was invited to join the Bauhaus School in Weimar, Germany, by Walter Gropius in 1919. During his time there, Hirschfeld-Mack studied form and colour under the tutelage of painter Johannes Itten, eventually becoming the head of the school's metal, wall painting and glass painting workshops. The exercises in colour theory are described on the reverse of each disc and include the ideas of Johann Wolfgang von Goethe, Arthur Schopenhauer and Adolf Hölzel. When spun, the top's colours blend to create varying effects. Among the most well-known toys to emerge from the Bauhaus, the Optischer Farbmischer (Optical Colour Mixer) has been reproduced by the esteemed Swiss wooden toy company Naef, based on Hirschfeld-Mack's original design, since 1977.

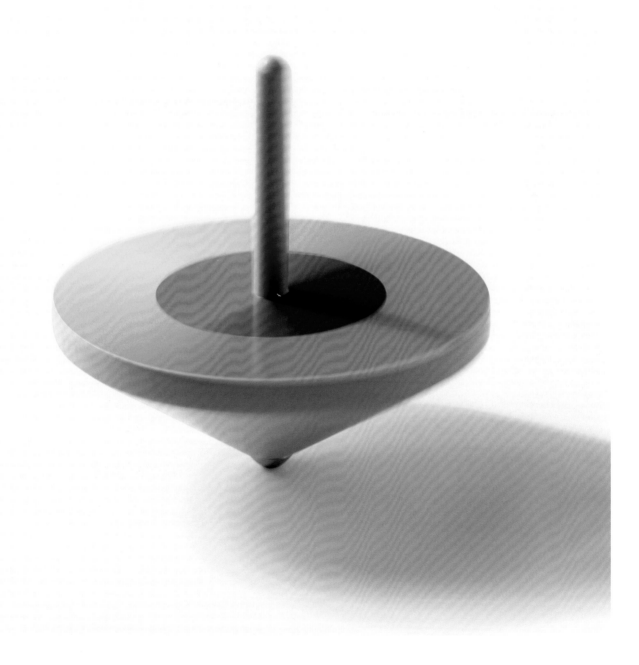

254 ⚏

Mercredi 12 Balance Bike, 2012
Moustache Bikes (est. 2011)
Moustache Bikes

Made using the same technologies as an adult bicycle, the Mercredi 12 (Wednesday 12) Balance Bike brings adult sophistication to Lilliputian scale. From its hydro-formed aluminium tube frame, to its 30.5 cm (12 in) inflated tyres, or its padded saddle with adjustable stem, the sporty bearing of the Mercredi 12 sets it apart from other training bicycles. Made by Moustache Bikes, a French company that specializes in electric-assisted two-wheelers, the Mercredi 12 is designed to introduce children to a lifetime of cycling. Without pedals, toddlers learn to balance by pushing off with their feet, eventually cruising with their feet off the floor for longer periods of time. With its moveable seat height, this mini Moustache accommodates children aged between twenty months and five years. Available in seven colours and weighing only 3.4 kg (7.5 lbs), the Mercredi 12 strikes a happy balance between the practical and the entertaining.

255 🐻

Classic Red Wagon, 1940
Antonio Pasin (1896–1990)
Radio Flyer

This iconic fire-engine red wagon with its shallow-sided steel tray, set of four robust black rubber wheels, pull handle and accompanying scrolling logo, has become as emblematic of American childhood as cream sodas and the sleep-over. Its creator, Antonio Pasin, was an Italian immigrant living in Chicago. The son of a cabinetmaker, Pasin dreamt of a business of his own, making his first wooden wagon, the Liberty Coaster, in 1917. Seeking to make his wagons affordable for every family in America, Pasin drew inspiration from the new automotive assembly lines of the 1920s to mass produce his wagons in stamped metal – a move that earned him the nickname 'Little Ford'. The Radio Flyer Classic Red Wagon was one of the safest toys of the period, with 'no-pinch' ball joints to keep children's fingers safe, and a controlled turning radius to prevent the wagon from tipping over. A century later, the company is still producing this timeless classic, now with Pasin's grandson at the helm.

256 🍴

Dinner, 2006
Naoto Fukasawa (1956–)
Driade

As a young teenager, Naoto Fukasawa decided his career path upon reading that a product designer made people happy through objects. 'I thought that's a great idea because I like to make things that make people happy,'[1] he explains. Fukasawa has certainly achieved that goal countless times throughout his career, designing with an elegance that the late Bill Moggridge, former director of the Cooper Hewitt, Smithsonian Design Museum in New York, characterized as 'modern international, combined with a deep sensibility to traditional Japanese beauty'.[2] That sense of simplicity and gracefulness is evident even in his design for infants. When the Italian furniture and interiors company Driade approached Fukasawa to create a line of tableware for children, he chose to celebrate a meal as a formal ritual within a child's day. The resulting seven-piece melamine set, Dinner, nestles bowl-within-plate-within-tray with a pleasing sense of poetry and balance. Its soft, rounded forms are both gentle to the toddler's grip and pleasing to the adult's eye.

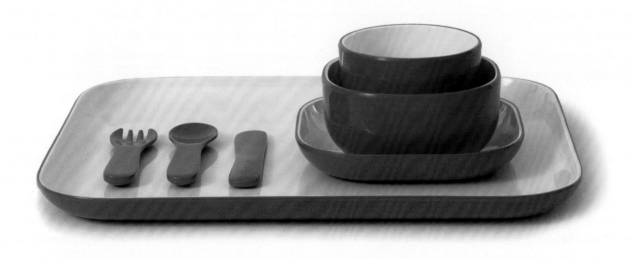

257 ☾

Bunky, 2012
Marc Newson (1963–)
Magis

Growing up in 1960s Australia, Marc Newson was captivated by the American television series 'The Jetsons' (1962), and the influence of the cartoon's cheerful space-age styling is evident in the Bunky bed – Newson's first design for children. Now London-based, the designer is known for his prolific output and his expansive portfolio features objects as diverse as watches, aeroplane cabins, shotguns, bicycles and cookware. The Bunky, made with Italian furniture company Magis, is a modular four-piece bunk bed that can be stacked or unstacked, as family needs change. The design is characteristic of Newson's materials-driven approach: made from rotational-moulded polyethylene, it is lightweight and easily assembled. Perforations in the frame allow for ventilation underneath the mattress and its surface can be easily wiped clean. Bunky displays all the hallmarks of Newson's graphic style, though here they take on a playful twist: voids become spaces for hiding, soft corners are child-friendly and its seamless forms can withstand even the most boisterous of playtimes.

258 🐻

Hula Hoop, 1958
Richard Knerr (1925–2008)
and Arthur Melin (1924–2002)
Wham-O

The Hula Hoop took advantage of new plastics technology to refashion an age-old toy in a colourful, lightweight, durable and affordable material. While the concept dates back to ancient Egypt, when children would weave together dried grape-vines to swing around their waists, the version that we are familiar with today was invented in 1958 by two Californians, Richard Knerr and Arthur Melin, of the successful toy company Wham-O. Inspired by hearing a visiting Australian recount how children in his country twirled bamboo hoops around their waists in their fitness classes, the pair quickly created a prototype for the American market. The motion necessary to keep the hoop spinning reminded them of Hawaiian hula dancers, thus the Hula-Hoop's name was born. Following advances in thermo-plastic research, the inventors were able to fashion a hoop that was both light and inexpensive enough to become a cult phenomenon. In their first four months of business, Knerr and Melin sold 25 million hoops.

Skwish, 1981
Tom Flemons (1953–)
Manhattan Toy Company

Few other baby toys can claim to have inspired rocket scientists, but Skwish's unique bounce and resilience caught the eye of NASA engineers working on the Super Ball Bot landing platform due to its ability to 'squish' under pressure, and then bounce back to its original shape. Created in 1981 by the artist and inventor Tom Flemons, this unusual rattle and teether toy applies the principles of tensegrity to create a dynamic and hardy toy for toddlers. 'Tensegrity' describes a structure whose integrity comes from the balance of its rigid elements being held in tension, rather than them remaining rigid. With Skwish, the wooden rods are held in formation by elastic, and can therefore be pulled, pushed and twisted – the toy always returning to its original shape – while brightly painted beads slide and rattle. Flemons has spent a lifetime exploring tensegrity through toys, furniture, sculptures and anatomical models. Designed for very young children, including newborns, this multi-award-winning toy has sold over three million units around the world.

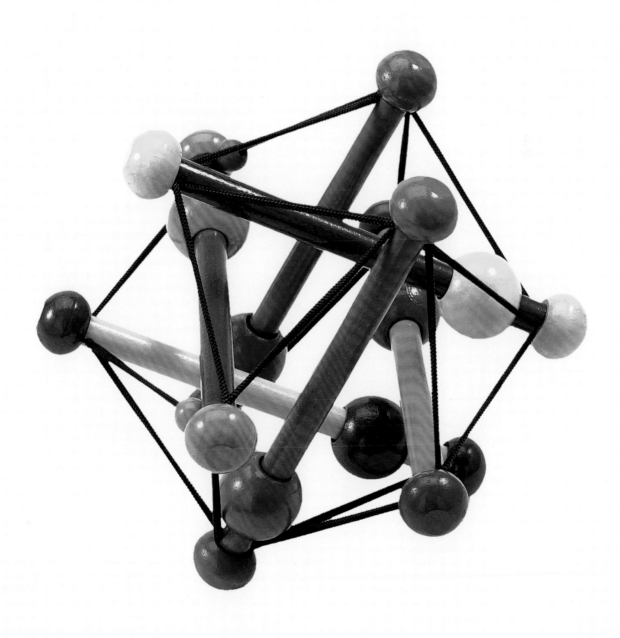

260 🐻

Omochi, 2011
Naoto Fukasawa (1956–)
Jakuetsu

Naoto Fukasawa's Omochi is as sculptural as it is playful. 'I believed that it was important for it to be aesthetically pleasing wherever it was placed, just like a large sculpture',¹ Fukasawa explains. Made of bright-red, fibreglass-reinforced plastic, the slide playfully references the traditional round Japanese rice cake, *mochi*, in both form and name. An unusually elegant piece of play equipment, Omochi seeks to encourage exploration and intuitive play, which is not directed or controlled by adults. While the centre of the sculpture incorporates the steps and ramp of a more traditional slide, Omochi's inviting shape and shiny surface invites children to climb and slide in any direction. The diminutive red slide is one of six sculptural pieces of play equipment that Fukasawa has designed for Jakuetsu, a Japanese company that has been designing for children's learning environments for over 100 years. Omochi was awarded Japan's Good Design Award in 2011 and a Kids Design Award in the following year.

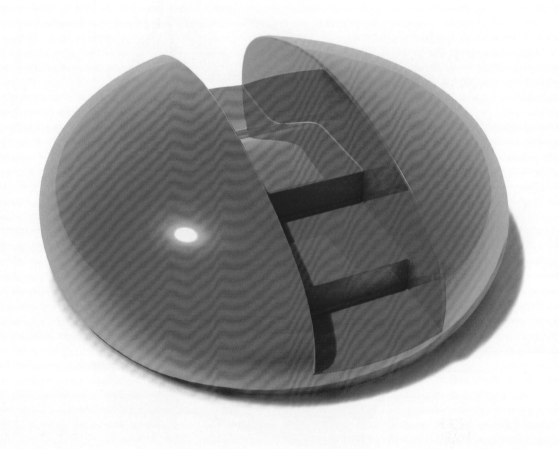

261 ♯ 🐻

Kapsule Chair, 2001
Karim Rashid (1960–)
Offi & Company

Designed by Karim Rashid, heralded by *Time* magazine as the 'Prince of Plastic',[1] and who – with over 3,000 designs in production – is known for his prolific output, the cheap and cheerful Kapsule Chair reflects Rashid's interest in catering to the masses. Like the toy-filled plastic eggs dispensed from arcade claw machines, the Kapsule Chair's shell separates into two pieces, providing the perfect space for children to store toys through a hole in the back of the chair. Made from injection-moulded polypropylene, Kapsule is sturdy, easy to clean and rendered in a range of candy colours, including neon green, purple, orange and electric blue. With its comfortable contours and youthful shape, the lightweight, multifunctional seat successfully combines Rashid's signature playfulness and fluid aesthetic. In 2002, the Kapsule was awarded Silver in the Industrial Design Excellence Awards.

262 🌙

Swing Low Cradle, 1998
Søren Ulrik Petersen (1961–)
SUP Design

Intended for babies less than two months old, the Swing Low is a soft sling that cradles newborns in a soothing embrace. Made to hang from the ceiling, the cradle is designed so that the dense wool felt pulls in closely around the baby, shielding it from noise, and yielding a sense of warmth and security similar to that of being swaddled. The Swing Low was designed and produced by Søren Ulrik Petersen, a cabinetmaker known for imbuing his designs with a craftsman's touch. Petersen exhibits this approach here through his careful choice of timeless and natural materials – wool felt and hemp yarn. The Swing Low has been exhibited at the Centre Georges Pompidou in Paris and is part of the permanent exhibition of the Design Museum Denmark. Petersen was also celebrated by the Danish Arts Foundation with a three-year working grant in 2000.

263 ♯

Mod Rocker, 2005
Lisa Albin (1967–)
Iglooplay

Lisa Albin designed this rocking chair, which she describes as 'a love poem for her first child, Anya',[1] with the knowledge that children often fidget while sitting in stationary chairs. Constructed from two bent-plywood pieces, and available in sustainably sourced maple or walnut veneer, Albin conceived the Mod Rocker to appeal to design-minded and environmentally conscious parents, as much as to children. The rocking chair's low, curved form was inspired by the shape of African stools, which are commonly contoured to cup the body. Albin trained as an architect before working as an interior designer on residential projects and feature films in New York City. After becoming a mother to two daughters, she designed a children's furniture line called Iglooplay. Like other pieces in the collection, the Mod Rocker is informed by a distinctly Modernist sensibility. Through its sculptural forms and textures, Albin aims to stimulate children's sensory development.

264 🪑

Lilla m, 1995
Caroline Schlyter (1961–)
Forsnäs Form AB

As an art student in Stockholm, Caroline Schlyter was tasked with creating a letter of the alphabet in three-dimensions. Selecting the lowercase 'h', Schlyter embarked on a multi-year alphabet furniture project, pushing materials such as bent plywood to their limits in an attempt to create 'a clean unbroken line, and avoid joints and connecting details'.[1] After several manufacturers told her that the design would be impossible to create from laminated-birch veneer, Schlyter produced the initial prototype of her h chair herself in her school's carpentry department. This design was soon followed by Schlyter's Lilla m (Little m) chair – this time intended for children – similarly made from a ribbon of bent plywood. Created in 1995, it has since been produced in many different finishes, including cowhide and shag. Over the course of her career, Schlyter's furniture designs have been recognized with many awards and exhibited at museums including the Louvre in Paris, and London's Design Museum.

265 🛴

Max Ride-On Car, 2000
Wolfgang Sirch (1964–)
and Christoph Bitzer (1964–)
Sirch

This elegant ride-on car pays homage to the legacy of its Swiss company, Sirch, which has produced steam-bent wooden designs since 1805. Here, the curved ash body allows children to tuck their belongings into the under-carriage, bringing them along for the ride. For tots with lots to tote, the Lorette, an equally refined birch trailer, can be hitched onto the back of the Max car. Both the car and trailer feature heavy-duty rubber wheels, for silent cruising around the house. Known for its craftsmanship and design sensibility, Sirch aims to create toys that are beautiful enough to be left out, rather than tidied away. The Max Ride-On was one of the first products conceived by Wolfgang Sirch and Christoph Bitzer, who have since gone on to produce an award-winning line of children's furniture and wooden toys, called Sibi. The Max Car and Lorette Trailer have since been acquired for the permanent collection of the Philadelphia Museum of Art.

266 🪑

Baby Bite, 2009
Karim Rashid (1960–)
XO

In his manifesto, aptly titled 'Karimanifesto', the Egyptian-born design visionary, Karim Rashid, states that beauty is a 'collective human need'.[1] One of the most prolific designers of his generation, Rashid launched his career by going against the current: he leveraged his designs for an $8 (£6) rubbish bin and a $45 (£34) stackable chair to parlay his way into designing for the elite. Having tackled everything from perfume bottles to hotels, Rashid caters to a world in which nothing lives forever, excelling at using digital-age materials to create design for the masses. The three-legged Baby Bite stool, part of his Extraordinary Family collection for French company XO, embodies his signature fluid aesthetic, which he terms 'Blobism'. Produced from rotational-moulded polyethylene, Baby Bite can be cleverly combined by inverting it and locking it into another stool to create a taller seat or table.

267 🐻 🪑

Bruchi, 2015
James Irvine (1958–2013)
Play+

So-called because of their bug-like legs and bendy bodies, these *bruchi* (caterpillars) are modular, foam elements that can be locked together in an endless variety of formations. With their comb-shaped contours, they are flexible enough to bend up against walls and squish into small spaces, providing seating or a colourful playscape. They exude the characteristic exuberance of their British designer, James Irvine, who gained an enviable reputation through his work for leading brands such as Artemide, Olivetti, Muji, Mercedes-Benz and Thonet. Irvine designed Bruchi for Play+Soft, a research project involving designers and teachers, which resulted in a collection of soft furnishings. The line is intended to enrich children's environments and to stimulate their cognitive development through sensory exploration. Able to be used alone or in a group, Bruchi is made from a fireproof polyurethane foam, which is easy to clean, odourless, water-repellent and mould-resistant.

268 🪑 🍴

High Chair, 1968
Piet Hein Stulemeijer (1941–2009)
Self-produced

With its carefully judged structure and modulated interior spaces, this high chair perfectly demonstrates Piet Hein Stulemeijer's training as a Modernist architect. Stulemeijer graduated from the Tilburg Art Academy in 1963, then worked at an architectural firm before stepping out on his own in 1967. This high chair was designed fairly early on in his career; he also produced other designs for children around this time, including a curved-beech rocker that displays a similar attention to sculptural form (218). Stulemeijer later became known for large-scale sculptures designed for public spaces, including hospitals, police stations and parks. Throughout his lifetime, he carried out extensive research into light and its effects, an interest that is evident in this chair's varied planes of light and shadow, highlighted by the uniform application of blue paint. From the mid-1980s, Stulemeijer turned his specialist focus to the use of glass in spatial design projects and he remained an active designer throughout the 1990s.

269 🪑 🐻

Junior Minus+, 2006
Arne Quinze (1971–)
Quinze & Milan

Part furniture, part building block, the playful Junior Minus+ collection is the work of Quinze & Milan, the innovative design company founded in 1999 by Belgian conceptual artist Arne Quinze and Yves Milan. Made from durable water-repellent foam (a material that the company has patented as QM Foam), the vibrantly hued set includes chairs, love seats and sofas with simple angular silhouettes. The Junior Minus+ perches are toddler-sized and, thanks to their elemental, block-like design, the collection can be assembled and reassembled in various configurations, making them a versatile solution for a variety of settings. The cult design brand is a self-ascribed 'creator of atmosphere' and has produced a wide range of furniture, including similar seating to the Junior Minus+ for adults. Quinze & Milan notably collaborated with celebrated American designer David Weeks and Areaware to produce a foam Cubebot (181), twenty times larger than its original size.

270 ⊟

High Chair, 1920
Gerrit Rietveld (1888–1964)
Gerard A van der Groenekan

Nothing fuels good design for children as much as a talented designer becoming a parent. Happily, such is the case with Gerrit Rietveld. Between 1913 and 1924, Rietveld and his wife had six children. With funds in short supply, particularly in the lean war years, work and home life became closely intertwined as the designer's growing family lived on the same premises as his furniture shop in Utrecht. With likely ample need for one, Rietveld set about designing a high chair that would be radically different to the conventional furniture of the day. Though conceived in the early 1920s, Rietveld's design wasn't realized until 1960, when it was built with the assistance of his personal cabinetmaker, Gerard A van der Groenekan. Echoing his Red and Blue Chair of c. 1918, the High Chair's distinctive criss-crossing joint would come to be known as the 'Rietveld joint'. Over the course of his career, Rietveld would go on to produce several other high chair designs.

271 🪑 🍴

Ovo High Chair, 2011
CuldeSac (est. 2002)
Micuna

Spanish design firm CuldeSac has a knack for reimagining everyday objects to make people's lives a little easier: a bicycle helmet that can collapse to fit into a day bag; a slender dining table, which effortlessly extends to over double its original length. The Ovo High Chair, created in 2011 for the Spanish children's furniture brand Micuna, is no exception. Conceived to transform from a baby's high chair to a desk chair for toddlers, Ovo's design comprises an easy-to-clean polypropylene seat, beech legs with white extensions that can be removed to shorten its height, an adjustable tray, a foot-rest and a leather harness strap that can also be removed. The chair's sleek, modern aesthetic makes it well-suited to contemporary living spaces and, coupled with its simple pragmatism, equally appealing to children and their parents alike.

Fabrik, c. 1920
Josef Hoffmann (1870–1956)
Wiener Werkstätte

Over the course of his long career, Josef Hoffmann created architecture, designed interiors and produced objects at a wide variety of scales. Among these was his Fabrik (Factory), a hand-painted child's assembly kit created around 1920. Comprising twenty-nine pieces of different building typologies, the miniaturized set offers a child the ability to construct not only a factory, but an entire industrial town, with living quarters and offices included. Carved architectural features, such as arches and doors, punctuate the miniature buildings, adding detail and definition. While at first glance the set appears to be painted in monochrome grey with black windows, closer inspection reveals the buildings to be dotted with tiny floral sprays, introducing a whimsical touch of nature into an otherwise industrial landscape. Despite its manufacturing theme, the play-set was in fact completely unique, produced meticulously by hand and sold for a not-insignificant sum.

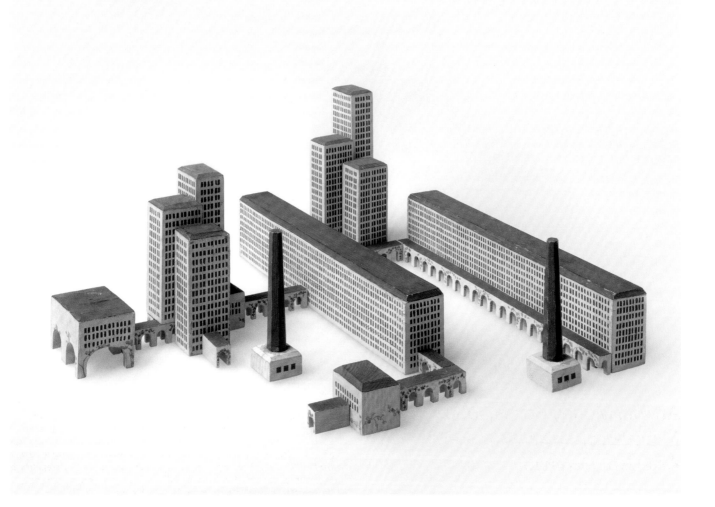

273 ✎

Animal Money Boxes, 1930
Minka Podhajská (1881–1963)
Artel Cooperative

While the exact origins of the piggy bank are uncertain, it is believed that the concept originated in the Middle Ages with the pygg clay used to create pottery. Created in 1930 by the Czech artist and designer Minka Podhajská, these stylized piggy banks also include a dog, squirrel, mouse and rabbit. Having trained in Vienna under the Wiener Werkstätte's founder, Adolf Böhm, Podhajská became known for the wide variety of toys she designed for Artel, a cooperative of prominent Czech avant-garde artists and designers that advocated for modern aesthetics in the applied arts. Created in the same year as her Personifications of Childhood Misdeeds (312), these money boxes demonstrate Artel's strong commitment to Cubism. With a dislike for naturalistic toys, which Podhajská felt did little to educate a child or stimulate their imagination, she developed a reputation for bringing artistic and modern form to traditional Czech toys, becoming one of the foremost toymakers in turn-of-the-century Vienna.

274

ABC Blocks, 1869
John Wesley Hyatt (1837–1920)
The Embossing Company
/ currently Uncle Goose

Based on traditional toys, these colourful alphabet blocks were first put into production by John, Charles and Isaiah Hyatt of The Embossing Company in 1869. The original blocks featured red and blue carvings of animals, and the letters of the alphabet were surrounded by ornamental borders. Although it's not entirely clear which of the brothers was responsible for the design, it was most likely John Wesley Hyatt, who was involved in no less than 236 patents in his lifetime, including these ABC Blocks. Best known for inventing celluloid, John served as president of the Embossing Company from 1871–85. The company closed its doors in 1955 and the blocks fell out of production until 1983, when Uncle Goose reissued the design. Today's blocks are now made from lime wood and maintain the original surface design, but feature an expanded colour scheme and a variety of alphabets, and are printed with child-safe inks.

275 🐻

Mice, 2005
Dorthe Mailil (1967–)
Maileg

Sweet and full of personality, the Maileg universe of animals is inspired by children's storytelling. Each diminutive creature – many of which come nestled in a large matchbox – wears a hand-sewn outfit that lends itself to imaginary play. Developed by Danish illustrator Dorthe Mailil, the charming collection began as a clay pixie figure for a class project while Mailil was still in school. She later translated the design into felt, founding Maileg with her husband, Erik, in 1999. The name Maileg (pronounced 'my'lye') is a portmanteau of the couple's surname with *leg*, the Danish word for play. With several collections of animals, ranging from Polar, Safari and Forest Creatures, to Bunnies and Mice, Maileg creatures have migrated far and wide, and are sold in thousands of stores internationally. 'In these days with all these screens, it has never been more important to have a retreat for kids, where they can dream and use their imagination,' Erik explains.[1]

276 ♟ 🪑

Build Up Table and Chair, 2009
Philippe Nigro (1975–)
Skitsch

Produced by the Italian company Skitsch, this cardboard chair and its accompanying table are deceptively strong, with a design inspired by the structure of aeroplane wings. While drawing on examples from real aircraft, the Build Up Table and Chair also adapt the interlocking principles used for easily assembled cardboard or balsa-wood model planes. The furniture set enables children to partake in building their own furniture, and they are further encouraged to decorate their new creations with drawings, collage and paint. Created by the French designer Philippe Nigro, Build Up's pieces are punched from sheets of corrugated cardboard, making the set both lightweight and recyclable. Nigro worked closely for many years with the influential Italian designer Michele De Lucchi, and continues to work in both France and Italy, producing his own furniture, interior and lighting designs. In 2014, he was awarded the Now! Design à Vivre title by the French furniture fair, Maison et Objet.

277 ⬒ 🐻

Villa Julia, 2009
Javier Mariscal (1950–)
Magis

Valencia-born designer Javier Mariscal is among the most prolific and versatile contemporary artists and designers living and working in Spain today. His bold, colourful expressiveness, and whimsical yet minimalist style permeates his furniture designs, as well as his typographic, cinematographic and even architectural repertoire. The Villa Julia is faithful to both his design language and experience in creating children's objects. With its brickwork, eaves, door style, porch light and chimney, Mariscal can be seen to have conceived of a play house in the style of the classic, mid-century, American detached dwelling. The DIY design comes flat-packed with assembly instructions, making children the designers, builders and inhabitants of the villa. Kids are encouraged to colour the sides and adorn the structure with stickers, which are included in the package – features that ensure each house is the unique product of its young owner's creativity. Part of Magis's Me Too collection, the endearing Villa Julia debuted at the Salone del Mobile, Milan, in 2009.

278 🛴

Baltic Rocking Horse, 1972
Furniers (est. 1957)
Furniers / currently Troja

Since its first appearance in 1972, this Latvian design has become something of a classic. Originating from the plywood production plant Furniers, the simple and elegant design quickly took off, eventually leading to the establishment of Troja – a sister company specializing in wooden toys – in 1992. While the Baltic Rocking Horse has inspired other versions, it is the spotted steed that has best stood the test of time. Made of birch plywood, its gentle curving rockers and supportive back rest make it the perfect partner in helping to develop a child's sense of balance before they can walk. The hand-painted horse continues to be manufactured by Troja in accordance with the original design, but it is also imported by the American-based company Offi & Company, which – thanks to the help of award-winning designer Eric Pfeiffer – offers a lovingly crafted version in Forestry Stewardship Council-certified ply.

Boris Cradle, 2009
Nika Zupanc (1974–)
Self-produced

Since her first highly successful collaboration with Moooi in 2008, Slovenian designer Nika Zupanc has garnered quite a following. 'In a world of design which is dominated by rationalism, minimalism and technology, it is a pleasure and a necessity to find a scarce and lonely soul who puts forward her power and sensitivity to create pieces with a smart aesthetic and feminine language,'[1] notes Moooi's co-founder, Marcel Wanders. Aiming to offer an alternative to those for whom 'parenthood has brought a rude introduction to the boredom of visually humiliating options',[2] Zupanc designed Boris (pictured), Vladimir and Alexander – three cradles with the same silhouette but made from varying materials. Created from laser-cut wood or acrylic and with brass legs, each member of Zupanc's proclaimed 'silent brotherhood of slightly arrogant cradles'[3] is meant to embody the timeless elegance and craftsmanship that will see it passed down between the generations. Their arrogance is not without reason: Zupanc's bassinets rock the world of cradle design.

280

Rosinante Kids Rocking Horse, 2013
Eero Aarnio (1932–)
Vondom

Captivated by the eternal allure of carousel horses, Finnish designer Eero Aarnio sought to design a rocking horse that both adults and children can delight in. His Rosinante, named after Don Quixote's patient and weary steed, comes in a range of colours and two different sizes so that parents and children can rock together. Unlike typical rocking horses, Rosinante not only rocks back and forth but also spins on its curved base. The sense of playful delight that Rosinante inspires is characteristic of Aarnio, who has been infusing modern design with a fun Pop sensibility since the 1960s. And, like the story of Don Quixote, Rosinante is a product of Spain, made in Valencia by Vondom, who have been producing contemporary outdoor furniture in collaboration with a range of iconic designers since 2010. Like all of the pieces that Vondom produces, Rosinante is durable and weather-proof, and made using rotational-moulded polyethylene resin.

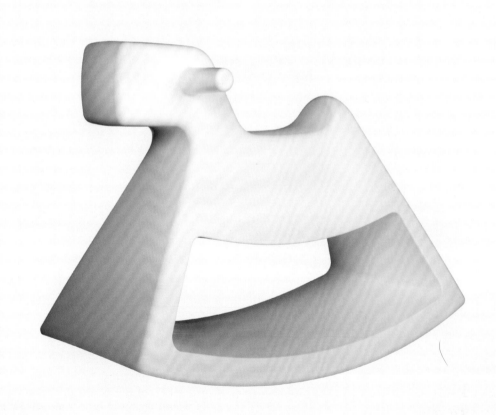

281 🛴

H-horse, 2016
Nendo (est. 2002)
Kartell

Since launching his company Nendo in 2002, Oki Sato has become one of the world's most prolific designers. Known to juggle some 400 projects at the same time, Sato enthusiastically takes on everything from bags to buildings. While his work exhibits the kind of elegant minimalism often associated with Japanese design, just as central to the designer – whose company's name references the clay of the children's Play-Doh brand – is making sure that each project is imbued with a sense of fun. When asked to create a rocking horse for the Italian furniture company Kartell, Nendo adapted the form of an architectural steel H-beam (or I-beam), known for its tensile strength, into a sleek, methacrylate riding toy. Referencing Kartell's historic pioneering of plastic, this simple yet playful rocking horse speaks to both children and adults alike.

282 🪑

USSR Sitzgruppe, 1949
Albrecht Lange (1908–n.d.)
and Hans Mitzlaff (1910–97)
Manufacturer unknown

This children's furniture series, which included a table, desk set and rockers, was designed in 1949 by the German architects Albrecht Lange and Hans Mitzlaff, and manufactured in the USSR. The pair worked together between 1938–61 in their own architectural office, Lange and Mitzlaff, becoming known as the 'Mannheim pair', after the German city in which they were based. In addition to their work as architects, the duo also became known for their furniture designs, such as these birch-plywood pieces for children. The low-slung form and curved frame of the rockers echo their adult designs, which feature similar shapes and cutout motifs. In profile, the chairs can be seen as plumped-up variations of the 'boomerang' form, which was popular during the mid-century and was more acutely referenced in other designs by Lange and Mitzlaff – hinting at the influence of wider design styles on their practice.

283 ♯

Me Rocking Chair, 2013
Jorge Frías Montes (1980–)
and Irene Zurdo Prieto (1979–)
Estudio Ji

Designed by Jorge Frías Montes and Irene Zurdo Prieto of Estudio Ji, a Spanish architecture and design studio founded in 2005, the Me Rocking Chair helps to make children feel enclosed and protected. The high sides of the chair extend to the ground, arcing gently at the bottom to form the rockers, while the upholstered seat curves upwards to act as a backrest, producing a streamlined design with a minimum number of pieces. Two eye-like cutouts offer playful details for children to hold onto or peek through, as well as to pass toys and secret messages through. Designed for children aged from one to six, Me's wide-set sides also enable it to be used as a stool by adults. Believing that the care with which you make something is evident in the object, Estudio Ji makes each Me rocker by hand from waxed-maple plywood, foam and organic cotton.

284 🪑 ◗

The Classics, 1974/2014
Enzo Mari (1932–)
Cucula

In 1974, Italian designer Enzo Mari urged consumers to create their own furniture with his publication, *Autoprogettazione?* (*Self-design?*), which he described as 'an elementary technique to teach anyone to look at present production with a critical eye'.[1] Including nineteen templates for furniture that could be produced inexpensively with readily available supplies, Mari's catalogue foreshadowed open-source design in the twenty-first century. In 2014, several designers teamed up to establish Cucula, a refugee association, education programme and workshop in Berlin. The word *cucula* means to do something together and to take care of one another in the Housa language of North Africa. Giving his project new life, Mari granted Cucula permission to make and sell his *autoprogettazione* designs. Each item in The Classics furniture series is made of waxed pine and features the signature of the refugee who made it.

285 🪑 🛴

Trioli, 2005
Eero Aarnio (1932–)
Magis

Legendary Finnish designer Eero Aarnio once said that 'a chair is the most diffi-cult and most fascinating thing to design',[1] a fitting statement from a creative best known for his iconic Ball (1963) and Bubble (1968) chairs, which remain just as fashionable and coveted today as when they first appeared. His style is charac-terized by a blending of geometric and organic shapes, producing innovative and forward-thinking items of furniture. Aarnio's portable Trioli resembles a piece of macaroni with an exterior slice removed, revealing its core. Manufactured in rotational-moulded polyethylene for Magis's Me Too collection, the durable child's seat can reside indoors and out, wherever playtime permits. Available in each of the primary colours, this multifunctional chair has two configurations: resting upright, it can be used as a seat; placed on its side, it becomes a simple rocker. Light and easy to move with small hands, children can arrange Aarnio's creation themselves, for either active play or for a spot to rest.

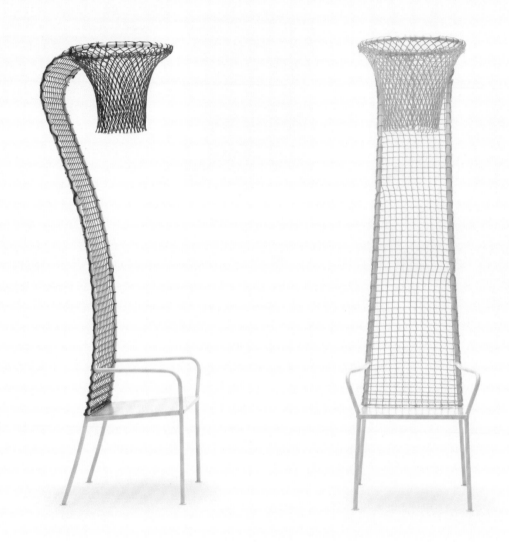

286 ♨ 🐻

Lazy Basketball Chair, 2013
Emanuele Magini (1977–)
Campeggi

The Lazy Basketball Chair is part Duchampian wit, part street-fair amusement and all sleek Italian design. Rather formal and unassuming on the bottom, the chair's back extends, like a giraffe's neck, to a basketball hoop suspended precariously above the seat of the chair. While the chair's name suggests that the user plays basketball while seated, a swish would likely make a person's head spin. Created for Campeggi by the Milan-based designer, Emanuele Magini, the Lazy Basketball Chair is one of a line of 'lazy' sporting chairs, including Lazy Football, a chair with goal netting stretched around its legs, and Siesta, a bench whose hammock-like seat appears to be a repurposed volleyball net. Passionate about football as a child, Magini wanted to create objects that would enable the sport to have a more constant presence in his life. Having worked as a set designer for Walt Disney in Italy, it is clear that Magini seeks to embrace both playfulness and whimsy, if not serious exercise.

287 🐻

Pogo Stick, 1919
George B Hansburg (1888–1975)
JM Originals / currently Flybar

The Pogo Stick's familiar frame and exhilarating bounce have ensured it enduring popularity throughout the last century. A popular account of the Pogo's origin tells of an anonymous German who came up with the toy following a trip to Burma, where he witnessed a young, shoeless girl, named Pogo, using a stick to hop along the rocky path on her daily trips to the local temple. The stick's origin might, however, be more reliably traced to two Germans by the name of Max Pohlig and Ernst Gottschall, who filed a patent for a 'spring-end hopping stilt' in 1920. Nevertheless, when the Gimbel Brothers Department Store in the United States ordered a shipment of these wooden hopping sticks in 1919, only to find them warped and unusable on arrival, they asked the American designer George B Hansburg to create a metal version; he was later credited with the toy's invention and patent that same year.

288 🐻 ◢◣

Las Sillas, 2007
Javier Bermejo (1954–)
Pico Pao

Las Sillas (The Chairs) is an open-ended game that invites children to follow their intuition, challenging them to stack, pile and hang tiny chairs in increasingly daring formations. Produced by Pico Pao, a games company based near the border of Spain and Portugal, Las Sillas not only hones a player's feeling for balance and refines their motor skills, but further encourages abstract and creative thinking in the pursuit of new ways to defy gravity. Las Sillas is part of the company's Ludus Ludi collection, which features games with no defined set of rules, helping players to tap into a sense of pure play and enjoyment. Designed by Pico Pao's Javier Bermejo, the compressed-cardboard chairs are available in sets of fifteen or twenty-nine, and come beautifully housed in a wooden box. Pico Pao, which is named after a local woodpecker, draws inspiration from timeless, multigenerational games that never lose their charm.

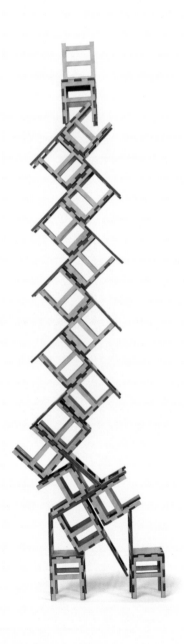

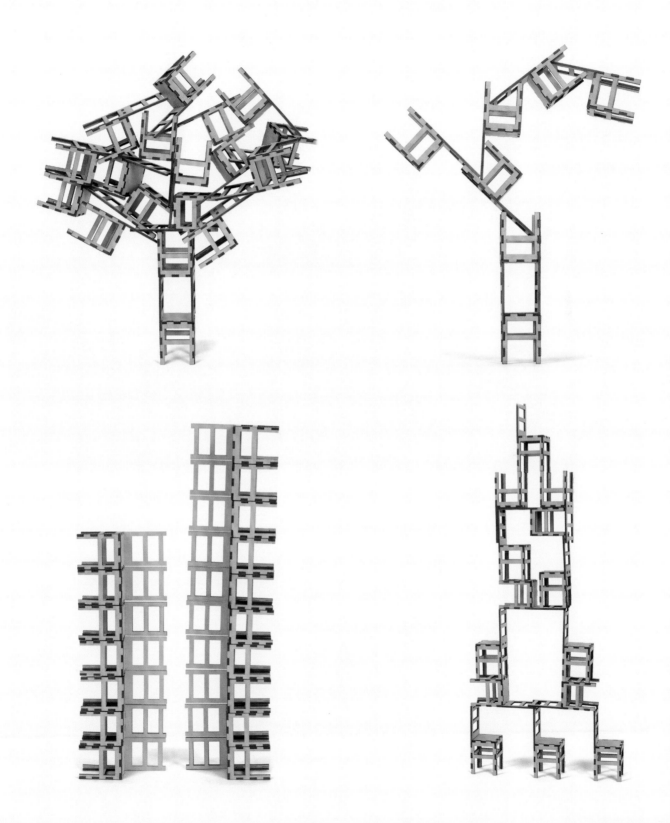

289 ☾

Snoo Smart Sleeper, 2016
Yves Béhar (1967–)
and Harvey Karp (1951–)
Happiest Baby

Although a robot nanny might sound like something from 'The Jetsons', the renowned Swiss industrial designer Yves Béhar has made it a reality – albeit without the cold, mechanical feel that you might expect. Standing on hairpin legs and accented with a wooden surround, the Snoo is the first smart crib; the sleek product of a five-year collaboration with top paediatrician Dr Harvey Carp, a recognized expert on how to lull infants to sleep. Snoo's sleek and simple look belies some serious bells and whistles. Using robotic technology, the crib is able to sense a baby's level of crying and fussiness, and to deploy any combination of rocking, jiggling or white noise techniques to soothe its unhappy camper. It also includes a sleep sack that swaddles the baby and keeps it on its back through the night. Over time, Snoo tracks a baby's patterns, thereby enabling parents to monitor its sleeping habits, while also getting more sleep themselves.

290 🐻

Doll's House, 2017
Jasmin Gröschl (1992–)
Prototype

Industrial designer Jasmin Gröschl considered the adult consumer as much as the child user when conceiving of this minimalist doll's house. Recalling her own mother's aversion to the chunky plastic aesthetic of her childhood Barbie playhouses, Gröschl set out to create a miniature home that could both stimulate a child's imagination and fit elegantly within their parent's carefully curated living spaces. Knowing that a simple shoe box with holes cut in it provides enough detail for a child to perceive it as a house, she produced a similarly reduced design: a mid-century modern maisonette crafted from walnut plywood and acrylic glass. The interior of the doll's house comprises only the most basic furnishings and characterless figurines, giving children the creative control to devise any scenario they like. When not in use, the house folds closed, more like a vintage gramophone cabinet than a toy.

291 🪑 ✏️

Rolltop Chair, 1994
Simon Maidment (1968–)
Offi & Company

The tambour – a sliding, flexible shutter generally composed of a number of closely set wooden slats – is often found on cabinet fronts. In this design by Simon Maidment, however, the tambour's gently rolling track serves dual purposes: when pulled down, it ingeniously forms the seat and back of a chair; when peeled back, it reveals a generous space for children to hide their treasured possessions in. Inspired by his own childhood memories of storing Lego pieces in deteriorating cardboard boxes, Maidment designed this more personal and durable toy-storage solution while studying at the Royal College of Art in London, in the early 1990s. Following graduation, he honed his skills working for the British designer Tom Dixon, before founding his own studio, Sam Design, in 1994. The design brand Offi & Company began producing the Rolltop Chair with a birch-plywood body and beech tambour in 2004.

292 ☾

Culla Cradle, 1973
Mario Ceroli (1938–)
Poltronova

Designed by the Italian sculptor Mario Ceroli, the Culla Cradle was produced in 1973 by Poltronova, as part of the Annabella series of bedroom furniture. Throughout the 1960s, Poltronova collaborated with designers and architects, including Ettore Sottsass, Massimo Vignelli and Superstudio, earning itself a reputation for iconoclastic furniture. Early designs were often rendered in wood, cultivating a uniquely Tuscan strain of Modernism that leaned on the region's tradition of craftsmanship, while fostering close association with the avant-garde artists and art movements of the time. For his part, Mario Ceroli was already a highly regarded Arte Povera sculptor in the 1960s. Like other artists of the movement, his work featured natural and commonplace materials, such as wood, fabric and aluminium. In the juxtaposition of a pre-industrial material with its clean application of geometry and pattern, Culla reflects Arte Povera's driving tension between tradition and modernity.

293 🐻

Polypops Cardboard Toys, 1968
Roger Limbrick (1933–)
Polypops Products

It's through imaginative free play that these cardboard toys come alive. In 1966, the London-based designer and artist Roger Limbrick was commissioned by the Reed Paper Group (Polypops's parent company) to explore new uses for corrugated cardboard. No doubt thinking of his own five children, Limbrick designed this series of five large toys, which were sold in kits containing pre-punched pieces that were embellished with printed designs and metallic finishes. Through folds and interlocking joints, children and parents were able to bring the toys into three dimensions, entirely without the use of glue. Limbrick's careful attention to construction techniques yielded exceptionally strong toys, including a geodesic dome that only became stronger as its pieces compressed beneath a child's weight. Reflecting the era's popular fixation with space travel and moon landings, the series included a space station, a rocket and the Lunartrack that children could crawl along the inside of as it inched forward.

Slinky, 1943
Richard James (1914–74)
James Industries
/ currently Alex Brands

Slinky's story began in the workshop of a naval engineer named Richard James, whose tinkering to develop a shipping spring resulted in one of the twentieth century's most recognizable toys. Noticing the way that one of his samples continued to flop about after it was dropped on the ground, James realized that he had hit upon something great. In that instant, a classic toy was born. Its first commercial success occurred during the Christmas season of 1945, when 400 Slinkys sold in minutes at Philadelphia's Gimbels Department Store. Traditionally made from 2.5 metres (8 feet) of wire compressed into a helical spring, the Slinky remains successful both as an entertaining novelty and as an educational tool, which guides children to ponder the principles of gravity. Its uncanny ability to 'walk' down stairs – a feat made possible through a principle of physics, known as Hooke's Law of elasticity – as well as its 'slinkety sound', was highlighted in the popular 1960s jingle, 'Everyone knows it's Slinky'.

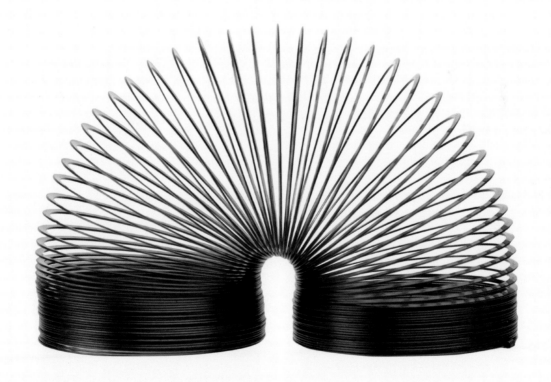

295 🐻

Playsack, 1968
Fredun Shapur (1929–)
Trendon

Fredun Shapur's enchanting children's designs deserve to be placed along-side those of modern masters such as Bruno Munari, and Charles and Ray Eames. Throughout his remarkable career, the South African born, British designer collaborated with an array of international manufacturers, including Naef, Trendon and Creative Playthings. Produced in 1968, this series of twelve animal disguises emerged from a last-minute need for Shapur to find his children costumes for a school event. Using large paper sacks intended for kitchen waste, he fashioned a strikingly modern set of characters that has since become one of his most popular designs. Each sack featured an animal on the front, small cut-outs for the wearer's face and arms, and his trademark combination of graphic and abstract shapes with warm, saturated colours. Unisex and adaptable to a broad range of ages and sizes, the Playsacks' spontaneity and flexibility were key to their success.

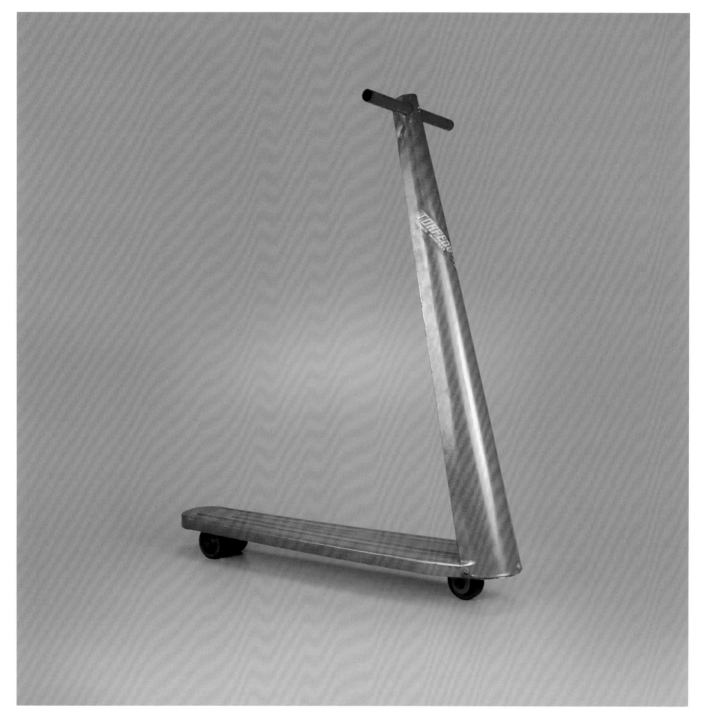

296 🛴

Torpedo Scooter, c. 1930s
O'Connor Industries (n.d.)
O'Connor Industries

This shiny red scooter, manufactured in Detroit by O'Connor Industries, hails from the austere years of the Great Depression. Made of pressed tin, the Torpedo recalls an era in which the steel and automotive industries dominated the American economy. It is therefore of little surprise that many popular toys of the era were made from steel, from the Radio Flyer Classic Red Wagon (255) to the Skippy-Racer (26). The Torpedo's name and streamlined profile further reflect the fact that Detroit was also quickly becoming a central hub for weapons production. The first scooter appeared over a century ago when children, in search of new diversions, attached roller-skate wheels to wooden planks, adding a handle for greater control. Thanks to Swiss banker Wim Ouboter, a scooter renaissance was sparked in 2000. As a way of speeding up his pilgrimage to his favourite sausage shop, Ouboter created a foldable aluminium version of the scooters he had so avidly played with as a child.

297

Children's Chair, 1956
Roger Fatus (1926–)
Lecel

This children's chair showcases the new materials that were shaping furniture design in the post-war period. Its gentle hourglass frame is constructed from bent-metal tubing, painted in a range of colours, while its seat is Formica, an American laminate that entered the European market through a licensing agreement after World War II. Produced by Lecel, this children's chair is an early work of French designer Roger Fatus, created just three years after he graduated from the École nationale supérieure des Arts Décoratifs in Paris, and one of several furniture designs that he would generate for the company. Fatus went on to build a successful career and a reputation based on his sensitive, curved forms, also serving as the director of the highly regarded École Camondo design school during the 1980s. The recipient of the Grand Prix du Meuble (Grand Prize for Furniture) in 1967 and the René Gabriel Prize in 1969, Fatus's work continues to be both collected and celebrated to this day.

298 🪑 🍴

Tripp Trapp, 1972
Peter Opsvik (1939–)
Stokke

A favourite of parents for decades, the Tripp Trapp is a timeless piece of Scandinavian design that has been in continuous production since it was first released in 1972. Conceived by one of Norway's best-known designers, Peter Opsvik, the genius of this iconic chair lies in its adaptability; the seat and footrest height can be adjusted in fourteen positions, allowing children of all sizes to sit at the table in comfort. The Tripp Trapp's angular construction is formally rooted in Gerrit Rietveld's Zig-Zag High Chair (210), resulting in a design that is both stable and lightweight. Produced by Stokke in solid beech, the chair comes untreated or varnished and in a variety of colours. 'It is satisfying to see that products that solve everyday challenges are appreciated,'[1] Opsvik has said of his design, noting that, nearly fifty years later, 'it does not look old-fashioned, and thus there is no reason to replace it.'[2]

299 🐻

Bagger, c. 1960
Konrad Keller (est. 1864)
Konrad Keller

Konrad Keller has been a household name in Europe for generations. Founded in Göppingen, Germany, in 1864, many of Keller's wooden toys continue to be sought by children and collectors alike. Among their line of products, the first version of this toy, the Schaufelbagger (meaning 'excavator'), stands out. With two cranks – one to open and close the excavator claws, and the other to manipulate the boom – the excavator encourages children to develop their hand-eye coordination as they play. Keller further developed the metal claws, which can be made to pick up sand, stones, objects and water, to be sold as a distinct marionette-style version called the Bagger (grabber). This version was included in *Play: Toys, Sets, Rules*, an exhibition by the London-based design practice Systems Studio, in 2015, which assembled notable toys from the 1960s and 1970s. The German toy manufacturer Ostheimer purchased Konrad Keller in 2011; however, the Schaufelbagger and Bagger are sadly no longer in production.

300

Bronco Scoop Truck, 2014
Neue Freunde (est. 2011)
Neue Freunde

The German brand Neue Freunde (New Friends) was founded in 2011 by Carsten Rosenbohm and Christopher Fellehner to create toys and lifestyle products that combine 'good design with funny ideas'.[1] Among their offerings is a sandcastle mould of Cologne Cathedral, a water pistol made from beech and the Little Salt Express – wooden train carriages that serve as salt and pepper shakers. The Bronco Scoop Truck embodies Neue Freunde's creative playfulness, while having children's motor development in mind. Made from beech, with robust skateboard-like rubber wheels adding stability, the Scoop Truck's most prominent feature is a large yellow plastic scoop, modelled on a kitchen accessory. The detachable scoop can be clipped onto the truck's simple wooden frame to resemble a dump truck or reoriented 180 degrees to become a front-loader. The scoop's design makes it a perfect tool for collecting everything from sand to Lego.

301 🐻

Wolf Pull Toy, 1988
Keith Haring (1958–90)
Vilac

One of the most iconic Pop artists to come out of New York, Keith Haring began drawing as a child, influenced by Walt Disney, Dr Seuss and his father's amateur cartooning skills. Haring gained acclaim as a graffiti artist in the 1980s, developing a vocabulary of simple graphics and symbols that spoke to the times. This pull toy, designed in 1988 but posthumously released by the French toy manufacturer Vilac in 1993, depicts a wolf – an animal that appeared repeatedly in Haring's work. Its whimsical, post-modern design and vibrant, primary colours capture the artist's instantly identifiable style. Made from a simple material palette of lacquered wood, rubber-rimmed wheels and a pull string, the toy's solidity lends it both a durability and an heirloom-like quality. Beyond entertaining them, the wolf's unmistakable character introduces children to Haring's central role in Pop and graffiti art, which was tragically cut short by his untimely death at the age of thirty-one.

302 🐻

Magnetic Building Blocks, 2009
Nate Lau (1978–)
Tegu

Unlike other block sets, Tegu's building blocks feature hidden magnets that enable pieces to connect and adhere to one another without the use of nesting grooves or connecting parts. This magnetic advantage means that children can take their constructions to new levels by adding features, such as extensions or cantilevers, which would typically take a tumble in a conventional building toy. The polarity of the magnets is also educational, encouraging children to exercise their critical thinking skills as they play. The original set of building blocks comprises twenty cubes, sixteen long planks, ten short planks and six jumbo planks. Founded by the New Zealand-born brothers Chris and Will Haughey, Tegu is a for-profit company that is intent on being environmentally sustainable and on creating meaningful economic change in Honduras, where it manufactures all of its toys. Tegu has now expanded its offering to include other sets and accessories, including Tegu Tints, a set of building blocks stained in a variety of pastel shades.

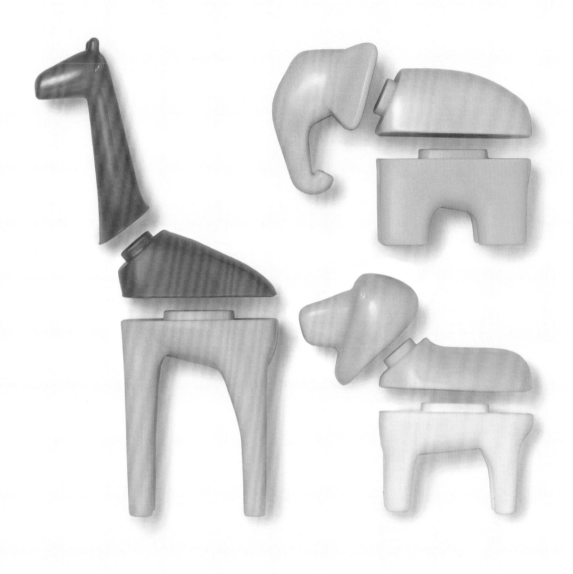

303

Mix & Match Animals, 2015
Lisa Mahar (1965–)
Kid O

Kid O creates vibrant plastic toys that rouse children's imaginations with their open-ended possibilities for play. The legs, bodies and heads of these mix-and-match zoo animals can come apart, be switched around and snapped together in new formations. Each set comes with six pieces, shaped to form a giraffe, a lion and an elephant, but are coloured in a way that means there is no obvious or definitive way of assembling them. Mix & Match thereby encourages children to think creatively, while developing their hand-eye coordination. Like the majority of Kid O toys, the plastics used are free from PVC, BPA, phthalates and lead, and the set has also been rigorously tested for safety. The pieces are easy to wash or wipe clean, and so make good bath time companions. Named Best Toy at the NY Now trade show in 2015, the versatility of these animal toys fosters early storytelling skills and puzzle-solving abilities in children.

304 🪑 ✏️

Le Chien Savant, 2013
Philippe Starck (1949–)
Magis

Philippe Starck began his career designing Parisian nightclub interiors in the 1970s, gaining recognition a decade later for his renovation of one of the private apartments of the then president of France, François Mitterrand. Since then, the internationally renowned industrial designer has turned his hand to everything from kitchen utensils and motorbikes to hard drives. Influenced by both the traditional and the far out, Starck's portfolio of work defies being placed into only one stylistic category. His designs are whimsical, taking on a wide range of forms and responding uniquely to their respective contexts. Produced for Magis, Starck's Le Chien Savant (The Wise Dog) is a children's chair and desk that was created in order to make schoolwork just that little bit more exciting. The inspiration for its form was simple: as a child, Starck never liked school, but he loved dogs. Made from rotational-moulded polyethylene, the desks come in a variety of matte colours and can be used indoors or out.

305 🪑 ✏️ 🐻

Animals, 2015
Stéphane Choquet (1973–)
IDM Design Library

IDM Design Library is a French interior design and architecture firm that specializes in creating dynamic and inspiring public and institutional libraries. Central to each project is a sense of joy and wonder, characteristics that IDM use to create different micro-environments and what they call 'quirky, charming objects'. This approach is exemplified by Animals, a spirited range of furniture designed by Stéphane Choquet, who trained at the Design Academy Eindhoven, and has collaborated with companies such as Habitat and Artek. Choquet's work often exhibits a simple yet playful aesthetic, as with these characterful wooden creatures, each of which come crowned with one of four different sets of uniquely hued headpieces, shaped to resemble ears, horns or antlers. The Animals, which can be accessorized with a book storage unit that can be attached, wagon-like, to their backs, serve alternately as chairs, benches, tables or fantastical library friends. The simple shapes, bright colours and open-ended quality of this charming range invite children to interact, teaching them the wonders of library learning.

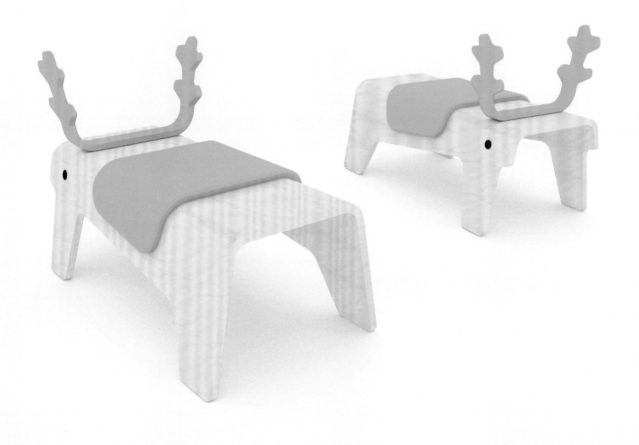

306

Rocking Ox, 1967
BRIO (est. 1884)
BRIO

BRIO's Rocking Ox simplifies its subject nearly beyond recognition, marking a significant departure from the more naturalistic approach of earlier rocking horses. Constructed of moulded plywood and accented with a blue felt seat, red horns that double as handles and pegs for the rider's feet, the ox's sturdy body is suggested by the stout, rolling design of the rocker. An abstract eye near the top of the form adds a final touch of character to this minimalist design. By the time of the Rocking Ox's creation in 1967, the rocking horse had long been a staple of childhood. The earliest rocking horses have been dated to the sixteenth century and by the Victorian era they had become regular fixtures of middle-class nurseries. Thanks to its moderate rocking arch, the Rocking Ox is both stylish and safe, allowing children to feel as if they are riding on the wild side, amongst a fantasy world of beasts.

307 🛴

BIT Bike, 2010
Glodos (est. 2010)
Glodos

With its low handlebars, neon colours and wide wheels, the BIT Bike is reminiscent of the futuristic high-speed bicycles often seen in science-fiction films. Decidedly more analogue than its fictitious counterparts, this balance bike is designed to introduce cycling to children between the ages of one and three by developing their balance and coordination without the added complication of pedals. The exaggerated width of the wheels makes the BIT Bike especially steady and the low position of the handlebars, which are cut from the chassis, encourages riders to adopt a position that protects their spine and back, while also doubling as a carrying handle for adults. Designed by the Spanish toy company Glodos, the BIT Bike is constructed from laminated plywood, with a rubber seat and plastic wheels. It's a stylish starter ride for toddlers who can't wait to get on a bicycle – although they'll have to scoot before they can pedal.

308 🐻

Hen, c. 1967
Klaus Michalik (1936–)
Juho Jussila

This simple, quirky, 'Hen' pull-toy comes from the workshop of Juho Jussila, a Finnish schoolteacher and designer. The youngest child of nine, Jussila studied carpentry and manufacturing in Germany, where he designed his first wooden toy set. On returning to Finland in 1923, Jussila established his own company – now a fourth-generation family business and the largest toy manufacturer in the country. Advocating a child-centric philosophy towards play, Jussila also recognized the educational value of toys. First appearing in the company's catalogue in 1967, Hen was the handiwork of Klaus Michalik, a designer more commonly known for his lighting products. Abstracting a bird's form to its most basic components – a triangular body, wheels for legs and a brilliant red comb – Michalik's original design came with string at its base, allowing children to pull it along as they went. In keeping with many of Jussila's early designs, Hen is made from unstained wood, revealing the natural pattern of its surface.

309 ☾

Danish Lucky Storks, 1953
Christian Flensted (1920–94)
Flensted Mobiles

Flensted Mobiles began in 1953 with cardboard, string and two sticks of straw. Conceived as a christening gift for his first daughter, the Lucky Storks mobile was Christian Flensted's first creation, which went on to be sold around the world. Christian and his wife Grethe launched their eponymous mobile business the following year in Aalborg. By 1956, Christian gave up his job to devote his efforts to his growing mobile business. His modern and dynamic designs earned him the nickname 'Uromager' roughly translating as 'the maker of mischievous things that are always on the move'. Still in the family today, Flensted was first passed to Christian's son, Ole, and his wife Aase, in 1982, before being handed over once more to his granddaughter, Christine, in 2017. Known for their elegant simplicity and sense of balance, Flensted Mobiles changed the perception of mobiles as simply nursery accessories, revealing them to be beautiful decorations for children and adults alike. While new designs are constantly being added, many of Christian's original designs still remain in production today.

310 🐻

Elephant, 1930
Ladislav Sutnar (1897–1976)
State Institute for Home Industry
/ currently Modernista

Ladislav Sutnar was a celebrated designer, pioneer of information architecture and central figure of the Czech avant-garde, whose designs for children can be considered key to his life's work. Like many of Sutnar's toys, this elephant references abstract art and gives a nod to the speed of modernity with its geometric shape, spring-mounted head and wheeled feet. 'Only the vitality of an imaginative toy design of high standards can help a child's creativity to grow and be fun to the adult as well,'[1] Sutnar expressed. Sutnar always designed his toys with industrial manufacturing techniques in mind. His prototypes consisted of simple pieces, which could be machine-produced, assembled on a conveyor belt and painted according to a template. By eliminating manual labour, Sutnar hoped to make his toys widely available and affordable. However, none of these colourful and masterfully proportioned toys achieved widespread distribution: his Elephant, Rhinoceros, Walrus and Camel were instead replicated by hand.

311 🐻

Racer, 1969
Fredun Shapur (1929–)
Creative Playthings

Formed by two American scholars and educators in 1945, Creative Playthings championed the simplicity and beauty found in well-designed toys, as well as their ability to promote a child's imagination and creativity in play. Fredun Shapur began collaborating with the company in the late 1960s, designing both toys and, notably, a new visual identity for the brand. The company's belief in semi-abstract designs, inexpensive materials and refined craftsmanship matched Shapur's own values. Made from wood, and with bright red detailing on the axles and driver, Shapur's streamlined Racer has no front, back, top or bottom. Even the detachable motorist can be made to sit to face both directions. With its oversized, wide-set wheels, sculptural shape and flexibility of use, the Racer is easily fuelled by a child's imagination. Shapur strongly believed that good design could be at once fun and educational, helping develop children's emotional intelligence, while also appealing to their parents' aesthetic tastes.

312 🐻

Personifications of Childhood
Misdeeds, 1930
Minka Podhajská (1881–1963)
Artel Cooperative

These mischievous and endearing little characters were created by the Czech designer Minka Podhajská in 1930. Trained at the Viennese Women's Academy, where she studied under Wiener Werkstätte founder Adolf Böhm, Podhajská became one of Vienna's leading toy designers of the early twentieth century. Her wooden toys were full of character, highly stylized and frequently humorous. An experienced painter, illustrator and graphic artist, Podhajská produced many of her toys for Artel, a cooperative of Czech avant-garde artists akin to the Wiener Werkstätte and Bauhaus, which existed in Prague from 1908–35. Disapproving of the more typically realistic toys that she saw everywhere in abundance, Podhajská's designs embody Artel's mission to bring a modern aesthetic to household design and applied arts. Through her toys, Podhajská sought to instil children with those same values. Complete with a disgruntled adult figurine, it is evident that these Personifications of Childhood Misdeeds are intended to be as instructional as they are playful.

313 🐶

My Sweet Dog, 2006
Yoshimoto Nara (1959–)
Vilac

Produced by the French toymaker Vilac, this pull-along pup was designed by the internationally acclaimed painter and sculptor Yoshimoto Nara. Nara gained recognition in the 1990s for his Japanese Pop aesthetic, alongside the super-charged flower-power artist, Takashi Murakami. Nara's work frequently uses childhood themes to speak to what he sees as a larger shared subconscious. From doe-eyed children to forlorn, cartoonish dogs, his work often expresses a sense of displacement or melancholy, despite its youthful themes. It is, perhaps, their uniquely adolescent bad attitudes that give the cartoonish characters featured in Nara's drawings such widespread appeal. While My Sweet Dog's pensive brow alludes to this, the spring-loaded bounce of his head and tail help to give him a more upbeat, jaunty air. The maker of award-winning toys since 1911, Vilac's canine curio is one of several artist-designed toys in their line, which also features works by Alexander Calder and Keith Haring.

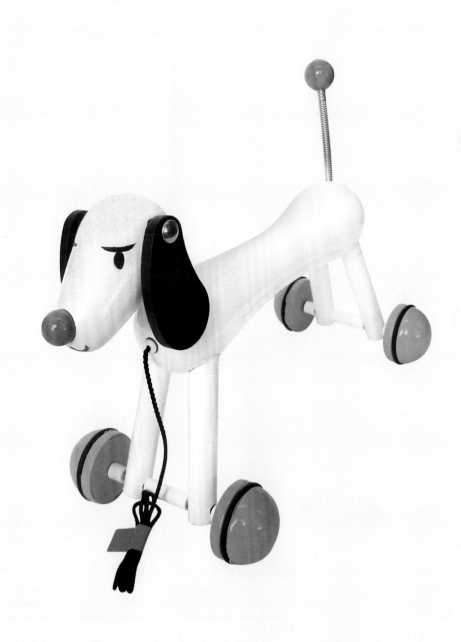

314 🐻 🛴

Petit Cheval, 1961
Pablo Picasso (1881–1973)
Self-produced

Pablo Picasso famously stated that 'every child is an artist. The problem is how to remain an artist once [they] grow up.'[1] Best known for his paintings, Picasso sculpted in a wide variety of media throughout his career. With Petit Cheval (Little Horse), Picasso imaginatively transformed a piece of furniture into a toy for his grandson, Bernard. Six metal table legs were simply but purposefully arranged to form a representational figure suggestive of a horse, with the shorter struts used for the back legs and torso, while longer ones at the front of the horse extended to become the neck. By using castors for the hooves, Picasso created a mobile toy that Bernard could easily interact with – and even ride. The figure is characteristic of Picasso's renowned abstracted forms and demonstrates his ability to create something dynamic from the simplest materials, while blurring the lines between art and play.

315 ⍾

Children's Chair for Peckham
Pioneer Health Centre, c. 1935
Christopher 'Kit' Nicholson (1904–48)
Manufacturer unknown

The interwar period saw Britain focus on preventive medicine for the working classes – particularly for children. Driven by this Modernist project of delivering healthcare to all, medical centres opened throughout the country. In Peckham, the movement reached an aesthetic apex with a concrete and glass building described as a 'factory of health', the Pioneer Health Centre, which opened in 1935 and recalled Le Corbusier's concept of the domestic space as a 'machine for living'. This chair was designed by British architect Kit Nicholson for the Pioneer. Formally echoing the building's pillars, the chairs could be clustered together in flexible and social arrangements. The chair's design further minimized waste through efficient production; two pieces cut from a standard-sized sheet of birch plywood were slotted together to form the base, with a flat seat and bent-wood back completing the chair.

Gicha, 2011
Seo Hyunjin (1982–)
and Kim Jaekyoung (1983–)
Kamkam

Gicha (meaning 'train' in Korean) is an elegantly playful, ride-on toy that can also cleverly serve as stools and storage. Designed by Kamkam, a Seoul-based design studio founded by Kim Jaekyoung and Seo Hyunjin, Gicha is one of four children's objects that make up their Protection Project. The collection debuted in 2011 at a furniture show, which was organized by the Arumjigi Culture Keepers Foundation in Seoul. Devoted to honouring and preserving Korean tradition and culture, Arumjigi invited ten design studios to create furniture for 'a new Bauhaus in Korea'. Alongside Gicha, Kamkam presented Ahye, a children's bed inspired by the shape of traditional Korean shoes; Duriban, a table that plays with the concept of the dureong-chima, a traditional skirt typically worn when carrying children; and Banjang, a wardrobe trunk with felt detailing, which was inspired by classical ornamentation. By artfully combining traditional Korean aesthetics with notions of physical and emotional security, the Protection Project demonstrated Kamkam's inherent talent for inventive design.

317

Steering Wheel and Reversible Chairs, 1937
Magnus Stephensen (1903–84)
Kay Bojesen

Designed by Magnus Stephensen and produced by Kay Bojesen – a collaboration of Danish design mastery – this reversible children's chair and table two-piece features a detachable steering wheel, enabling it to transform from a utilitarian furniture set into an imaginative vehicle for play. The simple, linear forms of the beech furniture set allow the pieces to be oriented in a number of different ways, so that they can function at different heights as chairs or stools, or even as tables. The set also fits together for easy storage. Following a trip to Japan in the early 1930s, Stephensen, who also collaborated with companies such as Thonet, drew inspiration for his subtle, paired-back designs from the traditional craftsmanship of the region. Bojesen collaborated with Stephensen for over twenty years, but would go on to become better known for his teak monkeys (04) and other wooden toy animals.

318 🛴

Rocking Elephant, 1940s
Elefanten Schuhe (est. 1908)
Elefanten Schuhe

Elefanten was the first company to create 'articulated' shoes that paid special attention to children's anatomy, rather than being miniature versions of adult footwear. The company was founded in Germany in 1908 by Gustav Hoffmann, who developed the width-measure system that is still used by shoe shops today. The revolutionary emphasis on measuring children's feet to achieve the best fit was accompanied by the launch of Elefanten's Torsana shoe in 1955, which featured an equally novel flexible sole. This rocking elephant, which could be found in shoe shops around the world, acted as a chair for children to sit on while their feet were being measured and their shoes fitted. Constructed from metal and wood, the elephant doubled as advertising, embodying the red elephant trademark that Elefanten adopted in 1928. One of these rocking elephants even found its way to the celebrated New York toy shop FAO Schwarz, where it was used in floor and window displays.

319 🪑

Side Chair, 2013
Lucas Maassen & Sons (est. 2011)
Kinder Modern

This child's table and chair was made with child labour, specifically that of Thijme, Julian and Maris, the three sons of Dutch artist and designer Lucas Maassen. At Lucas Maassen & Sons, the designer produces a line of wooden furniture that his children – one aged nine and two aged seven at the project's inception – then paint. The slapdash nature of the paint technique is an aesthetic developed out of consideration for production speed as, due to Dutch child-labour laws, the boys are only permitted to work for three hours a week. For each piece that they paint, they receive one Euro – a fee that each boy agreed to in a contract. 'My sons were the starting point for this project', explains the designer. 'I wanted to start a family business. But also this project looks at child labour. Many products around us are made by [child labour], but if we can't actually see it, we tend to ignore it.'[1]

320 🛴

Giulia Rocking Horse, 2008
Pininfarina Extra (est. 1986)
Riva 1920

If the sleek lines of this rocking horse remind you of a racing car, there's a good reason for that. Produced by Riva 1920, a revered Italian business known for its solid-wood furniture, the Giulia was designed by Pininfarina Extra. Since 1930, Pininfarina has been synonymous with exceptional automobile design, having given shape to many of the Fiats, Ferraris, Alfa Romeos and Maseratis that we've come to love over the years. In 1986, Pininfarina Extra was founded to bring their touch to things outside of the car sector – like Giulia. Carved from FSC-certified cedar, the rocker comes in both an 80 cm (31½ in) coupe and a 160 cm (63 in) sedan version. Unlike her turbo-charged counterparts, however, this ride celebrates the organic, using no unnatural finishes or toxic glue. Cracks and fissures that appear in the wood over time merely contribute to the unique look of each piece. Sporting the same name as the famed Alfa Romeo model, there's no denying that this rocking horse has a pedigree that's hard to beat.

321 ᵠ⁴

Baby Bottle, 2002
Philippe Starck (1949–)
Target

Tasked with designing an affordable baby bottle for the ubiquitous American retail chain Target, Philippe Starck sought to impart it with the elegance of a perfume bottle. The partnership between Starck and Target followed on the heels of the retailer's groundbreaking collaboration with architect Michael Graves in 1999. Starck, who is best known for producing iconic, high-end designs for companies like Alessi and Vitra, was inspired by Graves's efforts to make good design available to all, thus creating this bottle that sold for less than three dollars. Perceiving many children's objects to be overly bright and clumsy, the prolific French designer instead created items with simple shapes and soothing colours, including pale yellow, white and matte silver. Starck was particularly determined to restore a sense of femininity to the objects that new mothers are surrounded by, illustrated by Baby Bottle's refined dimensions. The rattle in its cap, meanwhile, keeps the baby entertained.

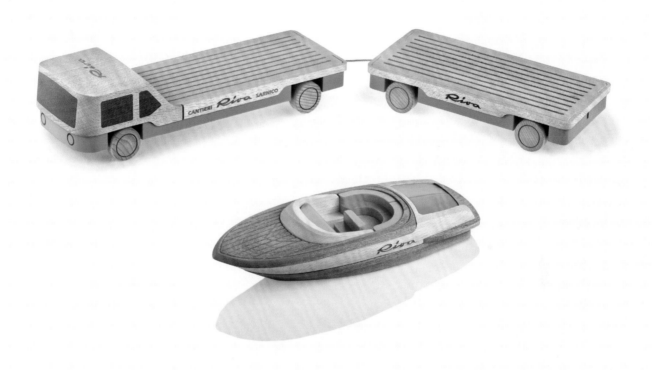

322

Aquariva and Truck, 2015
Madeindreams (est. 2004)
Riva

Established in 1892, the iconic Italian shipbuilding company Riva is a brand synonymous with luxury. Riva's yachts – typically owned by award-winning athletes, film stars and aristocrats – are characterized by their elegant forms, craftsmanship and quality materials. The company's set of miniature boats, imagined by Italian design studio Madeindreams, is no exception. Riva 5 Legends is a collection comprising replicas of the brand's most popular models: the Ariston and the Aquarama motorboats, and the more classic Aquariva and Rivarama. A Riva truck for transporting the yachts is also included. The pieces are made from the same types of wood found in their life-size counterparts – African mahogany, ash wood and Italian maple – and are hand-finished in Italy without the use of glue or other fasteners. Completely chemical-free, the boats come packaged in disassembled pieces, with individual compartments that can be swapped between models. When not in use, the handsome set can be displayed as a reminder of *la dolce vita*.

323 ☾

Thost House Crib, 1927
Marcel Breuer (1902–81)
Private commission

For most design enthusiasts, Marcel Breuer's name conjures images of chromium-plated, tubular-steel furniture. Posited as the first modern architect to introduce the chromium-plated surface into the home, Breuer was aged only twenty-three when he created the tubular-steel pieces that would later be considered his core contribution to the history of design. However, the famed Modernist also worked as an architect and interior designer. Breuer received his earliest residential design commission from the Thosts in 1926, while teaching at the Bauhaus in Dessau. The young Hamburg-based couple had an extensive pottery collection, for which Breuer designed several display vitrines. Breuer's love of standardization and modularity is on display throughout the Thost House, as evidenced by this perforated crib for the Thosts' nursery. Latches and hinges at the crib's sides suggest that it could also be converted in to a changing table.

324 ▲▼●

Building Zoo, 1965
Konrad Keller (est. 1864)
Creative Playthings

An unlikely menagerie makes up this set of wooden blocks, originally produced by the German manufacturer, Konrad Keller. Early sets featured seven animals that can be balanced atop one another to create a towering zoo. The animals are stylized, each with their own distinctive, expressive profile, much like the rocking horses that Konrad Keller produced from the mid-century onwards. From 1970, the American toy company Creative Playthings also sold a version of the Building Zoo blocks, which they imported from West Germany. The Creative Playthings set featured ten animals: a rhinoceros, bison, pelican, elephant, alligator, horse, ram, fox, polar bear and giraffe. The animal blocks are made from hardwood with a natural finish, allowing their colour to deepen over time and through use. Today, the sets remain in circulation, sometimes still in their original Konrad Keller or Creative Playthings cardboard boxes.

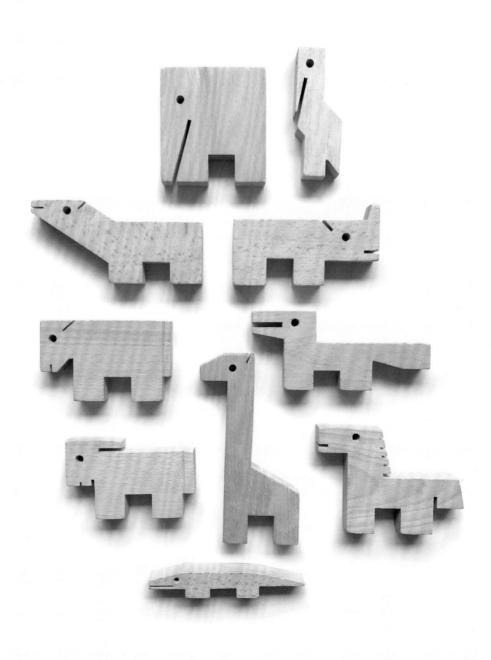

325 🪑

Kids-Rock, 2006
Alexander Taylor (1975–)
Thorsten van Elten

From 2002–14, the German-born, UK-based design enthusiast Thorsten van Elten, collaborated with young and emerging creatives to produce and sell punchy, smart design. Produced in 2006, the Kids-Rock chair by British designer Alexander Taylor, was one such collaboration. Its clean-lined frame is built from solid oak, which has been configured simply and without ornament. The exclamation mark, however, is to be found in its seat, which is made from a single piece of colourful Dalsouple rubber. Taylor's inspiration came from a vintage rocker spotted at a friend's house. 'I haven't made an adult's version,' he explains, 'as I believe that the purity of the design would be lost and I like the idea that it is designed just for children.'[1] Since his collaboration with Van Elten, Taylor has gone on to have a successful design career, with his Fold Table Lamp (2005) now included in the permanent collection of the Museum of Modern Art, New York.

326 ☾

Little Nest, 2016
Oszkar Vagi (1975–)
O-bjekt Design

The Little Nest cradle was very much a personal project for Oszkar Vagi of the Budapest-based studio O-bjekt Design. Inspired by his own child's restless nights, Vagi created a cocoon-like felt crib designed to reflect a baby's experience in its mother's womb. The cosy cradle offers a natural environment for sleeping, being handcrafted from a double layer of Merino wool using traditional felting techniques. Four leather straps suspend Little Nest from a wooden bar that hangs from a single point in the ceiling: this free-hanging design responds to movement with a gentle sway that is intended to calm and lull a restless child, helping them to sleep peacefully. Little Nest's soft tones, natural materials, blanket-stitched edges and handsome hardware make O-bjekt Design's cradle as beautiful as it is functional.

327 🪑

Plain Clay Children's
High Chair, 2011
Maarten Baas (1979–)
Den Herder Production House

It all started in 2002, when Maarten Baas set fire to his graduation project. For his degree show at the world-renowned Design Academy Eindhoven in the Netherlands, Baas took a blowtorch to pieces of second-hand furniture – some of which were flea-market junk, others were serious Baroque antiques – before covering the charred frames with epoxy resin to create Smoke. Picked up immediately by the Dutch furniture manufacturer, Moooi, it has become an iconic line, now in the permanent collection of several national museums. Clay followed in 2006, a surreally naive series of stools, chairs and tables, which are made of synthetic clay that appears to have been moulded like putty over a metal frame. Five years later, the Plain Clay collection emerged, to which this high chair belongs. A more robust version of the original series, Plain Clay sees pigment mixed directly into the synthetic clay, rather than being lacquered on. The collection's child-like simplicity is brought to bear by the fact that each piece is moulded by hand and is thus unique.

328 🍴

Twist Family Cutlery, 2012
Alfredo Häberli (1964–)
Georg Jensen

Featuring whimsical illustrations etched into mirror-polished stainless steel, the Twist Family tableware set is the product of a happy union between the Zürich-based designer Alfredo Häberli and famed Danish silverware company, Georg Jensen. Much of Häberli's work draws inspiration from his own childhood in Argentina, often beginning with extensive sketches and handmade models, before turning to digital tools. He highlights this process in the Twist collection by laser printing each piece with one of his sketches – mother, father, daughter and son – while the family's dog and cat can be found chasing each other on the set's double-handled cup. A celebrated designer, in 2014 Häberli was awarded the prestigious Swiss Grand Prix of Design by the Swiss Federal Office of Culture. This endearing set brings a sense of elegance and playfulness to mealtimes.

329 🪑 🍴

Henry IV High Chair, 2008
Wolfgang Sirch (1964–)
and Christoph Bitzer (1964–)
Sirch

Handmade in Bavaria, the Henry IV High Chair continues the Sirch family legacy of crafting high-quality wooden products. With a history dating back to 1805, the family-run woodworking company originally specialized in traditional, steam-bent, wooden sleds. In recent years, however, Sirch has become known for its beautifully crafted, clean-lined toys that are at once refined and rugged. The Henry IV High Chair was designed by interior designer Wolfgang Sirch and sculptor Christoph Bitzer, and forms part of the company's children's line, Sibi. Catering to kids from the age of six months to fifteen years, the strap and tray table can be removed, and the height of the seat adjusted, to become a stool as the child ages. The swivel seat is crafted from laminated birch, while the base is powder-coated steel, making it easy for parents to wipe clean after mealtimes. With its elegant lines and refined material palette, this high chair befits its royal name.

330 ☍

Children's Chair, c. 1908
Josef Hoffmann (1870–1956)
J & J Kohn

Originally founded in 1850 by the Austrian father-and-son team of Jacob and Josef, by the turn of the twentieth century, J & J Kohn had grown to be one of the largest furniture manufacturers in Europe, with stores all over the continent, as well as in the United States and Australia. They commissioned numerous iconic designers of the era to devise furniture for their line, including Koloman Moser, Adolf Loos, Otto Wagner and Josef Hoffmann, who would produce this handsome children's chair for them in 1908. Hoffmann was the leader of the blossoming Wiener Werkstätte (Vienna Workshop), a designers' cooperative in Vienna, where J & J Kohn was head-quartered. With a simple but elegant partial-bentwood construction, the chair was one of several productions made possible by the Hoffmann–Kohn partnership, including the Sitzmaschine Chair, which is among Hoffmann's most recognizable designs today.

331 🐻

No. 4 Elephant, c. 1921
Joaquín Torres-García (1874–1949)
Aladdin Toy Company

It was during his childhood in Montevideo that the eminent Uruguayan artist Joaquín Torres-García began constructing objects out of wood. Over his lifetime, his interest in the medium developed into a vast body of work that complemented his career as a painter. These elephants, which feature interchangeable parts that can be reassembled to create different poses, were produced through Torres-García's own Aladdin brand of wooden toys, which he founded in New York in the early 1920s. Inspired by the collections of ancient art from the Americas, which were on display in New York's American Museum of Natural History and the Trocadero Museum of Ethnography in Paris, Torres-García's figurines are at once rustic and avant-garde. After the Aladdin facility burned down in the mid-1920s, Torres-García relocated to Europe, where his toys continued to be commercially distributed. However, they were never again produced on the scale that they had been in New York.

Die Stadt, 1921
Lyonel Feininger (1871–1956)
Self-produced

The German–American artist and illustrator Lyonel Feininger had an extraordinarily creative career, showcasing his work through platforms as varied as the *Salon des Indépendants* exhibition of 1911, and the *Chicago Sunday Tribune*, to which he contributed cartoons. Like many artists and designers of children's toys, Feininger gained inspiration from his own sons, who he designed toys for as Christmas presents each year. Die Stadt (The Town), with its carved, colourful houses, cathedrals and charming stream of pedestrians, is one of his most beloved and playful designs. One of the first master teachers of the Bauhaus to be appointed by Walter Gropius, Feininger contributed the cover design of the 1919 Bauhaus manifesto. Like this toy set, and much of Feininger's two-dimensional work from this era, it presented a fragmented vision of architecture, the pointed spires of its Gothic cathedral set against a night sky.

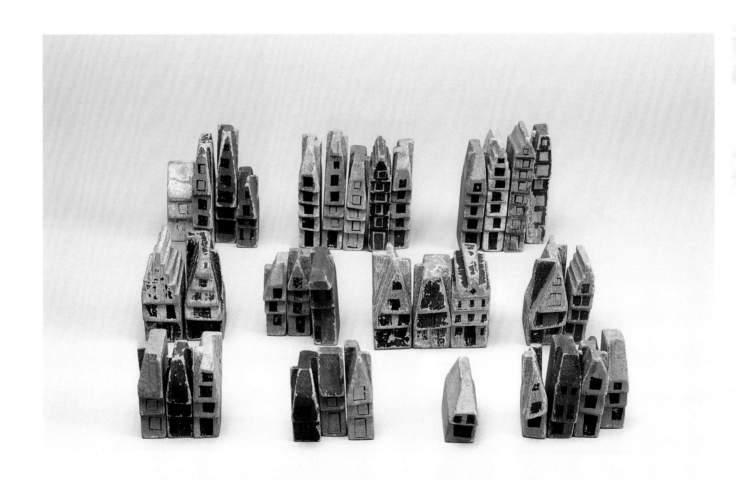

333 🐻

Ultra Modern Doll's House, c. 1937
Lines Bros (est. 1919)
Lines Bros

With its sculptural, geometric design, flat roof and ribbon windows, the Ultra Modern Doll's House, produced in 1938 by the British toy manufacturer Lines Bros, was one model in a line that also included a thatched cottage and a Tudor home. Drawing inspiration from contemporary trends in architecture, the Ultra Modern came out of a period in which Le Corbusier's Villa Savoye (1931) and Philip Johnson and Henry-Russell Hitchcock's exhibition *Modern Architecture: International Exhibition* (1932) had proclaimed the emergence of an International Style that favoured glass, steel and reinforced concrete. Hinged on one side, it could be opened to reveal two large rooms with parquet floors, a stairway, a garage and an open-air sun porch. The doll's house was also wired with electricity and had two fireplaces with modern detailing accenting the mantles. In the years immediately following the release of this toy, the company would temporarily convert their operations from toy production to military hardware.

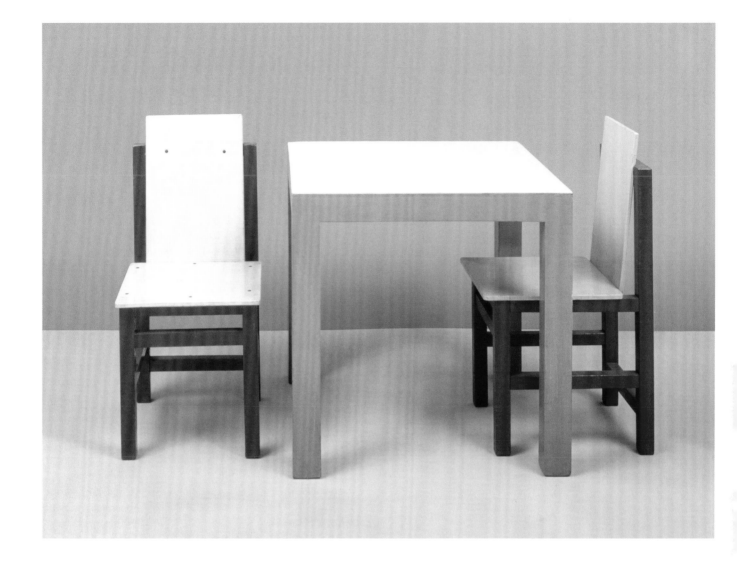

334 侰

Child's Table and Chairs, 1923
Marcel Breuer (1902–81)
Bauhaus Workshops

One of the most revered designers of the twentieth century, Marcel Breuer quickly ascended the ranks of the Bauhaus. A protégé of Walter Gropius, Breuer entered the school as one of its first students, and ultimately became one of its master instructors. The rectilinear design of this Child's Table and Chairs set displays the influence of Dutch furniture designer Gerrit Rietveld, who exhibited with the school in 1923. Much like Rietveld's chair designs of the late 1910s and early 1920s, Breuer's furniture set is defined by the intersection of its vertical and horizontal planes, as well as by the rectilinear frame of its base. Within a couple of years of fashioning this set, Breuer began his experiments in tubular-steel construction – tests that would yield one of his most iconic designs, the cantilevered Wassily Chair. Breuer's contributions to the Modernist movement eventually extended from the domestic interior to the form of the house itself, with architectural commissions that included the steel-frame Doldertal Apartment Houses.

335 🐻 🪑

Dollhouse Chair, 2014
Torafu Architects (est. 2004)
Ichiro

It seems only fitting that the idea to design a chair that doubles as a doll's house would come from an architect with a toy collection. In 2014, Koichi Suzuno of Torafu Architects collaborated with Polish designer Alicja Strzyżyńska to create Dollhouse Chair. The geometric, birch-plywood chair hinges down the middle, transforming into the shape of a home with a gabled roof when swung open like a book. Its red accent panels cleverly denote the roof of the house in its unfastened configuration, while the chair's interior compartments become toy storage when closed. Founded in 2004, Torafu Architects has built a reputation for bringing an architectural approach to a wide variety of disciplines, from film-making to product and exhibition design, and for its love of bringing an unexpected twist to familiar things. Dollhouse Chair fits seamlessly into the studio's ethos to 'design tools for living' that reimagine the relationship between furniture and the space that it inhabits.

336 🐻 ◢◣

Puzzle Carpet, 2005
Satyendra Pakhalé (1967–)
Magis

Offering up infinite possibilities, this carpet comprises puzzle pieces that can be endlessly reconfigured. Available in three printed patterns – water, sand or grass – the carpet's pieces can be bought individually, or as a set of seven, allowing parents to add to the puzzle over time. Made of expanded polyethylene and a polyester fabric, it is both soft and extremely durable, making it an ideal play surface for children. Part of the Me Too line for children by Magis, the Puzzle Carpet was created by Amsterdam-based designer Satyendra Pakhalé, who is recognized for his versatility, having produced everything from communication technologies and concept vehicles, to appliances and domestic interiors. Pakhalé is particularly well known for weaving elements of craft into designs for mass production, yielding unlikely combinations of material and form, as exemplified in his Mini Roll Ceramic Chairs. The playfully modular Puzzle Carpet is typical of his desire to create objects that restore the importance of the handmade in contemporary design.

337 🪑

Agatha Chair, 2013
Ágatha Ruiz de la Prada (1960–)
Vondom

The indoor/outdoor Agatha Chair, named after its designer, Ágatha Ruiz de la Prada, uses a frequent motif in her work – the endearing heart shape – to create a piece of furniture that is at once graphic and playful. Known for her sense of whimsy, and bold shapes and colours, it seems only natural that Vondom, the Valencia-based furniture company, chose the Spanish designer to lead its first foray into children's design. The daughter of both an aristocrat and an architect, Ruiz de la Prada debuted her eccentric fashion designs in 1981, later expanding into ceramics, toys, linens and make-up. With over 300 collaborations to her name, including Vitra, El Corte Inglés, Camper and Disney, Ruiz de la Prada is a household name in Spain. Her heart-shaped chair forms part of the Agatha collection, which also includes a flower-shaped table, a rug and a large flower-shaped plant pot. The Agatha Chair's youthful innocence and cheerful exuberance perfectly translate Ruiz de la Prada's vibrancy into child-friendly furniture.

338 🐻 🛴

Tumbling Animals, 2006
Bolette Blædel (1968–)
and Louise Blædel (1973–)
Bobles

Danish architect Bolette Blædel came up with the idea for furniture that would encourage children to move while she was on maternity leave with her first child, having been unable to find anything appropriate on the market. In 2006, she teamed up with her sister, Louise, a designer, to establish Bobles, the now award-winning design studio for children. Each Tumbling Animal was created with the help of a child physiotherapist to ensure that the design assists in the development of children's motor skills, by encouraging them to actively move and play. The toys are also suitable for children with special needs and motor difficulties. Made out of sheets of coloured EVA foam that have been fused together, the Tumbling Animals are soft, light and easy to clean. The collection features a wide array of characters to support what the Blædel sisters refer to as 'happy development', including a chicken, crocodile, anteater and elephant, which can be ridden like a rocker when turned upside down, or 'surfed' by older children, with a foot on either end.

339 🐻

Bimble and Bumble, 1968
Hans Gustav Ehrenreich (1917–84)
Hoptimist

It's hard not to smile when a Hoptimist toy springs into action. The playful design originated in 1968, when furniture designer Hans Gustav Ehrenreich decided that the Vietnam War and the start of The Troubles in Ireland had left the world in need of a little cheering up. Ehrenreich's first Hoptimist, Birdie, was quickly followed by Bimble, Bumble and Kvak, a frog. Each of the now iconic designs has the same spherical body and spring-loaded mouth, with varying colours and expressions. With a quick tap on the head they'll bounce away, seemingly chatting, swaying or dancing. Although manufacturing ceased in 1974, the buoyant figures remained a fixture of Danish cultural memory. In 2009, with an economic recession once again leaving Denmark down in the mouth, Danish fashion designer Lotte Steffensen tracked down Ehrenreich's son and asked for the rights to put the cheerful toys back into production. Thanks to her initiative, nearly every Danish home and office has its own Hoptimist again today.

340

Modulon, 1984
Jo Niemeyer (1946–)
Naef

The pared-down, geometric harmony of Modulon, consisting of white, red, yellow, blue and black blocks, echoes Piet Mondrian's De Stijl paintings in its use of the black segments to represent the dividing grid. The German artist Jo Niemeyer was commissioned by leading toy company Naef to create the desktop puzzle in 1984, decades after Mondrian's experiments in Neoplasticism. Modulon's sixteen blocks have been divided into seven different masses that can be rearranged to construct mini Gerrit-Rietveld-like creations. The blocks are harmoniously proportioned according to the ancient mathematical principle of the golden mean, which occurs when the ratio of two quantities is the same as the ratio of their sum to the larger of the two quantities. One of the most iconic art toys ever created, Modulon is a natural fit within Niemeyer's oeuvre: the artist first began experimenting with geometric painting in the mid-1960s and has continued to explore the golden mean in his work ever since.

341 🐻

Bath Duck, 1993
Patrick Rylands (1942–)
Ambi Toys / currently Galt Toys

As chief designer at Ambi Toys for more than thirty years, the British designer Patrick Rylands created products that were a staple of children's playrooms and bathtubs from the late 1960s through to the 1980s. Trained as a ceramicist at the Royal College of Art, Rylands combined his love for sculptural forms with the smooth materiality of plastic. With internal ballast to keep it upright and afloat, the Bath Duck has a beak that is designed to open and close as the duck bobs in the water. The moving beak also doubles as an escape route for any bath water that enters the toy. 'I love simple mechanisms,' Rylands notes, explaining that he often seeks to design toys 'with a little movement that doesn't cost much extra to include.'[1] Its elegant form and graphic simplicity lend this friendly bath toy a pleasing timelessness. Fittingly, Bath Duck is one of several of Rylands's designs for Ambi Toys to have been recently rereleased by Galt Toys.

342

Diabolo, 1904
Gustave Philippart (1861–1933)
Various

Commonly known as a juggling or circus prop, the Diabolo consists of a double-coned bobbin, or two cast-rubber domes, attached in the middle with a metal axle. Using a separate length of string, which is suspended between two sticks or wands, a series of gravity-defying tricks can be performed. By skillfully spooling the string around the toy's axle, the Diabolo can be made to spin, before being tossed into the air and then caught again by the string. The toy's design draws inspiration from the *Kouen-gen*, a traditional Chinese yo-yo originally made from bamboo and string, that dates back more than 3,000 years. Imported to Europe by traders in the eighteenth century, it became enormously popular and received different names, such as 'the Devil on two sticks', hinting at how difficult it was to master. When the French engineer Gustave Philippart patented significant changes to the toy's design in 1906, he called it 'Diabolo', from the ancient Greek *dia* (across) and *ballo* (to throw). Philippart's adaptation of the toy crystallized its form and established the Diabolo as a universal childhood activity.

343 ♯

Vipp Children's Rocking Chair, 1992
Verner Panton (1926–98)
PP Møbler

In 1992, Verner Panton, the maverick of Scandinavian design, began collaborating with the classic Danish joinery workshop PP Møbler, at the suggestion of fellow Danish designer, Hans Wegner. Based on Panton's vision for 'a piece of furniture consisting exclusively of rings',[1] they produced the Vipp, a children's rocking chair. If the lacquered bentwood and cane chair seems vastly different from Panton's more colourful designs of the 1960s, its perfect circles can be seen as an expression of his enduring fixation with exaggerated geometric forms, visible in the conical shapes and sinuous curves of his earlier work. Along with his renowned Panton Chair, the Vipp is a prime example of Panton's determination to continually push materials and manufacturing processes to their limits. In this case, the design was only made possible by the use of pre-compression, an experimental new steam-bending technique, which alters the very cell structure of wood, making it more elastic and thereby possible to achieve deeper curves.

344 ⛁

High Chair, 1978
Paul Wintermans (1950–)
Architektenburo Wintermans

Frequently a symbol of new life, the circle is celebrated in this curvilinear chair by Paul Wintermans. Reminiscent of Gunnar Daan's High Chair of 1966 (opposite), Wintermans's design was painted white, putting the visual emphasis on the child, while also recalling the widespread use of white in early twentieth-century nursery furniture. Alongside Frank Wintermans, Paul served as the director of Architektenburo Wintermans from 1980–95, before combining the practice with Wim Quist to form the Rotterdam-based firm Quist Wintermans Architects (QWA). Throughout his career, the Dutch architect has regularly turned his attention to furniture design, producing unique pieces, small series and work tailored to specific architectural projects, maintaining that the diversity of his projects keeps his mind sharp. This unusual chair, made from a combination of birch and three-ply plywood, forms part of the furniture collection of the Stedelijk Museum in Amsterdam.

345 🪑

High Chair, 1966
Gunnar Daan (1939–2016)
Self-produced

Dutch architect and designer Gunnar Daan created this children's high chair while living on a houseboat with his wife and four children. Daan's keen interest in geometry is evident in his ability to efficiently engineer the chair's four horizontal sections, which could all be cut from a single piece of plywood measuring 50 cm sq (7¾ sq in). A slightly thinner plywood was used for the chair's vertical supports. Although originally created for his own children, the chair would later find a commercial audience through the Dutch department store Metz & Co. Daan's love of the Dutch architect and designer Gerrit Rietveld, who also produced furniture for the store, is evident in its constructivist style. However, Daan's disappointment with profit margins reportedly led him to shy away from future collaborations with the store. In 2008, a limited number of reproductions were made for a small Amsterdam design store, named Huisraad.

346 ⊞

Anna Table and Chair, 1962
Otto Nielsen (n.d.)
IKEA

The 1960s saw IKEA pivot from producing heavier, traditional designs to more minimalist furniture – a move that followed trends of the period and shaped the company's reputation as a purveyor of modern Scandinavian design at an affordable price. With its bold colour and refined lines, this bent beech table and chair set displays the new sense of simplicity being introduced to home interiors. The base of the chair mirrors the arm and backrest, which cleverly enables it to be flipped, offering two different seat heights to accommodate children as they grow. Often incorrectly attributed to Karin Mobring, one of four in-house designers working at IKEA at the time of its release, the Anna Table and Chair set is, in fact, the brainchild of Otto Nielsen, who worked as an architect for the city of Copenhagen and was hired by IKEA as a freelance designer from 1959.

347 🪑 ✏️

Mullca 300 School Desk and Chair, 1949
Jacques Hitier (1917–99)
Mullca

Stackable, robust and light enough for a child to lift single-handedly, Mullca furniture was a fixture in the post-war French classroom. Designed by Jacques Hitier in 1949 and today deemed an iconic piece for its material efficiency and simplicity of form, the Mullca 300 chair and accompanying desk were among the first examples of tubular-metal furniture to be mass produced. Their combination of industrial and organic materials is typical of Hitier, who softened the image of metal furniture by offsetting it with wood or rattan and painting the tubes in enticing colours. He began his design training at the École Boulle in Paris at the tender age of thirteen, where he later served as director. Though well known for his work with Mullca, this design (a version of which, with curved back legs, was first produced by Mobilor) was for many years mistakenly attributed to his fellow French designer Marcel Gascoin, until close examination of both designers' archives proved otherwise.

Giffy Table Lamp, 2005
Markus Oder (1984–)
Leanter

Can decor make kids more creative? Leanter, the company behind the spirited giraffe-shaped Giffy table lamp, thinks so. The brand created Giffy as an extension of their ideology that an inspired environment can foster openness, a quality that they feel is especially important for children. Markus Oder found inspiration for the lamp in a photo of a giraffe on the savannah, believing the natural world excels at combining beauty and function. With its birch-plywood body, exposed hardware and aluminium shade, Giffy boldly pronounces the economy of its design, which – thanks to its modest materials and lean construction – makes a colourful, playful statement for a child's bedroom or study. The wooden body features voids that resemble the spots on a giraffe's back, while its lampshade becomes a head, which can be raised and lowered to create directional light. The shade, available in a range of colours, is matched by the lamp's cord, which weaves playfully through the wooden cutouts in the giraffe's body.

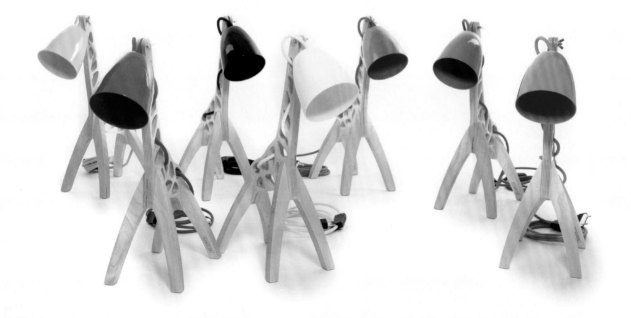

349 🛴

Konstantin B Toy Car, 2009
Nika Zupanc (1974–)
Self-produced

The Slovenian designer Nika Zupanc knows how to make an impression. 'Although it is an instrument of tiny proportions, this is a poisonous item,' Zupanc's website declares, 'because it efficiently grooms your vanity into an asset of unavoidable dimensions.'[1] With luck, your toddler will do more vrooming than grooming. Zupanc, whose work has been described as 'punk elegance' by *Elle* (US), has been turning heads since her Lolita lamp for Moooi catapulted her onto the design world's stage in 2008. Since then, she has become one of its most closely watched designers, and has collaborated with industry titans like Moroso and Dior. The sleek and playfully nostalgic outline of this ride-on toy recalls the teardrop-shaped vehicles of Norman Bel Geddes and the streamlined elegance of the 1930s and 1940s. Available in several colours, Konstantin B is composed of a lacquered-epoxy shell and aluminium or brass parts.

350 🪑

Saya Mini, 2013
Lievore Altherr Molina (est. 1991)
Arper

The Saya Mini, with its cinched waist and eye-catching colours, is as sophisticated as it is playful. The work of Lievore Altherr Molina, the celebrated Spanish firm that was honoured with the National Design Award in 1999, Saya also comes in an adult stool and chair version. One of the most prolific design firms in Spain, Lievore Altherr Molina has collaborated with many renowned companies, including Foscarini, Poltrona Frau and Driade. The stackable Saya Mini has a curved-plywood shell and chromed-steel sled base, the two pieces of which can be combined in a variety of colours – white, yellow, red and pink, or polished chrome for the base – to produce uniform or two-tone chairs. The adult version of the Saya also comes with options including wooden or metal legs and an upholstered seat. Produced by Arper, the leading Italian furniture manufacturer, the chair won the prestigious Red Dot Award in 2013.

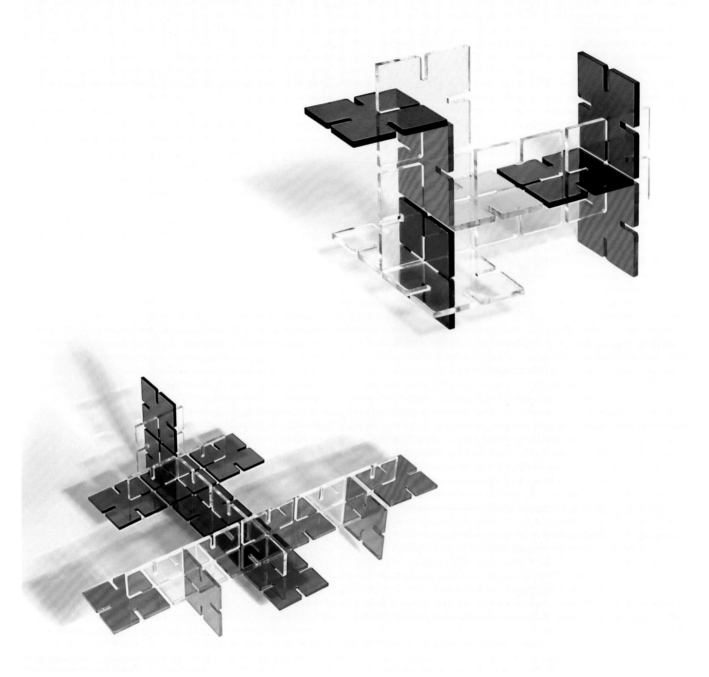

351 🎨 ✏️

PlayPlax, 1966
Patrick Rylands (1942–)
Trendon / currently PlayPlax

PlayPlax is a deceptively simple toy in its concept. Rather than building with dimensional objects, such as blocks, PlayPlax enables children to construct with flat, slotted squares. All forty-eight pieces are identical in size and shape, varying only in the hue of their translucent plastic. As children stack the colourful pieces to their liking (the set purposefully comes without instructions), the translucence of the polystyrene creates a kaleidoscopic, stained-glass-like effect. Patrick Rylands came up with the idea for the system while studying at the Royal College of Art in London, manufacturing the prototype during his summer holiday. Within three years of its first appearance in 1966, over a million sets of PlayPlax had sold and the toy was awarded a Design Centre seal of approval. Rylands went on to be the chief toy designer at Ambi Toys for over thirty years, his ubiquitous creations well-known to British children raised in the late 1960s, 70s and 80s.

352 🐻 ✏️

Famille Garage Collection, 2010
Alexander Seifried (1976–)
Richard Lampert

A child's nursery is reimagined as a workshop in the Famille Garage line of furniture from German manufacturer, Richard Lampert. The designer Alexander Seifried drew inspiration from his childhood memories of the everyday plastic boxes that had filled his father's garage. Seifried explained, 'Since I was old enough to think, I liked these plastic boxes. Everybody knows them and I thought maybe it is possible to do something with them.'[1] The collection, which includes a dresser/changing table, shelving unit, desk, bench and crib, applies a workspace mentality to children's furniture through modularity and adaptability. Elements within each piece can be interchanged in order to adapt to the evolving needs of a growing family: the dresser is easily transformed into a changing table through the addition of a desktop; its base can also be removed to form a bench and its drawers exchanged for the slide-out containers that Seifried loved as a child. Everything in the multifunctional set can be used and reused according to need, while offering a convenient and colourful storage solution when not in use.

353

Vintage Push Car, 2004
Vilac (est. 1911)
Vilac

This tiny metal ride-on racer rolls with major retro appeal. Its lozenge-shaped body, mini grille, large wheels, vertical steering column and gas cap, which sits behind the faux-leather seat, recall the exciting racing car designs of the 1920s – an era when companies such as Bugatti, Sunbeam and Austin produced sleek vehicles with a serious need for speed. While yesteryear's drivers sat in a sunken cockpit, tots are free to perch on top of this car, using their own two feet for momentum. Available in several colours, the rubber-edged tyres of this elegant racer make for silent and smooth cruising. A racing number and vents emblazoned on the car's body add the finishing touches. Designed by Vilac, the French company who have been producing wooden toys since 1911, this push car equally appeals to adventure-seeking kids and their style-concious parents.

354   🛴

Rocking Rabbit, 1988
Björn Dahlström (1957–)
Playsam

When commissioned to create a rocking toy for Playsam, Björn Dahlström noted that many historic rocking horses were so large as to render them too dangerous for a child to use without the assistance of a grown-up. His design, he determined, would be accessible on children's terms and the Rocking Rabbit, a playful reimagining of the traditional equine version, was his solution. Crafted at a scale that enables a child to safely mount, rock and dismount independently, it was designed in Playsam's signature palette of red, black and white, although it has since been produced in more colourful variations, too. The rabbit's perky leather ears double as reins that the child can hold onto tightly while rocking. Following the Rocking Rabbit's success, Dahlström also created a duck version and a hopping frog.

355 ◭

PlayShapes, 2010
Zoe Miller (1968–)
and David Goodman (1969–)
MillerGoodman

Setting out to concoct a toy for the twenty-first-century child, British designers Zoe Miller and David Goodman instead looked to the past. Their creation, PlayShapes, serves up a graphically charged block-set, which enables children to explore composition, representation, abstraction and collage in three dimensions, while evoking design-savvy toys, such as Alma Siedhoff-Buscher's Bauhaus Bauspiel of 1923 (130). Rather than providing uniform, simple shapes, the designers created a set of quirky and imaginative pieces, reminiscent of the remnants of a craft project. Large blocks that have been cut away at the sides, wide arcs and shark-fin sails are mixed with more anthropomorphic items, such as a Sgt. Pepper moustache and cylinder forms whose ends resemble eyes in a range of expressions. Brightly coloured on one side, each PlayShape is left in its natural unfinished rubberwood on the reverse, allowing children to determine just how much colour to include in their inventions.

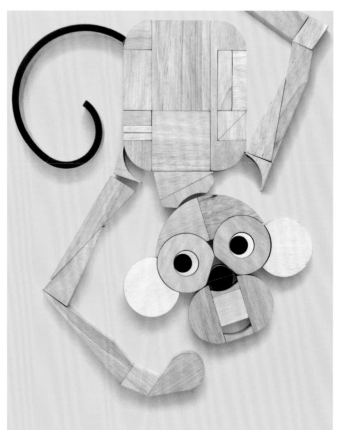

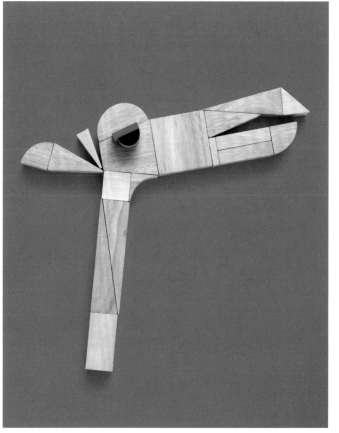

356 🐻

Spinning Tops, 2015
Piero Lissoni (1956–)
Porro

Nine decades might be considered a mature milestone, but the Italian design company Porro decided to celebrate their ninetieth birthday by issuing new variations on a youthful toy – the spinning top. With the help of the Italian architect and designer Piero Lissoni, Porro celebrated its legacy of beautifully crafted contemporary wooden design with elegance and lightness. Furthermore, as the third-generation family business changes its wood palette every year, these five spinning tops showcase the sixteen timbers that the company selected for their ninetieth year. Throughout its history, Porro has revived many artisanal traditions, such as slat work and wooden inlays, and these spinning tops explore the technique of turnery, which allows a craftsperson to execute fluidly sculpted shapes as the wood turns on a lathe. The material sensitivity inherent in the design of these spinning tops reflects the long-running partnership between Porro and Lissoni, who has served as the company's artistic director since 1989.

357 🐻

Pocket Dolls, 2011
Stephanie Housley (1975–)
Coral & Tusk

Stephanie Housley founded the beloved indie design company Coral & Tusk in 2007, with the dream of transforming her illustrations into embroidered textiles. What began with a single sewing machine in Housley's Brooklyn apartment has since grown into a business with significant global reach. Housley, a textile designer trained at the Rhode Island School of Design, comes from a line of American craftswomen, including a great-grandmother who made lace and a grandmother who created dolls. In 2011, Housley began producing her own intricately embroidered dolls, each one starting with a hand-drawn pencil sketch on paper. After digitizing her illustration, Housley traces every line of the drawing in a software program, and sends the image to production partners, who then sew and hand-embroider each object with her distinctive style. The end result is a testament to how new technologies enable handicrafts to scale-up, while maintaining the specific qualities that render them so unique.

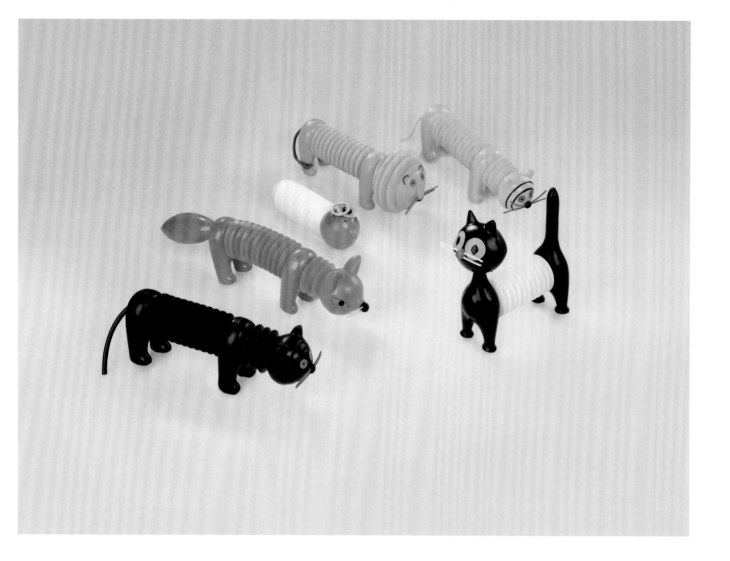

358 🐻

Accordion Animals, 1963–5
Libuše Niklová (1934–81)
Fatra

Libuše Niklová is an important figure in the history of modern Czech design due to her collaborations with the plastic products brand, Fatra. Though ubiquitous today, plastic only became widely available in the years following World War II. Niklová's pioneering plastic playthings were colourful, mass-produced, washable and affordable, helping to transform the public perception of children's toys, which until then had been mostly wooden and made in limited numbers. 'In the future, products from plastic matter will surround man just like the air, and they will become commonplace,' Niklová predicted in 1971. 'Increasingly, natural materials will be a luxury and the object of admiration. The future, however, belongs to plastic.'[1] The accordion bodies of these friendly animals cleverly celebrate a Fatra-patented technology. Suitable even for bath-time play, these musical animals were some of the first mass-produced toys in the country. Immensely popular in their day, Niklová's toys have since been celebrated in museums around the world.

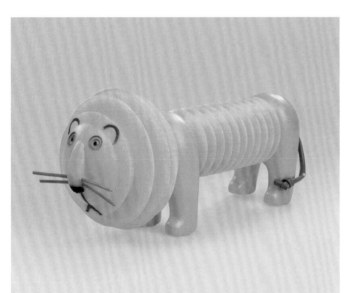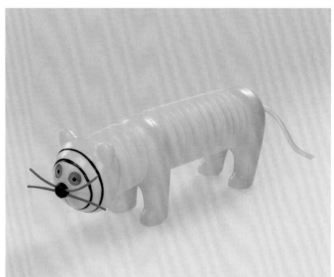

359 ✏️ 🔺🔵

ABC con Fantasia, 1960
Bruno Munari (1907–98)
Corraini Edizioni

Well-known as a designer of children's books, the acclaimed artist and designer Bruno Munari had a profound desire to understand and expand the world view of children. Munari's books were objects to be handled as much as stories to be read, and were among the most innovative of the 1950s and 1960s. Munari's storybooks jettisoned princesses, princes and monsters in favour of basic tales about people, animals and plants, which aimed to awaken the reader's senses. Believing in the power of simple design to stimulate the imagination, he combined pared-down illustrations, surprising materials and counter-intuitive sequencing to both physically and mentally engage young readers. Similarly, his *ABC con Fantasia* (*ABC with Imagination*) presents toddlers with a 'pre-book', designed to inspire a love of reading in pre-literate minds. With Munari's characteristic clarity of design, this 1960s letter-composition toy includes twenty-six brightly coloured, linear and curved, puzzle-like pieces of non-toxic plastic that can be combined to make a variety of capital letters.

360 ♯

Alfie Funghi, 2014
Philippe Starck (1949–)
TOG

'The only way to see life is no more trends', Philippe Starck has declared. 'The only trend that is acceptable is freedom, freedom to be different, freedom to choose what you want.'[1] Launched in 2014 by a friend of the celebrity designer, the short-lived Brazilian brand TOG (an acronym for All Creators Together) sought to provide this freedom by combining manufacturing excellence, technology and individualism. Offering a range of customization options both in-store and through a bespoke app, TOG invited customers to become part of the design process, creating pieces that were both affordable and unique. Alfie Funghi, a child's desk and stool, is one of eleven designs that Starck conceived for the company's launch collection. Moulded from a single sheet of durable plastic in a range of colours, this two-in-one desk echoes Nanna Ditzel's Trissen Stool of 1962 (123). Unlike Trissen, however, Alfie Funghi fell out of production when the open-source platform closed for business.

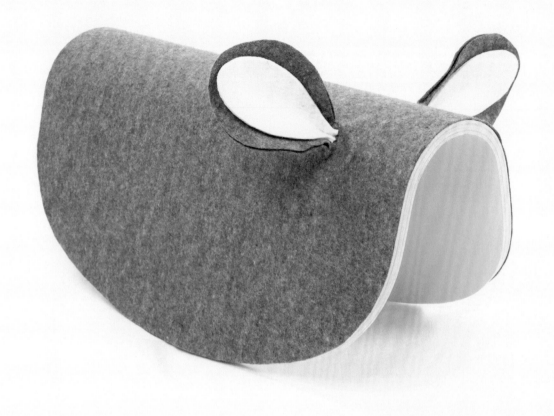

361 🛴

Buskas Rocker, 2008
Kaja Osholm Kjølås (1979–)
Trollkid Eventyrmøbler

With soft ears, a fuzzy-felt coating and a sunny yellow interior, the Buskas Rocker embodies the spirit of a friendly forest mouse. Buskas (meaning 'shrub' in Norwegian) is part of a three-piece furniture collection inspired by the Scandinavian forest, which also includes a tree that can be mounted on the wall and climbed, and a felt-walled fort shaped like a large beaver's head. The rocker's laminated wooden base enables smooth movement, while its contrasting colours and textures encourage the development of tactile and sensory awareness. Older children can hone their balance by sitting atop the rocker, the felt aiding with grip. Very young children can join in too, using the rocker as a tunnel to crawl through. Buskas was designed by Kaja Osholm Kjølås while she was still a student, in collaboration with the children's furniture company Trollkid Eventyrmøbler. Since graduating, the Norwegian designer has gone on to found Eggs, a multidisciplinary service design studio.

362 🛴 🐻

Watchawant, 2009
Charlotte Ryberg (1977–)
and Johanna Strand (1979–)
Prototype

Employing a timeless sensibility and minimal materials, the Watchawant stool teases at children's imaginations with its animal-like ears, body and tail. Created by Swedish collaborators, Charlotte Ryberg and Johanna Strand, Watchawant is made out of one sheet of elegantly curved plywood, with a multifunctional leather-covered rope that runs its length and can be pulled to create ear-like handles or a long animal-like tail. The stool can accommodate two children, encouraging them to sit side-by-side or straddle it widthways. Its adaptable design and simple shape foster active, imaginative play in children, with a silhouette that is sleek enough to be at home among adult furniture. Ryberg and Strand debuted their design at New York's International Contemporary Furniture Fair (ICFF) in 2009, modifying it into an upholstered version, called Imaginary Friend, the following year.

363 ◗▽◖

Dandanah, The Fairy Palace, 1919–20
Bruno Taut (1880–1938)
Luxfer-Prismen-Gesellschaft

For the renowned Expressionist architect Bruno Taut, glass was the material of spiritual transformation and political metamorphosis. His initiation, in November 1919, of the 'Crystal Chain' correspondence, is testament to Taut's visionary approach to design. It was during this period that the economic realities and material shortages of post-war Germany made smaller projects such as children's toys much easier to realize. Together with inventor Blanche Mahlberg, Taut designed Dandanah, The Fairy Palace; a realization in miniature of a world given new life by glass architecture. As the name Dandanah (an Indian word for a bundle of rods or pillars) suggests, the building set was inspired by India's colourful palace designs. Dandanah appeared on the German market in 1922 as a set of sixty-two multicoloured glass building blocks. It was intended for mass production, yet only a few were ever made. Nine sets are known to remain in existence.

364 ◱

Wright Blocks, 1949
John Lloyd Wright (1892–1972)
Self-produced

John Lloyd Wright, son of the famous American architect, began his career following in the footsteps of his father, Frank. After leaving his father's business, John created one of the most well-known toys in US history: Lincoln Logs (452). However, in 1943, he unwittingly sold the patent for the successful toy to Playskool for around $800 (£600). In an attempt to design another building-block winner, Lloyd Wright patented Wright Blocks in 1949. These rectilinear, cross-grooved blocks were sold in a variety of natural or stained woods. More versatile and modern than Lincoln Logs, Wright Blocks could be assembled into lighter and more open structures. With Wright Blocks, 'the child knows that the structure when finished will be stable and can be preserved as long as he wishes to have it remain intact,'[1] Wright asserted. Nevertheless, Wright Blocks failed to gain the widespread popularity of their predecessor and were never produced in large volumes.

365 ◨ ✎

PinPres, 2012
Nenad Katic (1977–)
and Vanesa Moreno Serna (1979–)
OOO My Design

Taking inspiration from sensory 'pin pressure' toys, this unique creation was developed by two architect–designers, Nenad Katic and Vanesa Moreno Serna. Lined with flat-headed wooden pins that can slide from one side of the device to the other, PinPres is as much large toy as it is storage unit. When a user presses on one side, the pin pops out of the other, enabling children to shape the piece to their liking, even creating a life-sized impression of themselves. Once extended, the pins can act as coat hooks, display platforms, bookshelves or simply as pure decor. PinPres is made in Spain, from locally sourced beech, and comes in both colourful and natural wood variations. Since its launch, the unit has been installed in day-care centres, offices and homes across the globe. Based on the popularity of this standing version, the design studio also released a miniature wall-mounted version for rooms with smaller spatial capacity.

366 🪑

Chair Thing, 1963
Peter Murdoch (1940–)
International Paper

The 1960s saw a shift towards youth and mass culture, consumerism and transience. These changes were visible in design that reflected the influence of Pop art, and which exploited new materials and industrial techniques to create furniture for more flexible, casual and nomadic lifestyles. Peter Murdoch's Chair Thing, designed in 1963 when he was a student, is one of the most famous children's chairs of the period. Made from a single sheet of industrial cardboard, the chair was at once inexpensive to produce and distribute (as it could be flat-packed), easy to construct (with the help of pre-scored lines), washable (due to a plastic coating), and surprisingly robust thanks to its sophisticated form. In 1967, Murdoch extended his range of furniture (tables, chairs and stools), marketed as Those Things: Fibreboard Furniture for the Young, which retailed for less than £1 each. Over 76,000 pieces were sold within six months of their release, yet Murdoch's dream of mass production was never realized.

367 🍴

Mother–Child Dining, 2005
Maartje Steenkamp (1973–)
Studio Maartje Steenkamp

For Maartje Steenkamp, the mother–child feeding experience represents a pro-
foundly intimate dynamic, for which she has created a dining set designed to celebrate this quotidian act. As both designer and parent, Steenkamp has conceived
a number of products for children, putting them to the test in her own home.
In designing Mother–Child Dining, Steenkamp affixed a baby's seat at high-chair
height, conveniently close to the dining surface. The leg-less seat aids access
to the floor beneath, simplifying the inevitable tidying up of dropped items.
An accompanying unfixed adult-sized chair comes with the table, which can be
repositioned to suit the parent's needs. After producing this set, Steenkamp also
designed the Child Child Chair, which includes two child-height seats at the table.
A minimalist and infant-friendly spin on a dining table, Mother–Child Dining
emphasizes the unique bond that exists between parent and offspring – although
one might reasonably ask, what of the Father–Child dining table?

368 🌙

Rockwell Bassinet, 2014
Monte Design (est. 2005)
Monte Design

Striking material contrasts come together in this streamlined bassinet, designed and produced by the Canadian furniture studio Monte Design. Walnut-wood rockers and a sleek chrome frame support a cosy upholstered baby basket, available in either white or grey micro-suede. Founded by Ralph and Michelle Montemurro following the birth of their son, Monte Design's range is produced in Toronto, combining fine craftsmanship with sustainable manufacturing. Each Rockwell Bassinet basket comes with a waterproof mattress and cotton sheets. The cradle's soft sides and calming rocking motion help babies to feel safe and secure, so that all members of the family can enjoy a restful night's sleep. The bassinet's removable basket enables parents to sleep safely alongside their newborn, or to transport the basket around the house, which transitions to function as a storage basket for toys or other children's items once a baby has outgrown it.

369

Robot Monkey Rocking Horse, 2015
Matt Monroe (1976–)
Monroe Worskshop Toys

With its generous wooden rockers, spindly legs and rope tail, this rocking horse perfectly embodies the sculptor and carpenter Matt Monroe's quirky, low-tech approach to design for children. A few years after founding his furniture studio, Monroe took inspiration from his two daughters to begin constructing what he called 'robot monkeys'. Using the pieces left over from his studio's larger furniture projects, he discovered that these idiosyncratic creatures had a charm all of their own and so decided to launch a line of handmade, collectible toys in 2015. The eco-friendly series includes a collection of endearing, abstract and quirky critters made from solid maple, with undyed rope accents – and his rocking horse is no exception. As a designer, Monroe states that he values minimalism and fun in his toys, and that his studio is committed to promoting imaginative play.

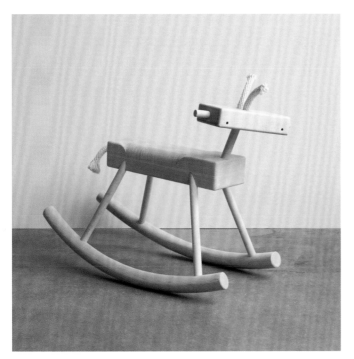

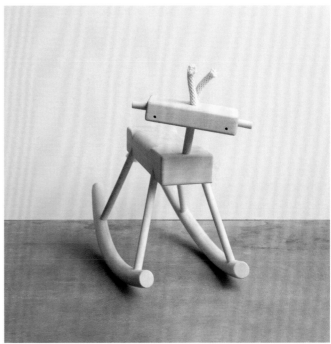

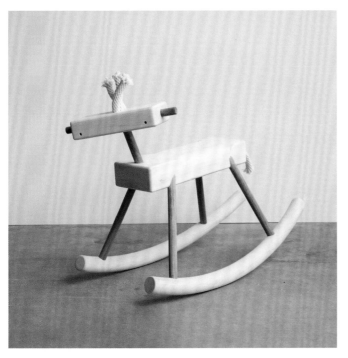

Blocky Cars, 2014
Libor Motyčka (1983–)
Nuxo

Libor Motyčka is a Czech designer who founded his own studio, Nuxo, after graduating with a master's degree in furniture and interior design from Prague's Academy of Arts, Architecture and Design, in 2014. The first designs that Motyčka produced through Nuxo were sets of wooden toy cars, including these brightly painted, angular ones – appropriately named Blocky. Made from maple wood, they are finished with non-toxic paint in red, green, yellow and blue. The subtle variations between the vehicles give them each a recognizable character – as a family car, a mini-bus or a saloon – despite their stylized form. Motyčka's finely honed skill in woodworking (a craft that he has enjoyed since high school) has resulted in him producing each set of cars by hand, and is evident in details such as their precisely inset wheels. Motyčka's designs have been presented at Milan Design Week.

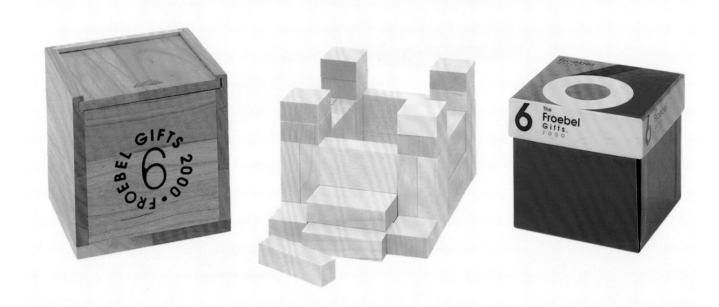

371 ▰ ✎

Froebel Gifts, 1837
Friedrich Froebel (1782–1852)
Milton Brady / currently Red Hen

The fact that we take building blocks and educational toys for granted is largely due to Friedrich Froebel, whose educational work in the 1800s continues to shape much of how we approach early learning today. In 1837, the German pedagogue invented the concept of kindergarten, conceiving of it as a place where young girls and boys could develop their own potential. Believing that children learn about the world through structured play, he created a series of wooden construction toys, which he called Gifts. Each Gift comes in its own box and is divided into five categories: solids, surfaces, lines, points, and lines-and-points. Specifically scaled to encourage children to manipulate and explore the world around them, each Gift is simple, yet open-ended, helping to develop awareness of structure, relationships, mathematics and science. While there is no shortage of modern educational toys, it remains difficult to find uncomplicated and modest ones, which perhaps explains why Froebel's Gifts have such enduring appeal.

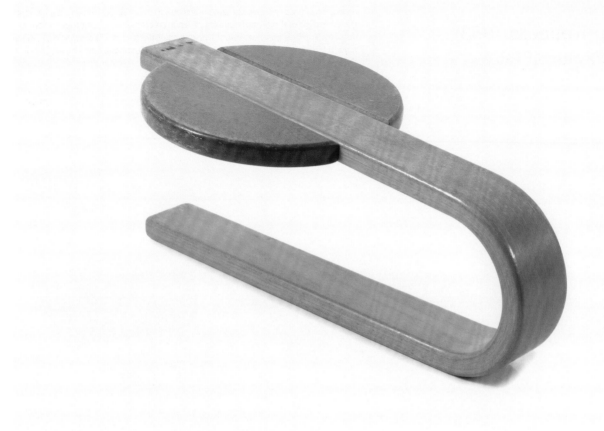

372 🪑 🐻

Children's Bounce Seat, 1960s
Alex Pedersen (n.d.)
Hukit

Created by Danish designer Alex Pedersen, the exaggerated U-shaped cantilever of this children's chair was achieved using beech plywood, lending it a natural bounce. A red wooden seat, also made from beech, hugs either side of the hairpin-shaped frame's top bar. Though Pedersen's later work went on to reflect historic shifts towards a postmodern, Memphis-style aesthetic, the sense of kinetic whimsy evident in his Bounce Seat persisted. The simple and elegant design was manufactured by Hukit, a Danish company founded by Hubert and Kitte Trojaberg, which produced other mid-century products for children, including a high chair from 1967 that is still produced today. Made from sustainable beech it is distinguished by its signature round cut-out in the back of the chair, a design equally refined and characterful as Pederson's bouncer.

373 ♟✏

Balancing Troupers, 1963
Fredun Shapur (1929–)
Naef

The graphic and toy designer Fredun Shapur was a great lover of puzzles and produced a number of them during his career, in formats that ranged from traditional jigsaw toys to his clever Four-Way Blocks (426). These Balancing Troupers from 1963 anthropomorphize jigsaw-puzzle pieces, transforming their positive extensions into tiny faces, and their voids into the curves of arms and legs. Shapur gave his pieces the dimensionality of wooden blocks, enabling them to be stacked like little acrobats into three-dimensional space. He crafted his earliest toys for his own children, Firoz and Mira, later graduating to sell his designs at the British department store, Heal's. The popularity of Shapur's products encouraged him to license his work through Naef, the Swiss toy manufacturer, as well as through the pioneering American brand, Creative Playthings. Carved from contrasting beech and rosewood, these shapely Balancing Troupers, exhibit Shapur's graphic sensibility and love of playful design.

374 🪑 🐻

Puzzel Furniture, 1988
Knut Hagberg (1949–)
and Marianne Hagberg (1954–)
IKEA

Knut and Marianne Hagberg are a brother-and-sister duo who have worked together as designers for IKEA since 1979. Of the thousands of designs they have produced over the years, the Puzzel collection is Marianne's favourite. With its bright primary colours, and combination of textures and shapes, the metal and plastic set is an example of the Hagbergs's knack for developing a stimulating collection of objects using a single, cohesive design language. The pair share a deep working knowledge of materials and production methods, having committed many hours to visiting the factories in which their designs are produced. At the other end of the production process, they often visit their local IKEA store to observe how customers react to their products. This range earned the Hagbergs an Excellent Swedish Design Award in 1988, and has featured in exhibitions including *Faces of Swedish Design* (1988) and *Kid Size* (1999). It is also included in the permanent collection of Stockholm's Nordic Museum.

375 ☾

Ozoo 600 Bed, 1967
Marc Berthier (1935–)
Roche Bobois

In the late 1960s, the French architect and designer Marc Berthier joined Günter Beltzig in designing furniture for children out of fibre-glass-reinforced polyester. Lightweight, durable and easy to clean, the material paved the way for the joyful designs of the 1970s. The Ozoo collection, which Berthier created for Roche Bobois in 1967–8, was the first affordable all-plastic furniture collection in France. Initially designed for children and teenagers, the range included desks, storage units and beds. Berthier's 600 Bed is reminiscent of Rolf Heide's Stacking Bed of 1966 (74), with an equally practical and versatile design, making it ideal for play dates and sleepovers. Berthier received the prestigious Gabriel Prize for the Ozoo collection and, to celebrate its fiftieth anniversary, Roche Bobois re-released the adult desk and chair in 2018.

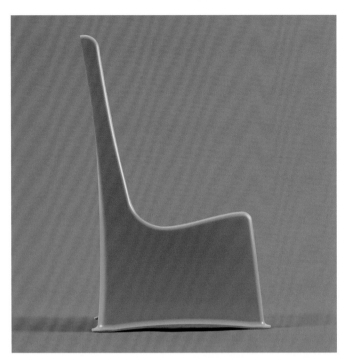

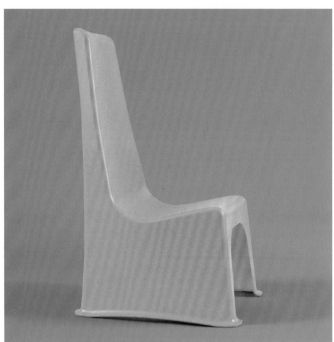

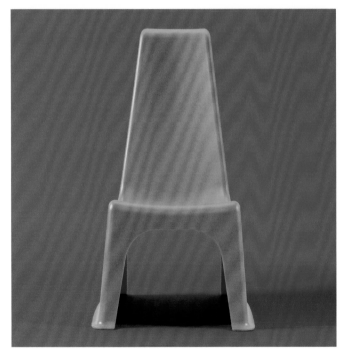

376 🪑

Juniör, 1966
Günter Beltzig (1941–)
Brüder Beltzig / currently Löffler

Thanks to designers like Walter Papst, Luigi Colani and Günther Beltzig, the 1960s saw Germany become a pioneer in plastic and fibreglass furniture for children. Beltzig began his career in 1966 in the design department at Siemens AG in Munich. That same year, the ambitious designer and his brother founded Brüder Beltzig, where for the next ten years they produced innovative plastic furniture and collaborated with other talented designers, like Colani. The Juniör children's chairs are part of a collection of moulded-fibreglass play furniture created in the same year that the company was founded. Intended for both indoor and outdoor use, the collection also included a table, a see-saw, a slide and a rocking tub-like piece. Organic and ergonomic in shape, each piece is durable enough to withstand rough play, and light enough for small limbs to carry. Back by popular demand, Beltzig's Juniör was reissued by German company Löffler in 2011.

377

Googy Rocking Horse, 2011
Wilsonic Design (est. 2000)
Novak

Wilsonic Design is a multidisciplinary design studio based in Slovenia, whose focus covers everything from buses and sailing boats to hospital equipment. As is often the case, the team turned its attention to objects for children when one of its designers became pregnant. Using only quality natural materials, the company launched 'ooh noo', a children's brand intended to create products that are practical enough to be used every day, beautiful enough to be treasured and durable enough to become family heirlooms. Googy reinterprets the conventional rocking horse into an organic shape that is soft and inviting to children, while also appealing to a more adult aesthetic. Made of linen, beech and foam, Googy is at once elegant and easy to clean. Made by hand in Europe, Googy comes in two sizes, the larger of which can even accommodate adults. It won a prestigious Red Dot Design Award in 2012.

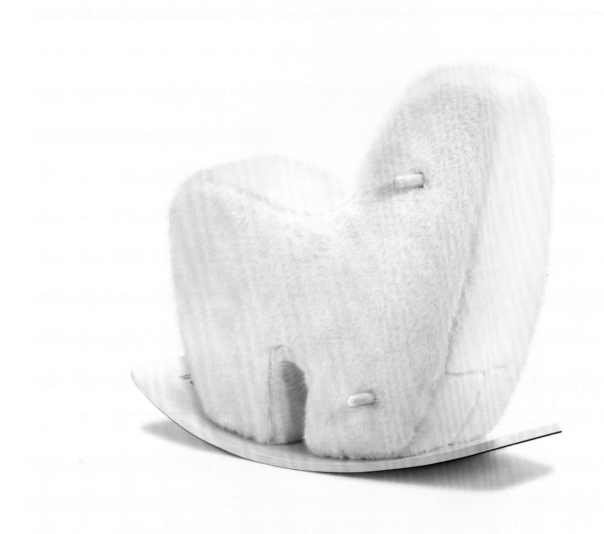

378 🐻

Steiff Teddy Bear 55 PB, 1902
Richard Steiff (1877–1939)
Steiff

Few toys conjure such a strong attachment as the teddy bear. Interestingly, it seems that the iconic stuffed bear first appeared on both sides of the Atlantic – entirely independently and almost simultaneously – in 1902. In the United States, a cartoon in the *Washington Post* had depicted a hunting outing on which President Theodore ('Teddy') Roosevelt refused to shoot a black bear cub; this led the toymaker Morris Michtom to create a soft toy, which he duly named Teddy's Bear. In Germany, the nephew of Margarete Steiff, a seamstress who had founded her own soft toy company in 1880 making felt elephants, came up with the idea for a toy bear following visits to Stuttgart's zoo. Richard Steiff called his bear 55 PB, with 55 referencing its height in centimetres, P its material, *plüsch* (plush), and B the *beweglichkeit* (movability) of its articulated joints. Still in production today, Steiff bears can be recognized by the hallmark brass button that they carry in their left ear.

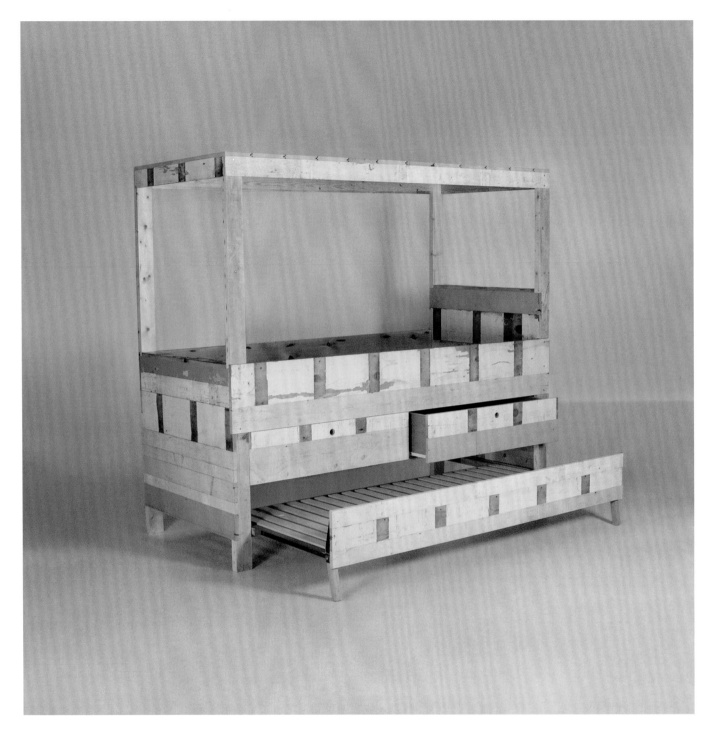

379 ☾

Bunk Bed, 2008
Piet Hein Eek (1967–)
Self-produced

Concerned with issues of mass production, design conformity, material waste and ostentation, Dutch designer Piet Hein Eek embodies many of the ideals of twenty-first-century design. While attending Design Academy Eindhoven in the 1980s, Eek visited a local scrapyard and saw beauty in the waste materials. For his thesis, Eek transformed discarded matter into high-end furniture, illuminating the potential for integrating reclaimed materials into product design. His project caught the attention of Gijs Bakker and Renny Ramakers, founders of the Dutch conceptual design company Droog. Including Eek in their 1993 debut show in Milan, the young designer earned a global following. Having gained renown for his patchwork, high-style approach, Eek has expanded his line to a wide range of products, fabricated at his large studio in Eindhoven. Often composed of available fragments, each item becomes a unique palimpsest of past use. Here, the designer applies his approach to a childhood favourite: the bunk bed.

380 ♯

Swivel Chair, 1952
Casala (est. 1917)
Casala

An oversized metal screw fixes the seat of this beech chair to its legs, allowing it to swivel. The same feature also enables the height of the chair to be adjusted by rotating the seat, making it to adaptable to children of different ages. The Swivel Chair was produced by Casala, a German company founded in 1917 to produce wooden-soled shoes in Hanover. In the following decades, they came to focus on the design and production of furniture, gradually expanding their material palette to include upholstered and metal-framed pieces. Today, the company is based in the Netherlands, and specializes in commercial and institutional furniture for churches, schools and universities. This particular children's chair is based on earlier Casala designs for swivelling adult chairs, which featured a more exaggerated curve in the seat and back.

381 🪑 🛴

Hokus Pokus 3-in-1 High Chair, 1967
Barnsängsfabriken (est. 1967)
Barnsängsfabriken

Form follows function in this high chair – and it is certainly rich with function. A Swedish classic, the Hokus Pokus 3-in-1 High Chair has been in continuous production since it was first designed in 1967. Without the need for reassembly or moving parts, the Hokus Pokus can magically convert from a high chair into a rocking car (complete with steering wheel), or a chair and table for a small child – all by simply flipping its orientation. Originally made of timber, the high chair has been produced in plastic with a padded seat since 1972, making it both durable and easy to clean. It is also produced in a huge array of over 200 colour combinations, to suit every child's taste. For safety, the high chair includes a strap to stop children from slipping, attachments to fix it to a table and no footrest, removing the risk that a child might stand up in the chair and tip it over. Now a cult favourite, the Hokus Pokus is also included in the prominent Delft Chair Collection, held at the Delft University of Technology.

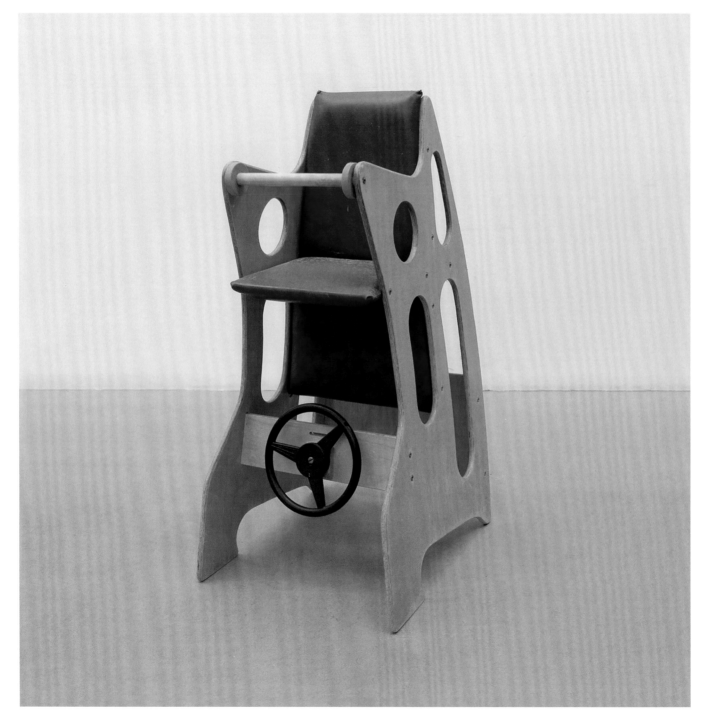

382 

Go-Kart, 2001
Piet Hein Eek (1967–)
Self-produced

Although best known for his distinctive furniture designs, the Dutch designer Piet Hein Eek is also well recognized for his dedication to craftsmanship and sustainable production practices. One of the many children's designs that Eek has created over the years, this nifty roadster is a pedal car that is one part industrial chic, one part Chitty Chitty Bang Bang. Originally created for the grandchildren of the Dutch designer Henk Vos, the car was later produced in a series of ten, the majority of which were sold to Cïbone (Eek's dealer in Tokyo) and the cutting-edge Amsterdam design store Frozen Fountain. The car's long metal body and large wheels recall early racing cars of the 1920s and 1930s, providing a touch of nostalgic appeal without veering into the kitsch. Through Eek's attention to materiality and construction, what could have been a humble racing car is instead elevated to a covetable design *objet*.

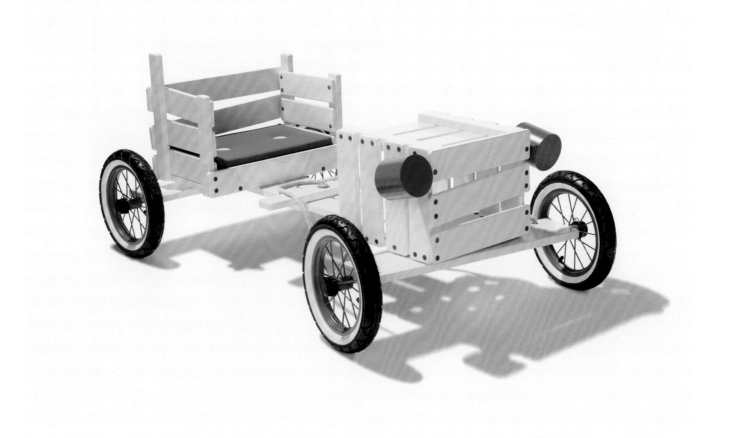

383 ⚙

Soapbox Cart, 2009
Jesper K Thomsen (1971–)
Normann Copenhagen

Jesper K Thomsen's Play range for Normann Copenhagen features a vivid-yellow children's bench, table, chair, easel and soapbox car, all built out of beech with humorously wonky angles. Combining homemade craft with a professional design sensibility, the soapbox car's gleaming, tightly spoked wheels betray the vehicle's otherwise ramshackle aesthetic, evoked through its off-kilter wooden frame and humble headlights. Built by hand in a local carpentry shop in Denmark, the car references the wooden soap (or apple) crates from which it was historically constructed. Soapbox cars, or 'gravity racers', are typically non-motored vehicles made by children to be raced against one another. Primarily known as an American tradition, downhill gravity racers have also long been a fixture of European play: the first soapbox car race was actually recorded in Germany in 1904. They have since gained popularity around the world. True to the soapbox tradition, Thomsen's version is powered solely by a friendly push and the force of gravity.

384 ◩ 🐻

Meccano, 1898
Frank Hornby (1863–1936)
Meccano

The twentieth century's archetypal construction toy was conceived by Frank Hornby, a British meat importer and father of two boys. Inspired by the cranes that fascinated his sons in the port of Liverpool, Hornby set out to create a miniature version using prefabricated elements. The first construction set of perforated metal strips and bolts that could build all manner of structures and vehicles using correct mechanical principles was named 'Mechanics Made Easy', before being shortened to 'Meccano' in 1907. It would take Hornby two years of farming the production out to local manufacturers before he could afford a workspace big enough to produce the toy himself. One of the oldest construction systems in the world, Meccano's impact would rival Friedrich Froebel's nineteenth-century wooden blocks (371), igniting the imagination of countless children and influencing the design of construction toys worldwide.

385 🪑 🛴

Julian, 2005
Javier Mariscal (1950–)
Magis

This characterful, dog-shaped chair is the work of the internationally renowned Spanish designer and artist, Javier Mariscal. Known for his love of cartoons and comics, Mariscal drew inspiration for the Julian chair from a dog of the same name, who starred in his comic series, *Los Garriris*, first published in 1974. As much a toy as a piece of furniture, the Julian chair fosters dynamic play, its sturdy frame ready to serve as a chair, car, pet or whatever else a young imagination might envision. Made of polyethylene in four basic colours, Julian is one of several objects created by the designer for the Me Too range by Magis: a high-concept line for kids with objects created by esteemed contemporary designers. Known for his playful and expressive designs, Mariscal designed this versatile seat to serve as a child's faithful companion, encouraging them to dream up as many options as they can muster for its everyday use.

386 🐻

Henne mit Küken, c. 1967
Antonio Vitali (1909–2008)
Werkstätte Antonio Vitali

Antonio Vitali disparaged the commercially available toys of his time, believing that they were too literal to truly engage the imagination. Instead, he drew on the folk tradition of handmade wooden toys and his own training as a sculptor, carving smooth, abstracted figurines that were designed to fit snugly in a child's hand. The Swiss craftsman began by making toys for his own children, before partnering with other companies to design for mass production. Throughout the 1950s, Vitali worked with Creative Playthings, a toy company whose philosophies were sympathetic with his own. The collaboration enabled his series of 'playforms' which, although industrially produced, still retained the sculptural qualities of his handmade toys. This Henne mit Küken – a 'hen with chicks' that nestle beneath her – was developed later in Vitali's career for his own self-titled studio. It demonstrates the timelessness of both his work's aesthetic appeal and his tireless belief that the creative latitude of children was best served by simple, open-ended toys.

387 ⬢

Golo, 1995
Věra Tataro (1966–2017)
Karel Makovský

As seen elsewhere in this book, many well-known Modernist toys (perhaps, most famously, those created by Artel Cooperative) originate from Czech artists and artisans. Golo, a toy developed in the 1990s by Czech designer Věra Tataro, continues this legacy. Reminiscent of Bruno Munari's ABC with Imagination from 1960 (359), Tataro's toy embraced the capacity for blocks to form graphic, geometric designs, as well as a bright, primary palette. The name 'Golo' is, in fact, a pun. In the Czech language, the word *kolo* means wheel. Tataro cheekily changed the 'K' to a 'G', as the letter's form reflects the shape of the puzzle. Through the tranches, wedges and semicircles of the Golo set, children can create colourful creatures brimming with personality, either on a flat surface or in conjunction with vertical space. The toy was produced through the Czech manufacturer Karel Makovský until 2013.

388 🐻

Greiflinge Allbedeut, 1939
Hugo Kükelhaus (1900–84)
Meistergilde KG / currently
Hohenfrieder Werkstätten

While these elegant and elemental baby toys may look familiar today, in 1939 they emerged into a toy world that offered babies only teethers and rattles. Their creator, Hugo Kükelhaus, was an architect, artist and philosopher who spent his life exploring the ways in which sensory experience shapes our understanding of the world. Inspired by the educational theories of kindergarten inventor Friedrich Fröbel, who foregrounded the 'touching experience' and proposed basic three-dimensional volumes as important pedagogical toys, Kükelhaus began to develop his own toys. Initially called Allbedeut (all meaning), his collection of wooden objects were abstract in form, thereby symbolizing many possible meanings for the child. Children, Kükelhaus believed, should grow into the world by playing, active touch and grasping for things. He therefore wanted his toys, later called Greiflinge (graspables), to underline the importance of touch in early brain development. Incredibly influential, the line expanded over the years, becoming synonymous with quality toys for babies.

389 ☾

Radio Nurse, 1937
Isamu Noguchi (1904–88)
Zenith Radio Corporation

In the wake of the highly publicized kidnapping of the twenty-month-old son of aviator Charles Lindbergh and his wife, Anne, in 1932, Zenith Radio Corporation's president hired Isamu Noguchi to design a one-way radio to help him keep an eye – or at least an ear – on his child. The device, named the Radio Nurse, was Noguchi's first industrial commission and has since been revered for its sculptural, Modernist form. One of the earliest examples of a baby monitor, the Radio Nurse was paired with a white-metal audio receiver, known as the 'Guardian Ear'. The biomorphic speaker, cast in the early plastic Bakelite, never achieved much commercial success. However, its formal sensitivity has earned it a position in the canon of beloved modern design and, today, the Radio Nurse is prized by collectors across the world. The device was also characteristic of Noguchi's sensibility as a designer, whose lighting and furniture are now considered to be Modernist classics.

390 ☾

Shell Crib, 2014
Luke Miller (1976–)
Luke Miller Studio

With its spiralling, panelled shell, this unusual crib by Luke Miller Studio recalls the gentle swirling form of a conch. Designed in 2014, it was fittingly dubbed the Shell Crib. But with this extraordinary design comes an extraordinary price tag: as of 2018, the unit retails for an astounding £14,360 (over $20,000). Still, this item is as much a work of contemporary sculpture as it is a functional bed for a child. The cradle's shell is constructed from laminated sycamore, which perches on four finely hewn, tendril-like legs. Its fine craftsmanship is the result of Miller's two decades in furniture design – a career that brought the British designer a three-year apprenticeship with Martin Patterson at the Furniture Workshop and the honour of being selected Triton Woodworker of the Year. Embodying Miller's penchant for biomorphic design and geometry, the Shell Crib provides a peaceful perch for a baby and offers a striking design piece for any interior.

391 🛴

Isetta Pedal Car, 1957
Velam (est. 1953)
Velam

This unusual pedal car is based on the Isetta, the iconic but short-lived bubble car, which was born during the micro-car craze that swept Europe during the 1950s. The Isetta's signature shape, bizarre but space-saving front entry door and single-seat occupancy made the vehicle instantly recognizable, and created its enduring design, which is still much-beloved by dedicated followers today. Originally designed in Italy by Iso, the Isetta was licensed to a number of companies across Europe, including BMW in Germany and Velam in France. Iso sold the body-making equipment to BMW prior to licensing the design, which encouraged Velam to create its own unique body shape in 1954. More pod-like than the original Isetta, the Velam version earned itself the nickname the 'yoghurt pot'. While this child-sized version lacks some of the original car's most notable features, including the front entry door and small motor, it perfectly captures the ride's quirky and distinctive form.

392 🐻

Animal Boxes, 2010
Karl Zahn (1981–)
Areaware

These charming beech boxes reflect the sensitivity to natural materials that runs through all of Karl Zahn's work. Born and raised in rural Vermont, Zahn's awareness of materials grew out of a childhood spent playing in forests and wood workshops. The handcrafted sensibility so present in his youth continues to inform his work as a product and furniture designer today. Each of these animal-shaped boxes swings open on a single hinge to reveal a small cavity for hiding precious objects. Zahn, a graduate of the Rhode Island School of Design in New York, now lives in Brooklyn, where the manufacturer Areaware is also based. Founded in 2004, Areaware works with a range of talented independent designers to bring their ideas for gifts and home accessories to life. Equal parts sculpture, toy and functional object, Zahn's Animal Boxes include a rhino, polar bear, bull, walrus, llama and whale.

393 ☾

Cloud Bed, 2015
Daniele Lago (1972–)
Lago

The Cloud Bed floats a short way above the floor, providing children with an intimate shelter akin to an indoor tree house. Its suspended appearance and minimal silhouette are achieved through a wall attachment system hidden inside the bed frame. Produced by the Italian furniture company Lago, the Cloud Bed was designed by Daniele Lago who, alongside two of his siblings, stewards the fourth-generation family business. The Cloud Bed exemplifies the company's remarkable evolution, from the artisan wood-work carried out by Policarpo Lago at the end of the nineteenth century to the contemporary domestic furniture designs produced by his descendants today. Despite having stores across Europe and global distribution, Lago maintains its meticulous attention to detail and penchant for timeless design. The Cloud Bed, for example, not only entices children with its one-rung ascent, but also makes it easier for parents to clean the bedroom floor.

394 🐻

Play Objects, c. 1919
Hermann Finsterlin (1887–1973)
Self-produced

As an influential figure in German Expressionist architecture and a member of the utopian Crystal Chain correspondence, the architect Hermann Finsterlin resisted rationalism in his designs. He intentionally rejected formal training in architecture, opting instead to collaborate with his children to explore ideas through toys, drawings and models. While the designer never erected any permanent structures, his work was nonetheless important in the movements of his era. Finsterlin's concepts for buildings were filled with swooping, colourful forms, biomorphic elements and impossible twists and turns. When a group of his works was displayed at the 1919 *Exhibition for Unknown Architects*, held in Berlin and Weimar, crowds took notice of Finsterlin's singular style. The architect felt that toys could equally be seen as vehicles for thought and speculation, and tools for discovery. These eight colourful, painted wooden objects, designed by Finsterlin, embody essential principles of design through their exploration of form, surface, colour and emotional resonance.

395 🐻

Kaleidoscope House, 2001
Laurie Simmons (1949–)
and Peter Wheelwright (1949–)
Bozart Toys

The artist Laurie Simmons first gained recognition in the late 1970s through a series of photographs shot within a vintage doll's house. Upon receiving a commission from Bozart Toys to design a doll's house of her own for commercial sale, she teamed up with Peter Wheelwright, then Architectural Chair at Parsons School of Design, to create the Kaleidoscope House. The toy company's founder, Larry Mangel, was a former private art dealer, who was interested in giving artists a chance to design better toys than those readily available on the market. Far from your typical doll's house, the Kaleidoscope House was a tiny shrine to contemporary art and design, accessorized with miniature furniture especially created by Jasper Morrison, Karim Rashid, Ron Arad and Michael Graves. A contemporary art collection by many of Simmons's friends – Cindy Sherman and Barbara Kruger included – was also provided. A commercial success, the house is in the permanent collections of the Museum of Modern Art, New York, and the Victoria and Albert Museum, London.

396 ♬

Babà-Jr Fluorescent Light Armchair, 2010
Andrea Radice (1979–)
and Folco Orlandini (1972–)
Domitalia

Inspired by the curved forms of Ancient Greek amphorae – the narrow-necked clay vessels used for transporting goods – Babà-Jr is a children's seat with a contemporary twist. Designed to be used indoors or out, translucent versions of the polyethylene chair feature an internal lighting system, which imparts a gentle glow. Babà-Jr is just one of several illuminated furniture pieces that the Italian design duo Andrea Radice and Folco Orlandini have produced since they began collaborating in 2008. Durable and lightweight, the chair can easily be moved using the handle that is moulded into its backrest. The Babà-Jr is made in Italy by Domitalia, the company that Radice and Orlandini have presided over as artistic directors since 2013. Functionality is always blended with humour and surprise in their designs, and the pair have garnered numerous awards including first prize in the 2007 MOV Design Competition and a Chicago Athenaeum Good Design Award in 2013.

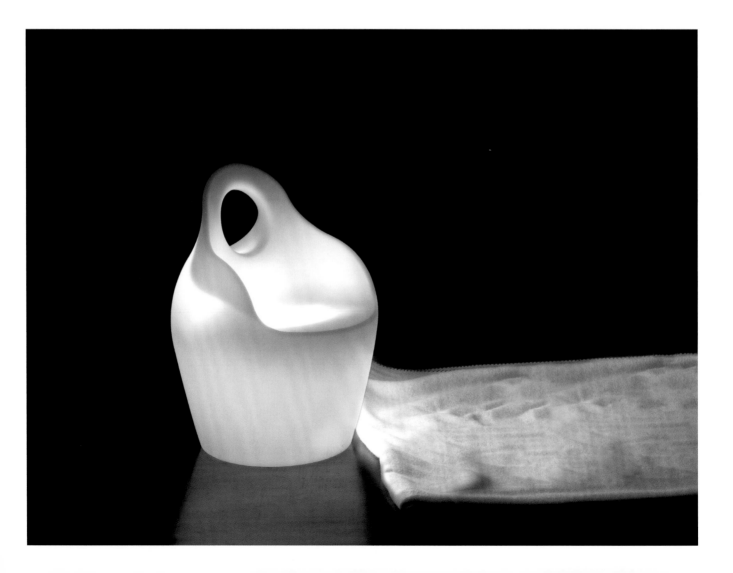

397 🪑 🐻

Mini Togo, 2007
Michel Ducaroy (1925–2009)
Ligne Roset

Born into a family of designers and furniture makers, Michel Ducaroy began working for Ligne Roset in 1954, quickly becoming one of the company's most important creatives. Ducaroy originally conceived the now-iconic Togo in 1973 as a three-seater sofa. Covered in generously quilted polyester, the sofa was made entirely of Dacron, a polyester fibre, with no frame of any kind. The world's first all-foam sofa, its low-slung, cocooned style led it to be compared to a caterpillar and, in Ducaroy's own words, a 'tube of toothpaste folded over on itself like a stovepipe and closed at both ends'.[1] Togo's enduring popularity expanded to a range of complementary pieces, including the Mini Togo. For children aged between five and twelve, its soft, lightweight form (less than 6 kg/13.2 lbs) making it ideally suited to youngsters. The Mini Togo is part of Ligne Roset's Les Minis collection, launched in 2007, which scales some of the company's iconic adult designs for children.

398 🪑

Sign Baby, 2017
Piergiorgio Cazzaniga (1946–)
MDF Italia

Sleek, clever and pop-like, the Sign Baby chair was produced by MDF Italia to celebrate the tenth anniversary of its adult counterpart, the Sign. Designed by Piergiorgio Cazzaniga, this ribbon-like chair is made of rotational-moulded plastic, rendering it lightweight, hardwearing, easy to clean, and suitable for use both indoors and out. Intended for children aged from three to ten, Sign Baby comes in a range of seven vibrant colours. The son of a cabinetmaker, Cazzaniga witnessed the processes of designing and manufacturing from an early age, and claims that they are part of his DNA. 'My reference is Scandinavian and American design from the 1950s and 60s,'[1] the designer explains. Known for his streamlined aesthetic, Cazzaniga has headed up his own studio since 1991, collaborating with a range of manufacturers, such as Living Divani, Andreu World, Desalto, Composit, Tribù and La Palma. His work has won numerous awards, making him one of the leading internationally renowned Italian designers.

Trebimbi Cutlery, 2011
Rivadossi Sandro (est. 1960s)
Rivadossi Sandro

Italian brand Rivadossi Sandro has made its name producing household items and tableware since the 1960s, including collections of cutlery with embellished and coloured handles. Influenced by different cultural aesthetics and cuisines, the brand's cutlery styles range from minimal to intricately ornate. The Trebimbi (meaning 'three children' in Italian) series was designed specifically for small hands with each cutlery set comprising a stainless-steel spoon, fork and child-safe knife, all decorated with a smiling face. The polypropylene handle of each piece is moulded in the shape of a figure, whose outstretched arms can snap together with the other handles, engaging children's tactile senses while ensuring that the set stays together when stored away. The dishwasher-safe cutlery can also be mixed and matched with other designs in the Trebimbi collection, making feeding easier for parents and more fun for toddlers.

400 ♯

Panton Junior, 1959/2008
Verner Panton (1926–1998)
Vitra

Verner Panton first envisioned a pint-sized edition of the Panton Chair in 1980, but it took another twenty-eight years for Vitra to bring the Panton Junior to life. Based on the original Panton Chair of 1959, the Junior, which is a quarter of the size, was launched in 2008, having finally been made economically viable thanks to improvements in plastic manufacturing. The Panton Junior is constructed from polypropylene and available in six different colours. Panton is remembered for pushing the possibilities of new synthetic materials to their limits: as the first plastic seat to be made from a single form, the Panton Chair was just one of the Danish designer's many experiments that rejected the conventional notion of a chair as a four-legged object. The Panton was the first product independently developed by Vitra and the Swiss company continues to produce many of Verner Panton's designs today.

401 ♯

Hiya Rocker, 2008
Robert Springer (1972–)
and Nicole Springer (1973–)
Spot On Square

As parents of three children, Robert and Nicole Springer launched their modern kids' furniture company, Spot On Square, with the desire to create safe, environmentally friendly and well-crafted pieces that promote an appreciation for good design. An industrial designer and primary school teacher by trade, the husband-and-wife team found that this creative output perfectly intersected both of their passions and knowledge. Each piece that they design responds to their own experience and needs as a family. Parents to twins, the Hiya Rocker is proportioned to be shared comfortably by two siblings and features a small compartment in the back for the light storage of books or art supplies. With its modern aesthetic, the rocker also fits in with a contemporary family household. Made entirely of recycled wood and painted with a non-toxic, UV-cured finish, the Hiya Rocker is a testament to the brand's dedication to using sustainable materials and eco-friendly processes.

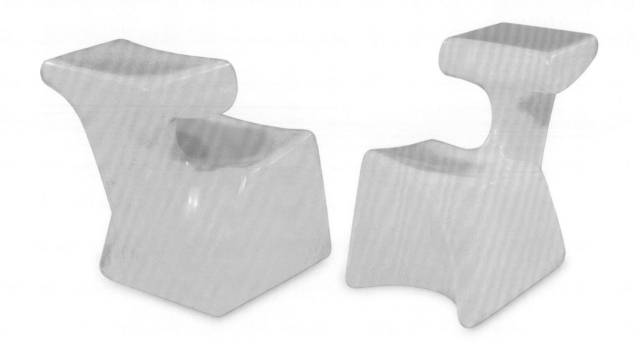

402 🪑

Zocker, 1972
Luigi Colani (1928–)
Top System Burkhard Lübke

With a background in aerodynamics, the German industrial design maverick Luigi Colani is best known for his futuristic car designs for the likes of Alfa Romeo, Fiat and BMW. Since the 1960s, however, he has also designed numerous collections of furniture and lighting. Inspired by a 1971 symposium on changing approaches to child rearing, the furniture maker Burkhard Lübke commissioned Colani to create a child-friendly piece that would function as more than just a scaled-down version of adult furniture. Colani's Zocker is a chair that seamlessly accommodates children sitting forwards or straddling it backwards, with the backrest doubling as a lectern-style desk or table. During play, its eccentric form can double as an animal to ride upon, a car or a cockpit. This multifunctional structure is also notable for its use of polyethylene, a plastic previously unused in furniture manufacturing. Zocker's hollow construction enables it to be lightweight but stable, while its smooth surfaces suit active play and facilitate easy cleaning.

403 🪑

Baby Ball Chair, 2008
Finn Stone (1971–)
XLBoom

The British deisgner and artist Finn Stone is defined by his unconventional and imaginative use of materials, and his spirited approach to his craft, be it painting, sculpture or furniture design. This Baby Ball Chair, perhaps his most well-known creation, is an ode to the exuberant furniture designs of decades past, drawing inspiration from the plastic fantastic visions of the 1960s and 1970s. Stone gives those synthetic stylings a twenty-first century update, manufacturing the chair from recycled ABS plastic and finishing it with a high-gloss paint that makes it suitable for use indoors or out. As the injection-moulded design is hollow, it is lighter than it looks, making it easy to move and adpatable to the changing environments of children. The Baby Ball Chair is manufactured by Antwerp-based XLBoom, which was founded by Ann De Cock and Geert-Jan Van Cauwelaert in 1997. In keeping with Stone's maximalist sensibility, the Baby Ball Chair is available in an extensive range of colours, and comes in both adult and child sizes.

Chicken Desk, 2015
Guillaumit (1980–)
Kinder Modern

Often featured in publications like *Le Monde*, Guillaumit is primarily known for illustration with a strong cartoon influence, characterized by geometric forms and saturated colours. 'My inspiration comes from the Bauhaus, electronic music from the 70s and comic books,'[1] the French designer states. The Chicken Desk, conceived for Gaîté Lyrique, a digital arts and modern music centre in Paris, boldly translates Guillaumit's signature style into three dimensions. This cheery fowl was originally one of a quartet of animals, which also included a horse, a fox and a whale, each serving as a functional desk. Its flattened back can be used for writing and drawing, while circular slots on its head can be used to store coloured pencils and also double as the bird's variegated plumage. 'My drawing tables just need paper and pencils,' the designer explains. 'Kids can interact with them for a long period and have fun.'[2] Since 2015, the vintage and modern children's design gallery Kinder Modern has produced Guillaumit's characterful chicken as part of their collection.

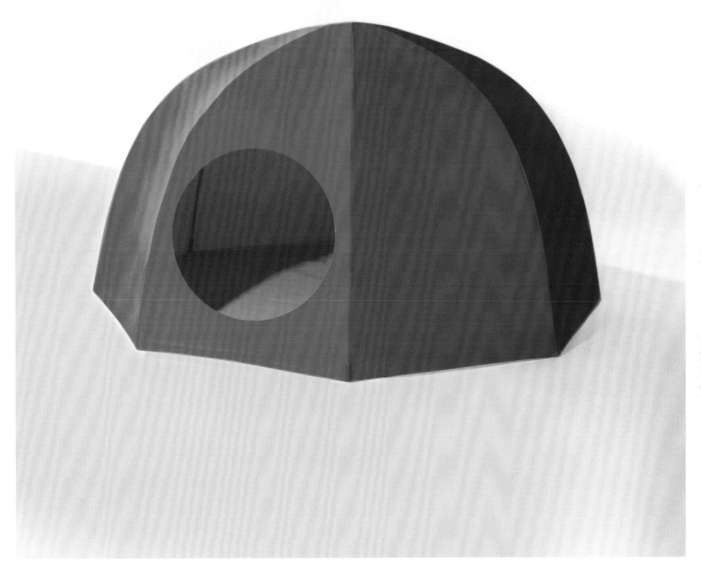

405 🐻

Iglu, 2015
Harri Koskinen (1970–)
Play+

When closed, the Iglu might easily be mistaken for an umbrella, but once released, Harri Koskinen's clever contraption transforms into a pop-up, child-sized shelter. With its water-repellent polyester covering and round cutout for entry, Iglu draws on the characteristics of a tent to provide children with a sense of security and privacy. The speed with which it can be set up or taken down matches the spontaneity of childhood, and its perfect meld of function and visual appeal are typical of Koskinen. The Finnish designer has produced a wide range of domestic products, including the iconic Block Lamp (1996), a bulb housed between two blocks of cast glass, which was acquired by the Museum of Modern Art, New York, for their permanent collection, in 2000. Iglu was created for the Play+Soft project, initiated by the Italian company Play+, which brought together designers and researchers to create soft furnishings that enrich children's play environments with colour and sensory variety.

406 🐻

Inflatable Toys, 2013
Jan Čapek (1976–), Anna Kozová
(1982–) and Jerry Koza (1976–)
Fatra

Facing stiff competition from other manufacturers, the Czech plastics company Fatra ceased making toys in 2000. But the popularity of their bright, bouncy, animal inflatables, designed by Libuše Niklová in the 1960s and 1970s, surged following their inclusion in several international design exhibitions a decade later. Spurred by demand, Fatra commissioned contemporary designers to come up with new toys that pay homage to Niklová's pioneering designs. Here, Czech designer Jan Čapek challenges the threatening stereotype of the bull terrier by rendering it instead as a jaunty inflatable toy, inspired by his very own pet terrier. Also by Čapek, Formula, a bright-yellow racing car with a cigar-shaped body draws inspiration from the shape of Niklová's Giraffe. 'The work for Fatra gave me a unique opportunity to become acquainted with entirely new technologies', Čapek remarked.[1] The trundling Tractor, meanwhile, was designed by Anna Kozová and Jerry Koza, a husband-and-wife team best known for their award-winning Torpedo push bike of 2009.

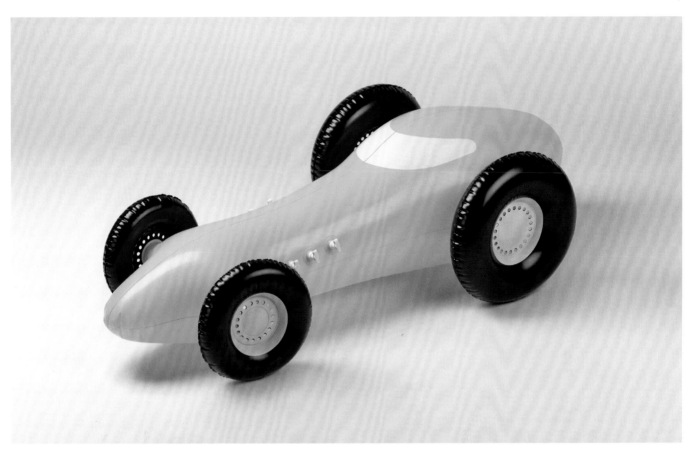

Discovolante and Testacalda, 2016
Piero Lissoni (1956–)
Kartell

It seems only appropriate that Kartell, a company which first introduced injection-moulded plastic furniture in 1964 with the child's chair K 1340 (14), should once again be at the forefront of design for children. For the inaugural collection of their children's line, Kartell Kids, in 2016, the forward-thinking company tapped designers such as Philippe Starck, Nendo, Ferruccio Laviani and Piero Lissoni. True to form, Lissoni, a renowned architect and product designer who has collaborated with the likes of Alessi, Flos, Knoll and Fritz Hansen, created two toy cars that are as sophisticated as they are playful. Part car, part hot rod, Discovolante (Flying Saucer) is an ironic nod to the Disco Volante, Alfa Romeo's famous racing car. This sleek racer is complimented by Testacalda (Hot Head), a jaunty tractor, which unfortunately didn't make it to production. Composed of a metal frame with transparent plastic of varying colours, Lissoni's nostalgic vehicles eschew pedals, instead encouraging children to push with their legs to propel themselves forward.

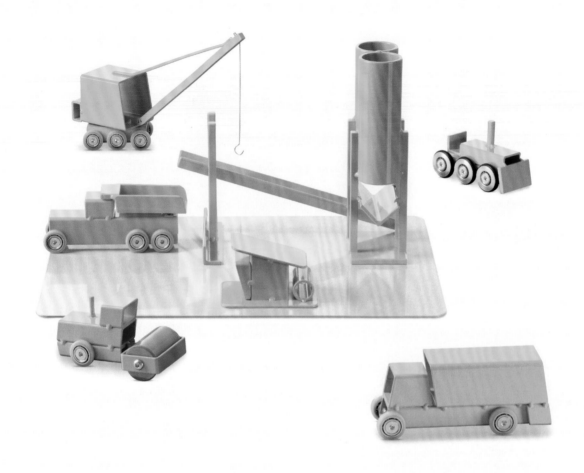

408 🐻

ArcheToys, 2013
Floris Hovers (1976–)
Magis

Known for his furniture, toys and interior design products, Floris Hovers has built a career on creating work that is playful and naive. As the name suggests, ArcheToys is a set of steel vehicles that invoke the archetypal shapes of everything from police cars to school buses and tractors. With its muted colours and traditional forms, the collection exemplifies the designer's interest in using techniques and materials that reveal how an object is made. The pared-down forms straddle the line between craftsmanship and mass production, appealing to adults through their sense of nostalgia and to children by the familiarity of their basic shapes. 'When I design toys, it is very important that there is room for imagination,' Hovers explains.[1] First presented at Eindhoven's Dutch Design Week in 2007, Hovers was commissioned to produce the collection for Magis's children's line in 2013. Two years later, he also added CARtools (248) to the Magis collection.

409 🪑 🐻

Filius, 1974
Günter Beltzig (1941–)
Brüder Beltzig

Günter Beltzig is best known for his work with playgrounds, both in Germany and around the world. In the late 1960s, the German industrial designer was fresh out of applied arts school when he formed a company, Brüder Beltzig, with his two brothers, which became synonymous with the bright, light, fibreglass-reinforced plastic furniture that was popular at the time. The company launched the Poly-Bel collection of children's seating, playground equipment and toys at the Cologne Furniture Fair in 1968, and continued to expand the series in the early 1970s, when the Filius table was introduced. The one-piece table and seat was one of two such combinations created. Filius was designed to be unconventional but also stackable and lightweight: the sculptural unit accommodates four children yet it takes only one to easily transport it. Later produced by Richter Spielgeräte, the table's durable, versatile and easy-to-clean material proved an excellent choice for play equipment, which could be kept both indoors and out.

410 🪑

Clay Children's Chair, 2006
Maarten Baas (1979–)
Den Herder Production House

Maarten Baas established himself as one of the most important designers of the Netherlands following the launch of Smoke, his graduate collection of charred furniture, which was created at Design Academy Eindhoven in 2002. Interested in overturning the conventional notions of beauty and value associated with perfection, Baas followed his debut release with Clay, a line of spindly, childlike furniture made from synthetic clay, that has been hand-moulded (with finger prints still visible) around a metal frame, before being lacquered in vibrant colours. Their wonky, naive appearance sits in marked contrast to the more forceful and weighty Smoke. 'I like that Clay came after Smoke', Baas remarks. 'It's like burning the fields on which you are going to grow new plants; Clay was, almost literally, a young plant coming out of the ground.'[1] Fittingly, each Children's Chair is made by hand at the designer's studio on a farm in the Dutch countryside.

411 🐻

Scimmietta Zizì, 1953
Bruno Munari (1907–98)
Pigomma / currently
La Permanente Mobili Cantù

Soft to the touch, but structured with a pliable wire skeleton, Scimmietta Zizì (Little Monkey) emerged out of Bruno Munari's experiments with foam rubber. The Italian tyre manufacturer Pirelli had recently started producing a new kind of rubber and approached Munari to design possible new products. Known for his innovative children's books, Munari immediately responded to the material's tactile and elastic qualities by experimenting in toy design. Gatto Meo Romeo, a cartoonish black cat with a copper-wire interior and foam-rubber body, was Munari's first Pirelli design. Developing the concept further, he produced Zizì two years later. Munari packaged the little monkey in a clear plastic bag printed with a wire-mesh pattern, a design that cleverly suggested that purchasing Zizì meant liberating the monkey from its cage. Zizì's wire skeleton enables it to assume any number of expressive positions, allowing the toy to swing from a child's arm – or to grab the nearest banana.

412 🐻

Slow Bus, 1972
Patrick Rylands (1942–)
Creative Playthings

Using a suggestive rather than a literal approach, the Slow Bus by British designer Patrick Rylands recalls the iconic red buses found on the streets of London. Over the course of his career, in which he served as the chief designer at Ambi Toys for more than three decades, Rylands helped to legitimize plastic toys in the eyes of the public. Early plastics were often of poor quality, earning them a negative reputation. The Slow Bus, designed by Rylands for Creative Playthings, sculpts the material into a minimal yet evocative form. Like many of the designer's toys, it uses a primary colour – red. 'A toy that does nothing, does everything for the child', Rylands claims. 'The main purpose of a toy is to enable children to enter into a world of make-believe, as it is in this way that children relate to reality.'[1]

413 🐻

Zic-Zag, 1980
Fredun Shapur (1929–)
Naef

Known for inventive toys made from simple materials, Fredun Shapur's career spans more than thirty years, multiple mediums and collaborations with a range of respected companies. Created for Naef in 1980, his Zic-Zag is a coordination game that requires the player to carefully manoeuvre a wooden ball along a series of jaunty paths, which are formed by eight slanted wooden rods. Characteristic of Shapur's toys, the Zic-Zag is not prescriptive with regards to age or gender. By the time of its production, Shapur had been collaborating with Naef, the Swiss company that has specialized in wooden toys since the 1950s, for decades. Indeed, it was Naef that first transformed Shapur's early toys, crafted by him and his wife, from handmade objects into mass-manufactured designs. Born in South Africa, Shapur studied in London before working in Prague in 1957, where he was exposed to the burgeoning toy industry, from which several icons of Czech Modernism emerged.

Little Helpers Children's Furniture, 2012
Elena Nunziata (1985–)
Prototype

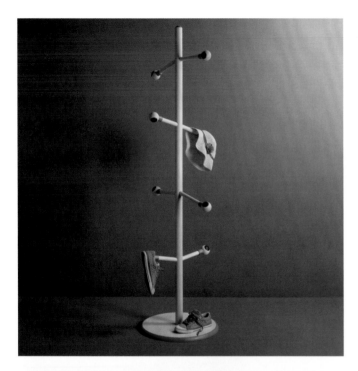

Italian designer Elena Nunziata created the Little Helpers furniture collection while studying at Central Saint Martins, University of the Arts, in London. Nunziata conceived of each piece by analyzing how children behave in domestic environments. Designed to encourage exploration, the series is exemplary of her creative approach, which is to produce furniture that is both engaging and educational. Paddy the coat rack, Charlie the hamper and Melvin the bedside table make up the Little Helpers, with each piece turning everyday chores into playful activities. Made from beech, the coat rack has adjustable rods with rotating 'eyeball' knobs, while the bedside table also features a set of eyes, shielded by wooden disk 'eyelids' that can be rotated to reveal built-in lamps. The hamper's visible Lycra sack is intended to provide a visual nod indicating when laundry needs to be loaded into the wash. By making chores fun, Nunziata's furniture wins fans in both children and parents alike.

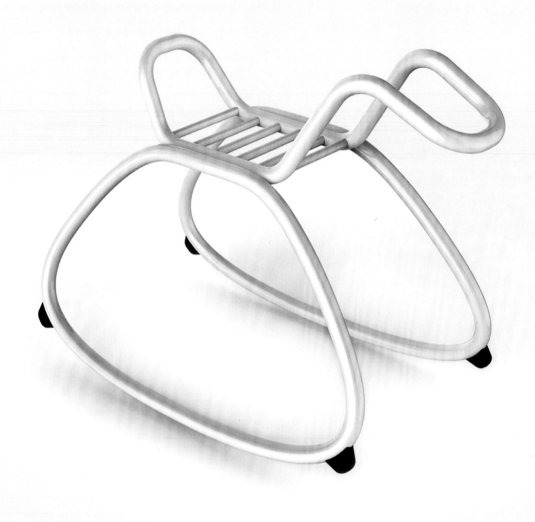

415 🛴

Hobbel Rocking Horse, 2012
Remko Verhaagen (1980–)
Blooey

The Hobbel Rocking Horse presents the type of minimalist approach to a traditional toy that fits seamlessly into a design-minded interior. Conceived by Remko Verhaagen for his Rotterdam-based studio, Blooey, this rocker is made from tubular steel that has been moulded into shape using a combination of machine and craft techniques. Its pared-down body takes on an equine appearance, but without the reins, stirrups, ears, saddle or even tail that one might expect to find on a more classic steed. Children hop onto its laddered back and rock away, gripping the sides of the frame to stay in place. Lest a rider get over-excited, 'horse-shoe' stoppers were added to keep the rocker from toppling over. Describing himself as a 'wholehearted dreamer, a creative optimist and a simplicity-loving beautifier',[1] Verhaagen donates fifty per cent of the profits from the sale of each Hobbel to Clini Clown, a children's charity.

416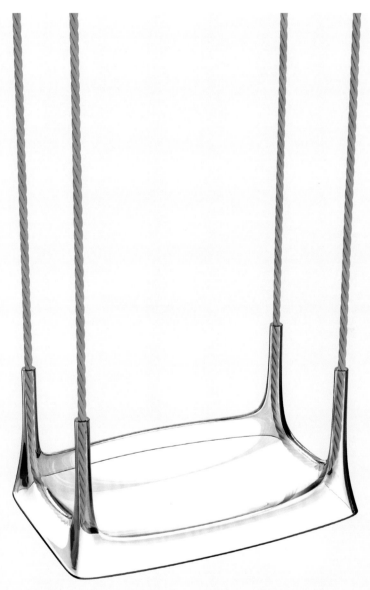

Airway Swing, 2016
Philippe Starck (1949–)
Prototype

In 1964, Kartell released the first chair in the world to be manufactured entirely from plastic, a child's stacking chair now known as the K 1340 (14). Conceived for Milan's schoolchildren by Marco Zanuso and Richard Sapper, the pioneering chair helped to convince the public that plastic was an appropriate material for the modern home. Kartell has since become synonymous with design-savvy contemporary plastic furniture. In 2016, the company launched Kartell Kids, a line geared to three to eight year-old children, featuring products created by celebrated designers including Nendo, Piero Lissoni, Ferruccio Laviani and many others. A Kartell collaborator since the 1980s, Starck is also no stranger to children's design. His Airway Swing features a transparent polycarbonate seat, held up by two coloured ropes that visibly loop through it at either end. When in use, this simple but surreal design creates the dramatic impression of its user floating on air.

417 🛋 ✏️

Kids@Work, 2008
Ora-ïto (est. 1997)
Habitat

As part of British furniture brand Habitat's VIP (Very Important Products) for Kids collection, the French design wunderkind Ito Morabito created Kids@Work, a scarlet-red desk and chair formed out of one moulded-plywood structure. Both bold and functional, its tilted desk functions like a drafting table, with a paper roll mounted on its underside that cleverly feeds continuously through a slot on its surface. Like all of the designer's products, which range from telephones to architecture, this two-in-one piece is both organic and futuristic in form. Morabito burst onto the global scene in 1997 when, at the age of nineteen, he mischievously declared himself the artistic director of global brands, including Louis Vuitton, Nike, Apple and Visa. Redesigning some of their flagship products, he presented his virtual creations on his website, which people quickly began clamouring to buy. Morabito has gone on to form a number of notable collaborations and was awarded the prestigious title of Chevalier de l'ordre des Arts et des Lettres in 2011.

418 ⛟

Olga Rocker, 2002
Wolfgang Sirch (1964–)
and Christoph Bitzer (1964–)
Sirch

With the fluid curve of its frame, Sirch's Olga Rocker abandons the traditional rocking horse form in favour of a delightful snail. Designed by Wolfgang Sirch and Christoph Bitzer, the Olga rocker is produced in Sirch's distinctive exposed birch wood. The plywood frame is soft to the touch and durable, making Olga a piece that can be passed from generation to generation. Its pared-back design makes the rocker both stable and lightweight, making it easy for children to move it around by themselves. Latticed webbing provides a comfortable seat and a bright pop of red: a visual signature that runs through the cars, bicycles and other wheeled offerings in the Sirch line. Suitable for children aged three and older, the Olga Rocker is another timeless object from Sirch that will enchant design-loving parents as much as it enthralls children.

419 🪑 ✎

Ozoo 700 Desk, 1967
Marc Berthier (1935–)
Roche Bobois

This children's desk, by the celebrated French designer and architect Marc Berthier, is part of his revolutionary Ozoo line, France's first collection of furniture made entirely from polyester and fibreglass. Produced in 1967 by Paris-based Roche Bobois, the collection won the prestigious Prix Gabriel. The Ozoo 700 reflects the decade's Pop art style in its colours – white, black, orange, red and green – and its all-in-one design incorporates a combined seat, a cubbyhole for books, a writing surface and a slot for writing utensils. Stackable and lightweight, the Ozoo 700 was purchased by the Parisian suburb of Créteil for use in its schools. Marc Berthier has received numerous awards and been honoured by his country as a Chevalier de l'ordre des Arts et des Lettres. His designs can be found in the permanent collections of the Musée National d'Art Moderne and Centre Georges Pompidou in Paris, and the Museum of Modern Art, New York.

420 ✎ 🐻

Rubik's Cube, 1974
Ernö Rubik (1944–)
Ideal Toy Company
/ currently Rubik's

In 1974, Ernö Rubik, a professor of architecture at the Budapest Academy of Applied Arts (now the Hungarian Academy of Arts), invented a multi-coloured 'magic cube' to help illustrate three-dimensional geometry to his students. Three squares long by three squares high, each of the cube's sides were attributed a different colour. The aim was to be able to scramble and unscramble the sides by turning the rows of cubes vertically or horizontally. While the current speed-cubing record stands at 4.59 seconds, many will take heart in the fact that it took Rubik more than a month to solve his own creation. With Hungary then behind the Iron Curtain, it would take five years before the Rubik's Cube was exported. Upon seeing it at the Nuremberg Toy Fair in 1979, games designer and entrepreneur Tom Kremer urged the Ideal Toy Company to distribute it. Licensed in 1980, it would become the biggest selling toy of all time, with over 400 million units sold worldwide to date.

421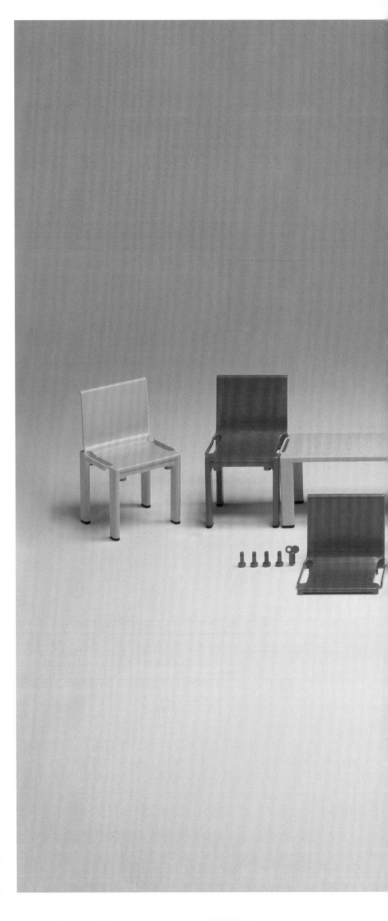

Sistema Scuola, 1978
Centrokappa (est. 1972)
and Masayuki Matsukaze (1942–)
Kartell

Designed in 1978, this modular furniture set by Kartell's research and development division, Centrokappa, is still in production today. The transformable Sistema Scuola (School System) consists of primary-coloured, plastic components that can be screwed together in varying combinations to produce four chairs, a bench and a table. Lateral perforations on either side of the seat and bench can function alternately as handles, hooks to connect one piece to another horizontally, or slots to enable vertical stacking. A similar element on the table-frame serves as an attachment for various specially designed accessories, such as a hook or a rectangular container for writing utensils. A sliding tray and tabletop that can double as a blackboard complete the versatile set. Led by Centrokappa's designer Masayuki Matsukaze, the system was designed for both educational and recreational purposes. By assembling and disassembling it to their own liking, the Sistema Scuola allows children to become the architects of their own space.

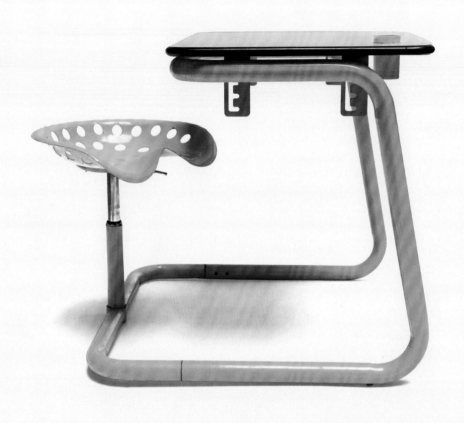

422 🪑 ✏️ �ై

Twenty Tube Desk, 1972
Marc Berthier (1935–)
Roche Bobois

The award-winning French architect and designer Marc Berthier is widely known for his pioneering work with new materials. His Ozoo 700 Desk (419) and 600 Bed (375) are part of a collection of playful, candy-coloured designs that were France's first affordable furniture line to be made entirely of polyester and fibreglass. Initially designed for children and teenagers, Roche Bobois rereleased the iconic desk and chair in an adult version in 2018. The Twenty Tube Desk, a prototype produced for Roche Bobois in 1972, was conceived as a self-build item for schoolchildren, resulting in the nickname 'Mecanotube'. Due to its innovative construction, the desk can be seen as a precursor to the 'do it yourself' (DIY) movement and it was included in the inaugural exhibition at the Centre Georges Pompidou in 1977. Berthier has been a pioneer of industrial design throughout his career, as evidenced by his now ubiquitous silicone-encased Tykho Radio, created for Lexon in 1997.

423 🪑 ✏️

Holzkufenstuhl School Chair, 1950
Karl Nothhelfer (1900–80)
VS

Introduced to classrooms across Germany during the 1950s, Karl Nothhelfer's skid chair heralded a new era for school furniture in the wake of World War II. Designed for the German company VS (Vereinigte Spezialmöbelfabriken), the chair was produced in the millions and the design widely copied. The chair was light enough for children to move themselves and marked a departure from the bench seats that had dominated classrooms before the war, reflecting a general turn away from Prussian military-style pedagogies. As well as showcasing the design industry's new interest in ergonomics, this chair introduced values such as flexibility and individualism to the classroom. Nothhelfer's other designs for VS included a skid desk, with similar sled-style legs, and a later version of the chair that was manufactured in tubular steel. Nothhelfer also designed two of the company's buildings in Tauberbischofsheim, Germany. Today, the VS headquarters are home to a museum, which is dedicated to the history of school furniture.

424 ✏️ 🧸

Thingamabobbin, 1975
Karen Hewitt (1940–)
Learning Materials Workshop

Inspired by a catalogue for the 1969 exhibition *Play Orbit*, which examined the relationship between art and play, Karen Hewitt combined her experience as an artist and early childhood teacher to become an award-winning toy designer and historian. Her first toy, Thingamabobbin, grew out of her work at a children's day-care centre. Originally made using the reject spools and bobbins from a local factory, it encapsulates Hewitt's belief in the power of open-ended toys: young children can match colours or move the bobbins on and off the dowels, while older children can build rolling cars, windmills, or even sailing boats. Thingamabobbin's generative nature fosters imaginative play, and encourages children to investigate cause and effect for themselves. The product's success launched Hewitt's career in toy design, which has gone on to last for more than forty years. Although her company, Learning Materials Workshop, is now closed, Hewitt continues to design and remains a sought-after authority on educational toys.

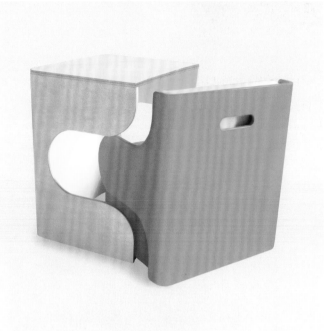

425 ♯

P'kolino Klick, 2008
Davide Cesca (1983–)
P'kolino

This desk-and-chair set fits together like two puzzle pieces to form a compact cube when not in use. In keeping with the 'playfully smart' philosophy of the American children's furniture company P'kolino, the Klick set provides children aged between three and seven with their own space for drawing, reading and playing. Designed by Davide Cesca, Klick is robust and non-toxic, and made using an unusual combination of plastic and baltic birch. The chair's vinyl padding offers a comfortable seat, so that children can sit for as long as their concentration span allows, while ample storage space underneath it makes for easy tidying up. P'kolino was founded by J B Schneider and Antonio Turco-Rivas in 2004, and works with both American and international designers to produce engaging toys and play furniture that supports children's developmental needs.

426

Four-Way Blocks, 1964
Fredun Shapur (1929–)
Naef

Four-Way Blocks are a hallmark children's game created by the graphic designer, Fredun Shapur. First inspired to build simple wooden objects by his own children, Shapur would go on to design innovative and distinctive products for a number of leading toy companies worldwide. Each Four-Way puzzle comprises six rectangular blocks that can be assembled to reveal the image of one of four animals – a cat, an elephant, a snake or a horse. The four long sides of each block features a different graphic pattern, so children can rearrange the order and rotation of the blocks to piece each animal together – or instead simply scramble them to produce a random combination of their own choosing. In keeping with Shapur's other creations, the simple puzzle was conceived to encourage and develop a child's sense of agency and also incorporates motifs common to his work: animal figures, flat planes, saturated colours and simple geometries.

427 🐻 ✎

Plus and Minus, 1970
Bruno Munari (1907–98)
and Giovanni Belgrano (1931–95)
Danese Milano / currently Corraini Edizioni

One of the most playful, inventive and influential Italian artists of the modern era, Bruno Munari was also a passionate advocate for active learning in children's art education. During the 1970s, Munari conducted a series of Tactile Workshops, in which he used highly sensory materials to encourage children to creatively explore their sense of touch. First developed in 1970 with pedagogist Giovanni Belgrano, Plus and Minus is a visual game in which children can explore countless environmental scenes and aesthetic arrangements. The kit comprises seventy-two square cards, each depicting a singular element such as a tree, a night sky or an ocean. Forty-eight of the sheets are transparent, encouraging children to layer and superimpose other images onto them in order to create complex compositions.

428 

Riverside, 2006
Baghera (est. 1999)
Baghera

The Riverside pedal car's streamlined form is inspired by cruising vehicles of the 1920s. Designed and produced by the French toy brand Baghera, the car has a smoothly curving metal body, making it both safe and durable. With a seat that can be adjusted to accommodate longer legs, the Riverside proves a versatile ride for children aged from three to six. Its large rubber tyres also mean that it can be driven on a range of surfaces, from lawn grass to wood floors to tarmac. The body of the car can even be customized with the driver's name using an accompanying sticker. Based outside Paris, Baghera has become a world-renowned producer of children's metal cars since being founded in 1999. Riverside is just one of many appealing models in its collection: the company focuses on producing a new vintage-inspired pedal or push car every year.

429 ⧠

Child's Chair, c. 1944
Charles Eames (1907–78)
and Ray Eames (1912–88)
Evans Products Company

Designers Charles and Ray Eames began experimenting with bent-wood techniques in 1941, creating splints and other medical equipment, which was used by the US Navy in World War II. Following this early development, the Eameses then sought to apply such processes to the creation of plywood furniture, establishing a form that could comfortably contour the human body without the need for a cushion. The couple considered themselves less as artists and more as tradespeople and engineers, combining ingenuity and technological progress to produce playful, useful and reliable designs. Their work would establish them as two of the most important designers of the twentieth century. Built from a single piece of moulded wood and sold in an array of colours, this little chair was one piece in a suite of kid-sized furniture that embodied the couple's sensitive approach to design. The heart-shaped cut-out in the centre of the chair back is a nod to Swedish folk art, highlighting the Eameses' appreciation of a variety of folk cultures.

430 ♯

Landleben Children's Table and Chair, 1967
Dieter Güllert (1923–)
Erwin Egel

The pared-down geometric forms of this children's table-and-chair set recall the work of Gerrit Rietveld, and the simplicity and abstraction of the De Stijl movement. Made of pine, this angular collection is constructed solely using wooden joinery, much like Hans Wegner's 1944 design for Peter's Table and Chair (29). Meaning 'country life' in German, the Landleben table and chairs are the most well known of Austrian-born Dieter Güllert's designs. Produced by the German company Erwin Egel, the chairs come in several variations, all with the same bold style. A version was included in the exhibition *Wrap Your Arms Around Me*, co-curated by children's furniture gallery Kinder Modern in New York and Miami's Gallery Diet, in 2016. One cannot help but wonder if Luigi Colani's Tobifant desk and chair set of 1977 (179) drew inspiration from Güllert's statement use of tenon and wedge joints.

431 🐻

The Arne Jacobsen House and Furniture, 2011
Linda Stenberg (1967–)
Minimii

The family home of Danish Modernist architect Arne Jacobsen goes pint-sized with this 1:16 scale doll's house from Minimii. The original Jacobsen house, built in 1929 in Charlottenlund, Denmark, still stands today, and is one of the designer's earliest known works. This tiny replica retains its spare, Bauhaus-influenced design, with its flat roof, maritime references and white plaster facade. In addition to the doll's house, Minimii also reproduced scaled-down versions of Jacobsen's well-known furniture, including the Egg Chair and the Ant Chair, as well as his carpet and wallpaper designs. The house features a detachable magnetic facade for section views and play within the interior. Children can even outfit the front door with a personalized sign for an extra homey touch. For smaller spaces, Minimii has crafted a space-saving solution: a wall-mounted doll's house that takes up half the footprint of the more conventional design.

432 🪑

Children's Chair N65, 1935
Alvar Aalto (1898–1976)
Artek

Celebrated for both his technical and stylistic innovation, Alvar Aalto worked as an architect and furniture designer, co-founding the iconic Finnish design company Artek in 1935. While Aalto experimented with a wide variety of construction materials, he is best known for his technical advancements with laminated woods, such as birch and plywood. In the early 1930s, Aalto collaborated with Otto Korhonen, his production plant manager, to develop a process using steam and resins that enabled him to bend wood at right angles. The 'L-Leg', first seen on his Stool 60 in 1932, is a defining feature of the Children's Chair N65. Its innovative technology allowed Aalto to solve the age-old problem of how to connect vertical and horizontal pieces of material. With its smart construction and organic, sculptural body, the N65 exemplifies Aalto's aesthetic, which combined nature and technology to give each piece an air of fine craftsmanship.

433

Sloop Cradle, 2018
Studio Irvine (est. 1988)
Yamakawa

In 1952, Hichiro Yamakawa established a rattan company in a small shed in his back garden, with the desire to provide employment for his two hearing-impaired sons. The company has since grown into one of the leading rattan manufacturers in Japan, producing beautifully crafted furniture designs, conceived by a host of talented designers. In collaboration with Marialaura Rossiello Irvine, of the Milan-based Studio Irvine, Yamakawa produced Sloop, a vessel-like crib that combines modern form with natural material. Named after the single-mast sailing boat, the cradle comprises a light blue rattan base and an oval basket with protective high rounded sides. Sloop's 'mast', a rattan-wrapped metal rod, can serve as a hanger for a mobile, a light, or a mosquito net. Irvine's adaptable cradle design enables it to sail easily into a child's toddler years, with the top and bottom separating to serve as a cozy armchair and a toy chest, or even a cubby for the family cat.

434 🪑 🍴

Children's Chair and Tray, 1885–1915
Gebrüder Thonet (est. 1853)
Gebrüder Thonet

The emergence of children's furniture as designer objects can be traced back to the Austrian bentwood furniture company Thonet, which began advertising mass-produced designs for children in 1866. The company continued to add models to its collection over the following decades, making the children's market an important contributor to the bentwood furniture industry. Like many of Thonet's designs for children, this chair is a miniature version of an adult design, yet it additionally features a built-in tray, thereby giving it a high-chair-like functionality with a surface for eating or drawing. Founded in 1819, Vienna-based Thonet is recognized for pioneering the mechanical steam-bending process, exemplified in designs such as the iconic Chair No. 14 (or, Vienna Coffee House Chair). The company would later divide into two distinct manufacturers, Gebrüder Thonet and Thonet Vienna. This particular children's chair is held in the permanent collection of the Cooper Hewitt, Smithsonian Design Museum.

435 🐻

American Modern Play Dishes, c. 1959
Russel Wright (1904–76)
Ideal Toy Company

Along with fellow designers Charles and Ray Eames, Eero Saarinen and Hans Wegner, Ohio native Russel Wright is known for his affiliation with the Good Design movement. The concept, which began to take shape in the United States in the 1930s, embraced the Modernist tenets of functionalism, simplicity and truth to materials, applying them to mass-producible everyday goods. Trained in art and sculpture, Wright created a number of commercially successful items, the most significant being the American Modern service, the most widely sold ceramic tableware set in history. During the 1950s, Wright did research on plastic tableware for restaurant use and designed several popular lines of Melmac melamine-resin plastic sets for the home, including these play dishes for children. Like its ceramic predecessor, this dinner set features curved organic shapes and a soft, metallic-like colour palette.

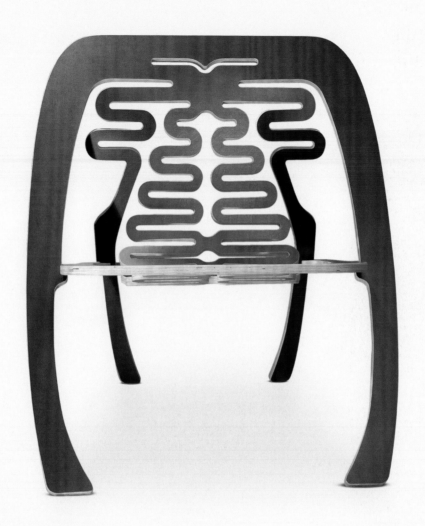

436 ⊓

One Eleven Children's Chair, 1985
Gregg Fleishman (1947–)
Self-produced

The key to this chair's springy but strong seat is its intricate cut-out pattern. Created from a single piece of plywood by the designer, architect and inventor Gregg Fleishman, the chair's subtractive design flexes to form a gently curved seat and can fold to be stored completely flat when not in use. As a designer, Fleishman is known for his mathematical ingenuity, which he has applied to a host of inventive playhouse structures and chairs. His collection of Sculpt Chairs features decades of iterations on the single-sheet chair, including this one for children. Cut from European birch, these designs eliminate the need for glue, screws or other fasteners, with some even featuring wooden springs and hinges. Fleishman studied architecture at the University of Southern California in the late 1960s; today, several of his designs are included in the collection of the Museum of Modern Art, New York.

Multi-View Puzzle, 1964/2014
Fredun Shapur (1929–)
Galt Toys / currently Piqpoq

Fredun Shapur's repeated presence in this book attests to his legacy in the field of design for children. Inspired to create toys by his own children, Shapur's remarkable creations carefully balance colour and graphic detailing to engage a child's agency. Originally called Four-Way Jigsaws, these four puzzles were first produced in 1964 by Galt Toys. The series interprets each scene – Traffic, Farming, Zoo and Seaside – using Shapur's characteristic style, which combines a minimal but distinctive colour palette with strong contrast and clear geometry. 'This puzzle was conceived with careful thought about the possibilities of play,' Shapur's daughter, Mira, explains. 'Shapur wanted it to be a social activity – it allows up to four children to play together, one on each side of the puzzle.'[1] Rereleased under the name Multi-View Puzzle by Piqpoq in 2014, the original can be seen alongside Shapur's entire toy collection at the Victoria and Albert Museum of Childhood in London.

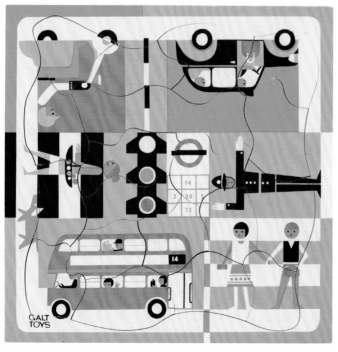

438 🐻 🛴

Schaukelwagen, 1950
Hans Brockhage (1925–2009)
and Erwin Andrä (1921–)
Gottfried Lenz / currently Werkform

Hans Brockhage and Erwin Andrä designed this unusual ride-on toy while Brockhage was a student at the Dresden Academy of Fine Arts, where Andrä worked as an academic assistant. As part of his studies, Brockhage presented his teacher, the influential Dutch designer Mart Stam, with a design for a rocking horse. 'When horse fall over, horse is dead', Stam is reported to have said in his best Dutch–German, challenging Brockhage and Andrä to 'make a horse that isn't dead when it fall over.'[1] The result is a rocking horse that inverts to become a car. Its plywood seat supports both modes of riding, while a laddered beech frame arcs over the wheeled base, offering a series of rungs for climbing or pushing. Once a standard feature of East German kindergartens, the Schaukelwagen (Rocking Car) is now in the permanent collection of the Museum of Modern Art, New York, and the Victoria and Albert Museum, London. In 2011, Werkform acquired the rights to its reproduction.

439 ӿ

Crosby Chair, 1998
Gaetano Pesce (1939–)
Fish Design

Over his fifty-year career, the Italian architect, designer and urban planner Gaetano Pesce, has amassed an extensive body of work, recognized for its materiality, emotiveness and unrestrained use of colour. His humanistic view eschews standardization in his work: 'perfection is very abstract, very neutral, very cold', he explains; 'the mistake, and the fault, are very human.'[1] Named after the street in New York City where his workshop is based, the Crosby Chair reflects Pesce's playful attitude towards design. The seat and back are constructed from a single sheet of moulded-polyurethane resin – an industrial, synthetic plastic – which is treated as if it is a craft material, celebrating its tactility and making each of the four designs unique in colour and detail. Furthermore, both planes of the chair provide the contours of a face, demonstrating the anthropomorphic qualities so characteristic of the celebrated designer's work.

440 ♯

UPJ Chair, 2014
Gaetano Pesce (1939–)
B&B Italia

Created in 2014, the UPJ is a junior version of Gaetano Pesce's UP5, the fifth in the 'Up' series of seven anthropomorphic chairs that B&B Italia debuted at the Salone del Mobile, Milan, in 1969. Made of polyurethane foam, the chairs were most noteworthy for their packaging: compressed under a vacuum, each chair came in a flat PVC envelope. The polyurethane took on the volume of each specified design only once the envelopes had been opened and the materials came into contact with air. *Donna* (woman), as Pesce named the curvaceous UP5, was inspired by the ancient Venus of Willendorf, layering the foam chair with female symbolism. Even the ball and chain are a statement against the historic oppression of women. 'In that design I was expressing my own view of women,' Pesce remarked. 'They have always been, against their own wills, prisoners of themselves.'[1] The UPJ comes with a removable cover of red stretch fabric.

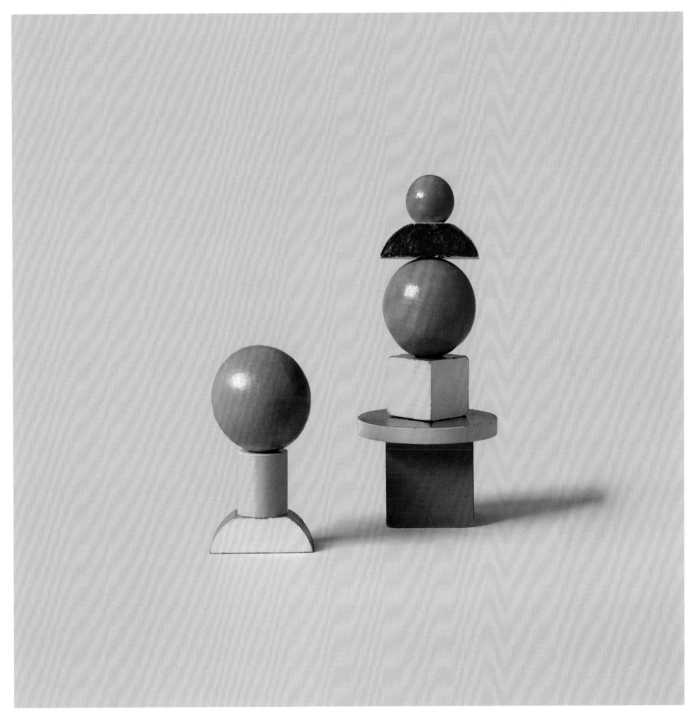

441 🐻

Kugelspiel, 1924
Alma Siedhoff-Buscher (1899–1944)
Bauhaus Workshops

As a sculptor at the Bauhaus in Weimar, Germany, Alma Siedhoff-Buscher maintained that design for children had the potential to benefit not only individuals, but also society at large. Toys, she believed, should be 'clear and specific' in their purpose and 'as harmonious as possible'[1] in their proportions. Among her first toy designs in the 1920s was this Kugelspiel (Ball Games) set, a series of wooden spheres, cubes and bisected geometric forms. Linking the cheerfulness of colour with the enjoyment of the user, Siedhoff-Buscher painted the set in red, yellow, blue, green and white – the same palette that she had used a year earlier when creating furniture and toys for the nursery at the Haus am Horn, a prototypical, modern show house. The balls in this set tacitly add a kinetic element, encouraging children to experiment with balance and movement as they stack, roll and build the pieces together. The result is a sculptural, beautiful toy that enhances its environment and stimulates the child's mind.

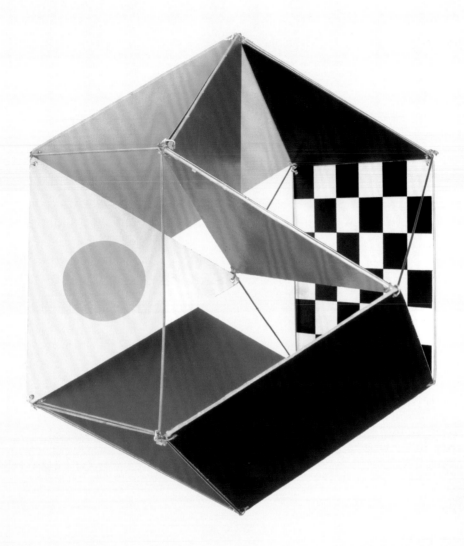

442

The Little Toy, c. 1952
Charles Eames (1907–78)
and Ray Eames (1912–88)
Tigrett Enterprises

The Toy and Little Toy, innovative construction kits produced in 1951–2, were among a series of playthings that Charles and Ray Eames would create for children, and embody the simplicity and playfulness of much of the designers' work. Sold by Sears, Roebuck and Company, each hexagonal box came filled with wooden dowels, pipe cleaners, and a set of square and triangular stiffened-paper in yellow, red, blue–green, magenta and black, which could be used to produce multiple structures, some large enough to inhabit. 'Toys and games are the preludes to serious ideas,'[1] Charles noted. By emphasizing composition, structure and building, the toy sets played into the mid-century desire to pro-mote a child's agency in the playroom. It also embodied the Eameses' interest in low-cost design produced from easy-to-find materials, an inclination that manifested itself most famously in their moulded-plywood furniture, which would forever transform our perception of the humble material.

443 🪑

Rodnik Shark Fin Chair, 2014
Philip Colbert (1979–)
Made

With an open sharp-toothed mouth and fins outstretched, the jaws of this shark are more inviting than evil. Designed by the Pop artist Philip Colbert, as part of his Rodnik collection for Made – a range that featured octopi-covered bed linens, submarine-inspired pillows and a fish-scale rug – this child-friendly armchair embodies the artist's irreverent, fantasy-laced aesthetic. 'For me, satire and humour are essential!'[1] Colbert explains. Dubbed 'the godson of Andy Warhol', Colbert is best known for his fashion label, Rodnik Band, which blurs the boundaries between music, Pop art and fashion. 'I think of myself as a Pop artist who runs an art brand,' he states.[2] Well known across the fashion and design worlds for his creative collaborations, Colbert's outlandish multidisciplinary art projects have been acclaimed by a number of fashion icons, including Karl Lagerfeld and Lady Gaga, and been exhibited in Saatchi Gallery, London.

444

Child's Chair, c. 1935
Piet Zwart (1885–1977)
Prototype

While best known for his contributions to the field of modern graphic design, Piet Zwart worked across multiple disciplines throughout the 1920s and 1930s, including architecture, photography and industrial design. Influenced by both De Stijl and Bauhaus principles, Zwart designed objects that were purposeful, simple and resolute. This noble little seat was conceived for Waassenaar Kindergarten, his children's school in the Netherlands. Inspired by an earlier design of 1919, its simple planar construction reflects De Stijl principles, as well as those of the Italian physician and educator Maria Montessori, who expressed a desire for 'light furniture, which is correspondingly simple, and economical in the extreme'.[1] Although Zwart had envisioned making the chair more widely available as an affordable flat-pack kit, he was unsuccessful in garnering interest from a manufacturer. In 2000, the Dutch designer's influence was recognized through the posthumous award of Designer of the Century, given by the Association of Dutch Designers.

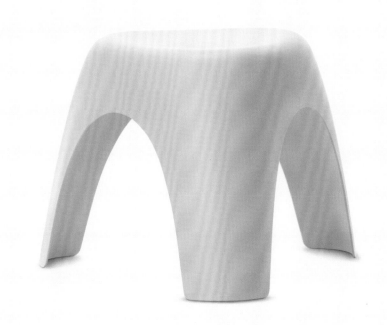

445 ♯

Elephant Stool, 1954
Sori Yanagi (1915–2011)
Kotobuki / currently Vitra

Created by Sori Yanagi in 1954, the Elephant Stool is one of the most famous objects of Japanese post-war design. Stable, stackable, lightweight, easy to carry, and suitable for both indoor and outdoor use, it has stood the test of time, and is today produced by Swiss manufacturer, Vitra. Born in Tokyo in 1915, Yanagi began his career working for the great French designer Charlotte Perriand when she was based in Tokyo in the early 1940s. Arguably his greatest influence, however, was his father, Sōetsu Yanagi, an important advocate of Japanese folk craft and the beauty of everyday objects. Dedicated to the Modernist principles of simplicity, practicality and tactility, Sori Yanagi championed 'anonymous design' over the course of his sixty-year career, believing that beauty emerged out of usefulness. Marrying Western industrial designs with Eastern artisanal traditions, Yanagi's prolific body of work proved influential to designers such as Naoto Fukasawa, Tom Dixon and Jasper Morrison.

446 🪑 ✏️

Maternelle Table No. 804
and Chair No. 805, 1951
Jean Prouvé (1901–84)
Ateliers Jean Prouvé

The French market for school furniture was booming in the 1950s. Companies such as Mullca, Mobilor, Tubauto and Delagrave were eager to produce furniture following the Ministry of Education's guidelines for desks and chairs to be lightweight and stackable. At the forefront of modern design in France, Jean Prouvé embraced the technological and industrial advances of his day. He exploited mass production and new materials – folded metal being a favourite – to create furniture that was practical, elegant and egalitarian. Committed to designing for learning environments throughout his career, Prouvé's 1951 Maternelle (Kindergarten) set came in several variations; a single or double table (with or without storage), and a chair with optional armrests. The set's innovations were subtle yet significant: the chair's form enabled efficient stacking while the triangular-shaped steel of its back legs splayed slightly to maximize balance and durability.

447 ✏

Swingline Children's Bookcase, 1952
Henry P Glass (1911–2003)
Fleetwood Furniture Corporation

This cleverly configured children's bookcase was part of a collection designed by Henry P Glass for the Fleetwood Furniture Corporation of Grand Haven, Michigan. The storage unit, like other components in his Swingline series, features vibrant colours and a wooden dowel pivot, which allowed the units to turn and the shelves to rest on intersecting planes. The range, which included a play table, room divider, wardrobe and toy chest, emphasized elements made to 'swing' playfully into different positions. Glass emigrated to the United States in 1939 and began working for the celebrated designers Gilbert Rohde and Russel Wright, before studying under László Moholy-Nagy. With fifty-two patents to his name, he quickly established a reputation in his own right. Today, Glass is perhaps most recognized as the inventor of the iconic hairpin leg in 1941. The Swingline series was awarded a gold medal from the Industrial Designers' Institute in 1952.

Railwayman, c. 1928
Joaquín Torres-García (1874–1949)
Self-produced

Wood was a favourite medium for Joaquín Torres-García, one of Uruguay's most beloved artists, and over the course of his career he produced more than 200 wooden toys – ranging from animals to vehicles to dioramic café scenes. In recent years, these painted wooden figures have come to be appreciated as more than just supplementary to his work as an artist. Following several large survey exhibitions featuring his *maderas* (wooden work), they are now seen as a form of research, through which Torres-García explored how he might introduce three-dimensional form into his paintings. Torres-García was keen to test the relationship between abstract forms and concrete depictions by fragmenting familiar things, such as this railwayman, into puzzle-like pieces that can then be reconfigured in different ways. This particular design, which is composed of five pieces, was made during a period in which Torres-García was living in France and painting toys by hand in large quantities for commercial distribution.

449 ◧

Animal Puzzle, 1963
Fredun Shapur (1929–)
Naef

Fredun Shapur is widely admired for his contributions to toy design. Perhaps best known for his work with the American institution Creative Playthings, Shapur made his mark on the company by crafting its graphic identity (its logo and packaging), and by producing memorable objects for children. He opened an office in 1959, focusing primarily on graphic design, although his own children inspired him to also work in three dimensions. A gifted artisan, his earliest toys were constructed out of wood, which were then sanded by Shapur and his wife, and later by a group of craftspeople. As the scale of production increased, Swiss manufacturer Naef helped the designer to meet the growing demand. Introduced in 1963, his Animal Puzzle is a unique toy comprised of sets of animals, which are cut from a single square block of wood and can interlock in an intricate manner. Shapur's sophisticated use of shape and colour produces a delightful optical effect in the six pairs of animals contained in the set.

450 ☾

Sebra Bed, 1942–3/2016
Viggo Einfeldt (1900–55)
Sebra Interior

Inspired by a newspaper story that recounted how a child had been injured by the bars of their cot, the Danish designer Viggo Einfeldt set about creating a crib that prioritized children's safety. His resulting Juno bed of 1942–3 could cleverly adapt as a child grew. Its removable sides, and adjustable height and length enabled the bed to evolve through two cot sizes and two bed configurations – and ultimately to even transform into a sofa. Instantly popular, Juno was featured in eight family films during the 1950s, quickly becoming a Danish design icon. In 2016, Einfeldt's family collaborated with Sebra, a children's design company, to reissue the bed under their brand name. The revised design maintains the character of the original, although the curve of its legs have been adjusted and its overall proportions enlarged to meet current safety requirements. Today, both Viggo Einfeldt and the Juno Bed are listed in the Danish Cultural Canon, which catalogues essential contributions to Denmark's cultural heritage.

451 🛴 🪑

Bunny, 2013
Kateřina Zemánková (1990–)
Prototype

The traditional rocking horse is given a run for its money by Czech designer Kateřina Zemánková, in favour of a playful bunny-rabbit-inspired rocking chair. Its cantilevered form has been created using laminated plywood, finished with a non-toxic, water-resistant paint that allows the natural variations in the wood to show through. Children can sit on the chair with the bunny ears as a backrest, or sit astride it, holding onto the ears for extra security while they bounce and rock. Two felt strips on the base of the chair keep it from damaging the floor and soften the rocking motion with a little cushioning. Designed for children between the ages of three and six, Bunny's solid construction means that older children can join in on the fun too. The design earned Zemánková the Czech National Award for Student Design in 2013.

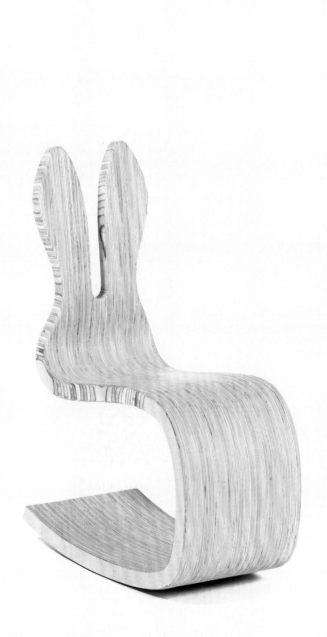

452 ⬛▲

Lincoln Logs, c. 1916
John Lloyd Wright (1892–1972)
Red Square Toy Company
/ currently K'nex

Designed over a century ago, these miniature logs by John Lloyd Wright (Frank Lloyd Wright's second son) have become one of America's most iconic toys. Named after President Abraham Lincoln's fabled childhood cabin, the toy's structure of interlocking wooden beams was inspired by the Imperial Hotel in Tokyo that Frank Lloyd Wright designed to be earthquake-proof. The product launched in 1918 and its original packaging featured a simple drawing of a log cabin, a portrait of Lincoln and the matter-of-fact slogan, 'Interesting playthings typifying the spirit of America'. Building on a growing interest in the value of construction toys, as well as a wave of patriotism in the wake of World War I, the toy was an instant success. Popularity peaked in the 1950s, when shows like the 'Pioneer Playhouse' and 'Davy Crockett' led Lincoln Logs to be among the first toys that were mass-marketed on television. The toy was inducted into the National Toy Hall of Fame in 1999, with more than 100 million sets sold worldwide.

453 🛴

Pegaso Rocking Horse, 2006
Enzo Berti (1950–)
Saba Italia

The Italian designer Enzo Berti began his career studying under the revered sculptor Alberto Viani at the Academy of Fine Arts in Venice. His interest in form and the influence of Viani's modern swooping shapes is evident in Pegaso, Berti's amorphous rocking horse, made from wood and felt. The recipient of both a Compasso d'Oro and Red Dot Design Award, Berti studied Industrial Design while part of the architecture programme at the IUAV University of Venice. He has since gone on to have a prolific career in design, collaborating with brands such as Artemide and Magis. Manufactured by Saba Italia, his Pegaso (Italian for 'pegasus') embodies the designer's signature sparseness and restrained colour palette, while playfully adapting his style for a younger audience. The frame reduces the flying horse to its most basic form, a hallmark concept of Modernism, while its handles and coloured wool upholstery add graphic boldness.

454 ᨒ

Peter Rocking Horse, 1950s
Konrad Keller (est. 1864)
Konrad Keller / currently Ostheimer

With its striking, simplified profile, the Peter Rocking Horse reflects the influence of European Modernism on mid-century toys. Peter's flat shapes and graphic clarity reveal a shift away from naturalism towards a more stylized form. The rocker was conceived and produced in the 1950s by Konrad Keller, a wooden toy company founded in 1864 in the German town of Göppingen, which became well known for its rocking and hobby horses. The design is most likely the work of sculptor Hermann Schwahn (1927–2003), who lived in Göppingen for most of his life. Today, mid-century versions of the horse can be found in both a natural finish and lacquered in a Bauhaus-inspired palette of primary colours. The timeless design continues to be manufactured by the German toy company Ostheimer, who acquired the license to the Konrad Keller collection in 2003, and the company in 2011.

455 🐼

Puffin, 1954
Kay Bojesen (1886–1958)
Kay Bojesen Denmark

The Puffin, or 'Sea Parrot' as it is known in Danish (on account of its colourful bill), lives in large colonies in Norway, Iceland and the Faroe Islands, now and then making an unexpected appearance in Denmark. Bojesen's winged wooden creature took flight in 1954, originally appearing in two sizes. Full of character and humour, Bojesen's Puffin can change expression with a simple tilt of its head. Its wonderfully graphic red, blue and yellow striped beak was designed in collaboration with the great scenographer and painter, Svend Johansen. Known for his naive painting style, Johansen decorated several of Bojesen's figures from his studio on Bredgade, the same street on which Bojesen's shop was situated. With over 2,000 designs to his name, Bojesen was unable to keep Puffin in continuous production and it was sadly forgotten for a time. Happily, it was resurrected in 2013, and continues to be a much-beloved possession for both children and adults alike.

Endnotes

00

1. Alain de Botton, interviewed by Andrew Lawless, 'Staus Anxiety – an interview with Alain de Botton', Three Monkeys Online (accessed 30 April 2018), <threemonkeysonline.com/status-anxiety-an-interview-with-alain-de-botton/3/>

2. Charles Eames, quoted in Daniel Ostroff, 'The Playful Designs of Charles and Ray Eames', Eames Official Site (1 September 2005), <eamesoffice.com/blog/the-playful-designs-of-charles-and-ray-eames/>

09

1. Kristian Vedel, quoted in Architectmade Child's Chair press release, einrichten design (2015), <einrichten-design.de/de/amfilerating/file/download/file_id/1265/>

11

1. Richard Hutten, 'Dombo mug (aka Domoor cup) by Richard Hutten "makes people happy"', interview for *dezeen* YouTube channel (1 February 2016), <youtube.com/watch?v=plJAtZEkMIA>

16

1. Tom Evans, quoted in 'Winner, Consumer Product Award: Suzy Snooze', *Core77* (accessed 16 September 2017), <designawards.core77.com/Consumer-Product/63436/Suzy-Snooze>

21

1. Alex Hochstrasser, 'Interview with Alex Hochstrasser, inventor of Bilibo', interview for Moluk press release (March 2007), <moluk.com/press/press_releases/Interview_AlexHochstrasser.pdf>

22

1. Mina Panic, 'IO Pod Bunk Bed by Mina Panic', interview with Frank Scott for A'Design Award and Competition (24 February 2017), <competition.adesignaward.com/design-interview.php?ID=54293>

2. Mina Panic, 'Love for Kids, Mina Panic', interview for dogtrot Vimeo (accessed 9 November 2017), <vimeo.com/128301648>

26

1. Harold Van Doren, *Industrial Design: A Practical Guide* (New York, 1940), 26.

33

1. Torafu Architects, quoted in Dan Howarth, 'Torafu Architects Designs Multi-functional Dice Furniture for Children and Adults', *dezeen* (12 August 2014), <dezeen.com/2014/08/12/torafu-architects-multi-functional-dice-furniture-adults-children/>

36

1. Author's email correspondence with Michaele Simmering.

39

1. Patrick Rylands, quoted in 'The Captivating World of Toy Design: How Patrick Rylands Inspired Children Worldwide with Award-winning Ambi Toys', *PR Newswire* (27 May 2015), <prnewswire.com/news-releases/the-captivating-world-of-toy-design-how-patrick-rylands-inspired-children-worldwide-with-award-winning-ambi-toys-300088665.html>

64

1. Emily Fischer, quoted in Dickson Wong, 'This Design Studio Is Bringing Us Closer to the Stars', One Kings Lane (accessed 24 March 2018), <onekingslane.com/live-love-home/haptic-lab-studio-tour/>

68

1. Pete Oyler, quoted in Katja Runge, 'Rip + Tatter: Chair for Children by Peter Oyler' afilii: Design for Kids (8 December 2016), <afilii.com/en/rip-tatter-chair-for-children-by-pete-oyler/>

69

1. 'About', Monogoto website (accessed 31 December 2017), <mono-goto.com>

70

1. Author's email correspondence with Mark Venot.

2. Ibid.

74

1. Rolf Heide, quoted in 'Design Icon (06) Stackable Beds by Rolf Heide', DW English YouTube channel (1 February 2010), <youtube.com/watch?v=7ohvMAE4-oU&feature=youtu.be>

75

1. Author's email correspondence with Vlad Dragusin.

79

1. Amy Ogata, quoted in Gregg Allen, 'Spectacular Creative Playthings Wooden Family By Antonio Vitali', daddytypes website (14 September 2006), <daddytypes.com/2006/09/14/fine_ill_post_them_spectacular_creative_playthings_wooden_family_by_antonio_vitali.php>

83

1. 'Designs for Independent Living, the Museum of Modern Art, New York, April 16–June 7, 1988', exhibition press release (Museum of Modern Art, New York, 1988), <http://moma.org/documents/moma_catalogue_2152_300062856.pdf>

84

1. Naoto Fukasawa, *Naoto Fukasawa* (London, 2007), 208.

85

1. Renate Müller, quoted in Monica Khemsurov, 'Renate Müller at R & Company', *Sight Unseen* (19 March 2014), <sightunseen.com/2014/03/renate-muller-at-r-company/>

93

1. David Weeks, quoted in 'Lucy the Crocodile', designy things (3 December 2011), <designythings.com/2011/12/03/lucy-the-crocodile/>

96

1. Stefano Giovannoni, quoted in 'Rabbit Chair by Qeeboo, the latest chair by Giovannoni', *designbest* (24 December 2016), <magazine.designbest.com/en/design-culture/objects/rabbit-chair-by-qeeboo/>

100

1. Floris Hovers, quoted in Riya Patel, 'Floris Hovers' Design Toys', *Icon* (19 August 2011), <iconeye.com/design/features/item/9490-floris-hovers-design-toys>

2. Ibid.

101

1. Eero Aarnio, quoted in 'Pingy – design Eero Aarnio, 2011', Magis press release (accessed 21 November 2017), <magisdesign.com/wp-content/uploads/2015/03/pingy_en.pdf>

103

1. Maria Monstessori, *The Absorbent Mind* (Adyar, Chennai, India, 1949).

105

1. Katie Sout, quoted in Alex Ronan, 'Keep Your Eye On: Brooklyn Designer Katie Stout', *dwell* (26 January 2015), <dwell.com/article/keep-your-eye-on-brooklyn-designer-katie-stout-c92bbbc0>

2. Katie Stout, quoted in 'Katie Stout and Zev Schwartz Make Stuffed Chairs', *Architectural Digest* (31 May 2015), <architecturaldigest.com/story/katie-stout-zev-schwartz-stuffed-chair>

106

1. 'Magis World: Me Too', manufacturer website (accessed 29 November 2017), <magisdesign.com/magis-world/me-too/>

112

1. Bruno Taut, 'The Crystal Chain and Architectural Play', in *Century of the Child: Growing by Design 1900-2000*, Juliet Kinchin ed. (New York, 2012).

114

1. Heikki Ruohu, designer website (accessed 10 February 2018) <jarvi-ruoho.com/company/bio-ruoho.html>

138

1. Takeshi Sawada, designer website (accessed 2 January 2018), <kamina-c.com/about/>

139

1. Author's email correspondence with Povl Kjer.

151

1. Atelier Sans Souci, product description on company website (accessed 26 March 2018), <sanssouciatelier.com/furniture.html>

2. Ibid.

152

1. Eglantine Charrier, quoted in Kelsey Keith, 'A Cramped Attic Became a Sunny Dining Room in this Renovation of a Copenhagen Tudor', *dwell* (15 August 2015) <dwell.com/article/a-cramped-attic-became-a-sunny-dining-room-in-this-renovation-of-a-copenhagen-tudor-3e0636a0>

154

1. 'Shapemaker Original', designer website (accessed 2 January 2018),

<millergoodman.com/creations/shapemaker/>

157   1.   Author's email correspondence with Frederik Roijé.

159   1.   Paolo Rusconi and Giorgio Zanchetti, *The Thirties: The Arts in Italy Beyond Fascism* (Florence, 2012), 158–9.

162   1.   Lucan Boscardin, interviewed in 'A talk with Luca Boscardin', *Polpettas Mag* YouTube channel (3 December 2014), <youtube.comwatch?v=C0umVmdhuzw&feature=youtu.be>

163   1.   Andrew Gelller, quoted in 'Andrew Geller: Architect of Happiness, 1924–2011', *Alastair Gordon Wall to Wall* (26 December 2011), <alastairgordonwalltowall.com/2011/12/26/andrew-geller-architect-of-happiness-1924-2011/>

164   1.   Thomas Laurens, interview with Morgana Matus, 'Thomas Laurens Designs a Play Table/Coffee Table Hybrid That Will Stand the Test of Time', *inhabitots* (1 March 2014), <inhabitat.com/inhabitots/thomas-laurens-designs-a-play-tablecoffee-table-hybrid-that-will-stand-the-test-of-time/>

167   1.   Sarit Shani Hay, designer website (accessed 6 February 2018), <http://shanihay.com/about/auto-draft/>

170   1.   Martí Guixé, quoted in 'Office/Zoo at Milan 2011', Design Indaba (24 April 2011), <designindaba.com/articles/creative-work/officezoo-milan2011>

177   1.   'Magis World: Me Too', Magis manufacturer website (accessed 29 November 2017), <magisdesign.com/magis-world/me-too/>

178   1.   Rui Alves, quoted in Rose Etherington, 'Welcome to the Jungle by My Own Super Studio', *dezeen* (20 June 2010), <dezeen.com/2010/06/20/welcome-to-the-jungle-by-my-own-super-studio/>

181   1.   David Weeks, quoted in Ben Hobson, 'David Weeks' folding wooden Cubebot toy «has a life of its own» on Instagram', *dezeen* (29 February 2016), <dezeen.com/2016/02/29/video-interview-cubebot-folding-wooden-robot-toy-david-weeks-areaware-movie/>

193   1.   Tammy Everts, 'Pippocampus Rocking Horse', *Apartment Therapy* (24 October 2008), <apartmenttherapy.com/pippocampus-rocking-horse-66995>

194   1.   Author's email correspondence with Peter Hiort-Lorenzen.

197   1.   Eero Aarnio, quoted in 'Happy Bird – design Eero Aarnio, 2015', manufacturer press release (accessed 29 November 2017), <magisdesign.com/wp-content/uploads/2015/11/happy_bird_s_en.pdf>

200   1.   Author's email correspondence with Scott Klinker.
2.   Ibid.

205   1.   Patrick Rylands, quoted in 'Patrick Rylands: Classic Toys From A Toy Design Hero', Mumfidential (25 August 2015), <mumfidential.com/patrick-rylands-classic-toys-from-a-toy-design-hero/>

209   1.   Frederik Roijé, quoted in Fiona Db, 'Frederik Roijé', *designboom* (1 June 2014), <designboom.com/design/frederik-roije/>

212   1.   William B Fageol, 'Wheeled vehicle for children', Google Patents (accessed 16 August 2017), <google.com/patents/US2423590>

222   1.   Donna Wilson, quoted in Rachel Leedham, 'Interiors: Donna Wilson's colourful London Home', *Telegraph* (15 May 2014), <telegraph.co.uk/lifestyle/interiors/10830865/Interiors-Donna-Wilsons-colourful-London-home.html>

224   1.   Cas Holman, 'Cas Holman; Identity in Play', Cas Holman YouTube channel (23 January 2015), <youtube.com/watch?time_continue=179&v=IL1n6LuUIcQ>
2.   Cas Holman, quoted in 'The Case for Letting Kids Design Their Own Play', *Fast Company* (13 July 2015), <fastcodesign.com/3048508/the-case-for-letting-kids-design-their-own-play>
3.   Ibid.

236   1.   Dor Carmon, quoted in 'A Duck for Life', Normann Copenhagen manufacturer website (accessed 6 Febraury 2018), <normann-copenhagen.com/product/product-collections/ducky>

237   1.   Bruno Munari, quoted in Bruno Munari and Paolo Fossati, *Codice ovvio*, 1st ed (Turin, 1971).

241   1.   'Company Profile', Danese Milano manufacturer website (accessed 17 January 2018), <danesemilano.com/company-profile/>

243   1.   Author's email correspondence with Louise Campbell.
2.   Ibid.

256   1.   Naoto Fukasawa, quoted in Diana Budds, 'Naoto Fukasawa On Designing with Objectivity and Interaction in Mind', *Fast Company* (22 October 2015),

<fastcodesign.com/3052429/naoto-fukasawa-on-designing-with-objectivity-and-interaction-in-mind>
2.   Bill Moggridge, quoted in *Naoto Fukasawa* (London, 2007), 166.

260   1.   Naoto Fukasawa, *Naoto Fukasawa: Embodiment* (London, 2018), 222.

261   1.   Belinda Luscombe, 'The Prince of Plastic Karim Rashid Wants to Change the World One Ordinary Object at a Time', *Time* (17 September 2001), <http://content.time.com/time/world/article/0,8599,2047730,00.html>

263   1.   Author's email correspondence with Lisa Albin.

264   1.   Charlotte and Peter Fiell, *Chairs – 1,000 Masterpieces of Modern Design, 1800 to the Present Day* (London, 2012), 607.

266   1.   Karim Rashid, 'Karimanifesto', designer website (accessed, 24 November 2017), <karimrashid.com/karimanifesto>

275   1.   Author's email correspondence with Erik Mailil.

279   1.   Marcel Wanders, quoted in 'La femme et la maison Nika Zupanc', Northern Icon (accessed 12 September 2017), <northernicon.com/s-260-nika-zupanc.aspx>
2.   Nika Zupanc, 'Boris, Vladimir & Alexander', designer website (accessed 12 September 2017), <nikazupanc.com/personal-collections/copy-of-boris-vladimir-alexander>
3.   Ibid.

284   1.   Enzo Mari, quoted in Paul Pettigrew, 'Enzo Mari Autoprogettazione Milan 1974 – Chicago 2008', MIT Architecture website (Fall 2008), <architecture.mit.edu/architecture-and-urbanism/project/enzo-mari-autoprogettazione-milan-1974-chicago-2008>

285   1.   Eero Aarnio, quoted in 'Eero Aarnio', exhibition press release, Designmuseo, Helsinki (accessed 7 December 2017), <designmuseum.fi/en/exhibitions/eero-aarnio-2/>

298   1.   Peter Opsvik, quoted in Aileen Kwun, 'How the Iconic Tripp Trapp High Chair Came to Life', *dwell* (16 August 2015), <dwell.com/article/how-the-iconic-tripp-trapp-high-chair-came-to-life-30098e55>
2.   Ibid.

300   1.   'Über uns', Neue Freunde designer website (accessed 20 February 2018), <http://neuefreunde.bigcartel.com/uber-uns>

310   1.   Ladislav Sutnar, quoted in Iva Knobloch, 'Mental Vitamins for the Future – Ladislav Sutnar's Toys', *Toys of the Avant-Garde* (Málaga, 2010), 226.

314   1.   Pablo Picasso, quoted in R P Davidson, 'Modern Living: Ozmosis in Central Park', *Time* (4 October 1976), Vol. 108, No. 14, <content.time.com/time/magazine/article/0,9171,918412,00.html>

319   1.   Lucas Maassen, quoted in Cassandra Prizzey, 'Furniture Factory by Lucas Maassen & Sons', *design.nl* (4 January 2012), <design.nl/item/furniture_factory_by_lucas_maassen__sons>

325   1.   Alexander Taylor, quoted in Helen McKay-Ferguson, 'Style Profile: Alexander Taylor', *Junior* (5 October 2010), <www.juniormagazine.co.uk/interiors/style-profile-alexander-taylor/3822.html>

341   1.   Patrick Rylands, quoted in Billy Langsworthy, 'Patrick Rylands of Ambi Toys, Technology and the Day-to-Day Life of a Toy Designer', *toynews* (17 June 2014), <toynews-online.biz/interviews/read/patrick-rylands-on-ambi-toys-technology-and-the-day-to-day-life-of-a-toy-designer/042561>

343   1.   'Verner Panton 1992', PP Møbler manufacturer website (accessed 28 October 2017), <pp.dk/index.php?page=gallery&cat=11&id=106>

349   1.   Nika Zupanc, 'Konstantin B Toy Car', Nika Zupanc designer website (accessed 12 September 2017), <nikazupanc.com/objects/konstantin-b>

352   1.   Alexander Seifried, quoted in 'IMM 2011 – Alexander Seifried for Richard Lampert', Architonic AG YouTube channel (3 February 2011), <youtube.com/watch?v=XEeNygFHHHc>

358   1.   Libuše Niklová, quoted in Juliet Kinchin, 'Manufacturing Poetry: The Toys of Libuše Niklová', *Inside/Out*, a MoMA/MoMA PS1 Blog (13 September 2012), <moma.org/explore/inside_out/2012/09/13/manufacturing-poetry-the-toys-of-libuse-niklova/>

360   1.   Philippe Starck, quoted in Dan Howarth, 'Customisable Furniture Means "no more trends" says Philippe Stark', *dezeen* (8 April 2014), <dezeen.com/2014/04/08/tog-customisable-furniture-no-more-trends-philippe-starck-milan-2014/>

364   1.   John Lloyd Wright, quoted in 'Building Block', US Patent 1894605 (accessed 26 October 2017), <google.com/patents/US1894605>

397   1.   Michel Ducaroy, quoted in Aaron Britt, 'Togo Sofa by Ligne Roset Celebrates Its 40th Anniversary', *dwell* (16 May 2013) <dwell.com/article/togo-sofa-by-ligne-roset-celebrates-its-40th-anniversary-299dc66e>

398   1.   Piergiorgio Cazzaniga, quoted in Selina Denman, 'In the DNA: The Design Language of Piergiorgio Cazzaniga', *The National*, Arts and Culture (3 December 2015), <thenational.ae/arts-culture/in-the-dna-the-design-language-of-piergiorgio-cazzaniga-1.103982>

404   1.   Author's email correspondence with Guillaumit.
      2.   Ibid.

406   1.   Jan Čapek, quoted in Tereza Kozlová, 'Inflatable Czech Design, Continuing the Tradition', *Visegrad Insight* (22 December 2014), <http://visegradinsight.eu/inflatable-czech-design22122014/>

408   1.   Floris Hovers, quoted in 'Duotone Serie, Dutch Design Wood Toy Cars by Floris Hovers', Ikonic Toys YouTube channel (20 June 2017), <youtube.com/watch?v=qFXKlviUAS8>

410   1.   Maarten Baas, quoted in Ben Quinton, 'Dutch Designer Maarten Baas is Setting the Design World On Fire – Literally', *Newsweek* (14 February 2017), <newsweek.com/2017/02/24/dutch-designer-maarten-baas-furniture-industry-556666.html>

412   1.   Patrick Rylands, quoted in 'The Captivating World of Toy Design: How Patrick Rylands Inspired Children Worldwide with Award-winning Ambi Toys', *PR Newswire* (27 May 2015), <prnewswire.com/news-releases/the-captivating-world-of-toy-design-how-patrick-rylands-inspired-children-worldwide-with-award-winning-ambi-toys-300088665.html>

415   1.   Remko Verhaagen, 'Create Beauty Do Good', Blooey designer website (accessed 15 November 2017), <blooey.nl/blooey/>

437   1.   Author's email correspondence with Mira Shapur.

438   1.   Mart Stam, quoted in 'Der Schaukelwagen', translated from artist website Hans Brockhage (accessed 18 September 2017), <hansbrockhage.com/#schaukelwagen>

439   1.   Gaetano Pesce, quoted in Nina Azzarello, 'Designboom Goes Inside Gaetano Pesce's Studio in New York', *designboom* (27 March 2017), <designboom.com/design/gaetano-pesce-studio-visit-new-york-soho-03-24-2017/>

440   1.   Gaetano Pesce, quoted in *Phaidon Design Classics* (London, 2006), object 714.

441   1.   Alma Siedhoff-Buscher, quoted in 'Bauhaus: Modernist Toy Icons', Maammo (accessed 17 October 2017), <maammo.com/blogs/stories/bauhaus-modernist-toy-icons>

442   1.   Charles Eames, quoted in Daniel Ostroff, 'The Playful Designs of Charles and Ray Eames', Eames Official Site (1 September 2005), <eamesoffice.com/blog/the-playful-designs-of-charles-and-ray-eames/>

443   1.   Philip Colbert, quoted in Tish Weinstock, 'Introducing the Crown Prince of Pop Art: Philip Colbert and the Rodnik Band', *i-D* (15 October 2014), <i-d.vice.com/en_uk/article/gygg34/introducing-the-crown-prince-of-pop-art-philip-colbert-and-the-rodnik-band>
      2.   Ibid.

444   1.   Maria Montessori, *Spontaneous Activity in Education* (New York, 1917), 144.

1. Index by Category

2. Index by Designer

3. Index by Product

Picture Credits

Author's Acknowledgements

In the spirit of the proverb 'it takes a village to raise a child', *Design for Children* would not have happened without the help of my wonderful team at Phaidon and my crackerjack research assistants Lila Allen, Emma Ng, Alexandrea Klimoski, Lauren Palmer and Akiva Blander. Thank you to Molly Heintz, William Myers, Alan Rapp, Lora Appleton and Aidan O'Connor for their generous and insightful guidance, to Jon Rossman for his creative eye, to Kai Barry for keen editing, and to my friends and family for their support. This survey would not have been possible without those design curators and champions who paved the way before me, Greg Allen, whose blog, Daddy Types, proved an invaluable resource, and of course the talented designers who made this book such a joy to write.